ST. PETERSBURG

ARCHITECTURE OF THE TSARS

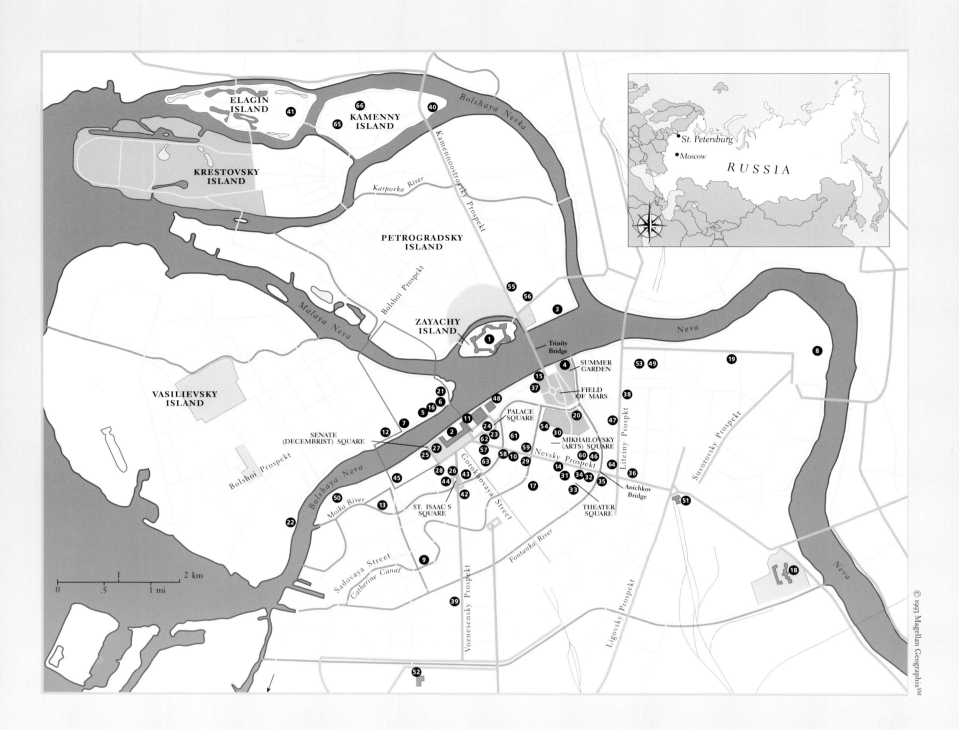

ELAGIN
ISLAND

KAMENNY
ISLAND

KRESTOVSKY
ISLAND

Bolshaya Nevka

Karpovka River

PETROGRADSKY
ISLAND

Bolshoi Prospekt

Kamennoostrovsky Prospekt

Malaya Neva

ZAYACHY
ISLAND

VASILIEVSKY
ISLAND

Neva

Trinity
Bridge

SUMMER
GARDEN

FIELD
OF MARS

SENATE
(DECEMBRIST) SQUARE

Bolshaya Neva

PALACE
SQUARE

MIKHAILOVSKY
(ARTS) SQUARE

Nevsky Prospekt

Liteiny Prospekt

Suvorovsky Prospekt

Bolshoi Prospekt

ST. ISAAC'S
SQUARE

Moika River

Gorokhovaya Street

Anichkov
Bridge

THEATER
SQUARE

Sadovaya Street

Catherine Canal

Voznesensky Prospekt

Fontanka River

Ligovsky Prospekt

Neva

1	2 km
0	.5	1 mi

© 1993 Magellan Geographix℠

St. Petersburg

Moscow

RUSSIA

1. Peter-Paul Fortress
2. Admiralty
3. Peter's Little House
4. Peter the Great's Summer Palace
5. Twelve Colleges
   (St. Petersburg University)
6. Kunstkamera
7. Menshikov Palace
8. Smolny Convent
9. Cathedral of St. Nicholas of the Sea
10. Stroganov Palace
11. Winter Palace/Hermitage Museum
12. Academy of Fine Arts
13. New Holland
14. Gostiny Dvor
15. Marble Palace
16. Academy of Sciences
17. Currency Bank

18. Alexander Nevsky Lavra
19. Tauride Palace
20. Mikhailovsky Castle
21. Stock Exchange
22. Academy of Mines
23. General Staff Headquarters
24. Alexander Column
25. Senate and Synod
26. St. Isaac's Cathedral
27. Monument to Peter the Great
28. Horse Guards Manège
29. Kazan Cathedral
30. Mikhailovsky Palace/
    Russian Museum
31. Public Library
32. Anichkov Palace
33. Alexandrinsky Theater
34. Monument to Catherine the Great

35. Beloselsky-Belozersky Palace
36. Yusupov Residence
37. Pavlovsky Regiment Barracks
38. Cathedral of the Transfiguration
39. Cathedral of the Trinity
40. Kamenny Island Palace
41. Elagin Palace
42. Mariinsky Palace
43. Astoria Hotel
44. Ministry of State Property
45. Nikolaevsky Palace
46. Shuvalov Palace
47. Bureau of Departmental Affairs
48. Grand Duke Vladimir
    Alexandrovich Palace
49. Kochubei Residence
50. Stieglitz Residence
51. Moscow Station

52. Baltic Station
53. Kelkha House
54. Cathedral of the Ascension, or
    of the Savior of the Blood
55. Lidval Building
56. Kshessinskaya Residence
57. Vavelberg Bank
58. Mertens Fur Store
59. Dom Knigi Bookstore
60. Eliseyev Building
61. Headquarters of the Guards
    Economic Society
62. Azovsko-Donskoi Commercial Bank
63. Russian Bank of Commerce
    and Industry
64. Commercial Galleries
65. Meltzer House
66. Rozenstein Apartment House

ST. PETERSBURG

ARCHITECTURE OF THE TSARS

PHOTOGRAPHS BY Alexander Orloff

TEXT BY Dmitri Shvidkovsky

Translated from the French by John Goodman

ABBEVILLE PRESS PUBLISHERS

New York · London

Dedicated to the memory of Svetlana, who gave us so much.

❧

ACKNOWLEDGMENTS

First and foremost, my profound gratitude to Boris Ometov, former director of the government bureau for the inspection and protection of the historical and cultural monuments of St. Petersburg, as well to his staff, especially Elena Grinevich. This book would have been impossible without the assistance of Boris Ometov, whose vast knowledge of the cultural patrimony and architectural history of St. Petersburg proved invaluable.

The project was undertaken in collaboration with UNESCO's Cultural Heritage Division. I would like to express my thanks to Federico Mayor, the general director of UNESCO; the much regretted Abdelkader Errahmani, formerly director of PATRICOM and head of promotion at the Cultural Heritage Division, as well as Lydie Perdereau; Giancarlo Riccio, assistant director of the World Heritage Center; Christine Gossa; Marie-Christine Bercot; Paola Antolini; Alla Murashova; and especially Elena Orlova. At the permanent delegation of the Russsian Federation to UNESCO, I would like to thank the permanent delegate Mikhail Fedotov, the former delegate Vladimir Lomeiko, Albert Roganov, and Evgeny Yagotkin.

I would also like to thank Anatoly Sobchak, former mayor of St. Petersburg; A. Konstantinov, representative of the St. Petersburg Committee for Culture; Evgeny Belodubrovsky of the St. Petersburg Cultural Foundation; Sergei Denisov and Valery Veliki, directors of the Center for Support of UNESCO in St. Petersburg; Sergei Klokov, former member of the USSR Committee for UNESCO Affairs; and Igor Shabdurasulov of the Russian Federation Cultural Department.

I would also like to express my gratitude to the following for their cooperation: Mikhail Piotrovsky, director of the Hermitage Museum, as well as Georgi Vilinbakhov and Dmitri Varygin; Vladimir Gusev, director of the Russian Museum, and Ivan Karlov. At the Russian Museum's annexes: Sergei Lyubimtsev, director of the Stroganov Palace, and Sergei Kuznetsov; Elena Kalinitskaya, director of the Engineer's Castle; Lyudmila Listskaya and Irina Tkatcheva at the Marble Palace; Natalya Metelitsa at the National Museum of Theater and Music; former artistic director Oleg Vinogradov and Maxim Krastin at the Mariinsky Theater; Viktor Veshnitsov and Mikhail Anikushin at the Academy of Arts; Galina Khvostova, director at Peter the Great's Summer Palace Museum; Larisa Anisimova, director of Grand Duke Vladimir's Palace; Ninel Kalazina, director of the Menshikov Palace Museum; Nikolai Lubushkin at the Anichkov Palace; Albert Magalashvili at the Beloselsky-Belozersky Palace; Larisa Peterskaya, director of the Elagin

Palace Museum; Galina Sveshnikova, director of the Yusupov Palace; Natalya Dementeva, director of the National Museum of the Peter-Paul Fortress; Valentina Bashylova, director of the Tauride Palace; Zakhar Suponitsky, director of the Polovtsov house; Marta Potoforova, director of the Kshessinskaya House Museum; Franz Sedelmayer at the Meltzer house; Igor Mazur at the Alexander Nevsky Lavra; Yuri Kudinkin at Nikolsky Cathedral; Georgi Butikov, director of the Museums of St. Isaac's Cathedral and the Cathedral of the Ascension, or of the Savior of the Blood; Ivan Sautov, director of the Tsarskoe Selo National Museum, as well as Nikolai Nagorsky, Viktor Faibisevich, Alexander Zhuravlev, Larisa Bordovskaya, Galina Khodasevich; Yuri Mudrov, director of the Pavlovsk National Museum, as well as Leonid Lyubimov; Nikolai Tretyakov, director of the Gatchina National Museum, as well as Galina Kondakova and Lidia Strizhova; Nikolai Karmazin, director of the National Museum of the Palace and Park of Oranienbaum; Elena Denisova at the Peterstadt Museum; Tatyana Kislashko at the Katalnaya Gorka Museum; Vladimir Klimentev at the Chinese Palace Museum; Vadim Znamenov, director of the Peterhof Palace National Museum, as well as Elena Kosterova and Svetlana Kuzmich; Valentina Tenikhina and Natalya Sharanskaya at the Cottage Museum; Elena Mikhalyova at the Monplaisir Palace Museum; Elena Bundina at the Hermitage and the Marly Palace Museums. I would like to offer my special thanks to the many staff members of these museums and palaces who accompanied me and waited patiently while I went about my work.

I would also like to express special gratitude to all those whose generous support and encouragement made it possible for me to complete this project: my parents; the Kasem-Beg, von Schweder, De Gioanni, Kaufman, and Porotsky families; with special thanks to Michiko Kokubun and Vera and Natan Petchatnikov for their warm hospitality and enthusiastic support from the project's inception; Dora Friedman; William Brui; Nadia Rosanova; Galina Demitrienko; Elena Bespalova; Marina Kuznetsova; Boris Petrov; Yuri Yarmolinsky; Sophie Julien; Ray-Güde Mertin; Jean-Pierre and Sylvie Pappis; Tom Tiberii; Bruce MacMahon; Lee Kok Kwang; Nobuki Kuroda; Ellen de Ludinghausen; Pierre Merle; Rosamond Bernier; and John Russell.

Finally, I would like to thank the Independent Agency of St. Petersburg for their coordination services, as well as Aeroflot, Air Len, and Kodak-Pathé France for their generous support.

— ALEXANDER ORLOFF

JACKET FRONT *Smolny Convent cathedral (see also page 103).*

JACKET BACK *Green Dining Room in the Great Palace at Tsarskoe Selo (see also page 215).*

ENDPAPERS *View of the Saltykov and Betsky residences on the Palace Embankment of the Neva.*

FRONTISPIECE *Map copyright © 1993 Magellan Geografix,ᔆᔆᴹ 6464 Hollister Avenue, Santa Barbara, California 93117.*

PAGE 8 *View of the Neva River. To the right, the English Embankment with St. Isaac's Cathedral in the background. To the left, the University Embankment on Vasilievsky Island.*

PAGE 10 *The architectural ensemble at the tip of Vasilievsky Island with, from left to right, the Academy of Sciences, the Kunstkamera (now the Museum of Anthropology and Ethnography), the Stock Exchange, and the Customs House, as well as the two rostral columns.*

PHOTOGRAPHY CREDITS

© Sinii Most: pp. 44, 60, 84, 128, 172; © Sinii Most / V. Terebenin-Hermitage: pp. 12, 13 (2), 54, 60, 66, 138, 150, 204, 229, 342; © Sinii Most / V. Terebenin-Heyfets: pp. 56, 80, 242; © Sinii Most / V. Terebenin-Museum of the History of the City: pp. 16, 29, 120, 137, 140, 143, endpapers; © Sinii Most / Russian Museum: pp. 45, 112; © Kurt Goebel / Zefa Agency: p. 342; © Alain de Gourcuff: pp. 268, 282, 306.

Book Concept: Alexander Orloff
Captions: Brigitte de Montclos
Graphic Design: François Caracache

FOR THE ENGLISH-LANGUAGE EDITION
Editor: Jacqueline Decter
Jacket and Interior Typographic Design: Barbara Sturman
Production Editor: Owen Dugan
Production Manager: Lou Bilka

Excerpt from "Less Than One" from *Less Than One: Selected Essays* by Joseph Brodsky. Copyright © 1986 by Joseph Brodsky. Reprinted by permission of Farrar, Straus & Giroux, Inc.

Excerpt from "The Admiralty," reprinted with the permission of Scribner, a Division of Simon & Schuster, from *Osip Mandelstam: Selected Poems*, translated by Clarence Brown and W. S. Merwin. Copyright © 1973 by Clarence Brown and W. S. Merwin.

Compilation, including selection of text and images, copyright © 1995 Editions Mengès, Paris. English translation copyright © 1996 Abbeville Press. All rights reserved under international copyright conventions. No part of this book may be reproduced or utilized in any form or by any means, electronic or mechanical, including photocopying, recording, or by any information storage and retrieval system, without permission in writing from the publisher. Inquiries should be addressed to Abbeville Publishing Group, 137 Varick Street, New York, N.Y. 10013. The text of this book was set in Electra and AT Burin Roman. Printed and bound in Hong Kong.

First edition
10 9 8 7 6 5 4

Library of Congress Cataloging-in-Publication Data
Dmitri Shvidkovsky
   [Saint Pétersbourg. English]
   St. Petersburg : architecture of the tsars / by Dmitri Shvidkovsky ; photographs by Alexander Orloff ; translated from the French by John Goodman.
       p.   cm.
   Includes index.
   ISBN 0-7892-0217-4
   1. Architecture, Baroque—Russia (Federation)—Saint Petersburg. 2. Neoclassicism (Architecture)—Russia (Federation)—Saint Petersburg. 3. Architecture—Russia (Federation)—Saint Petersburg. 4. Saint Petersburg (Russia)—Buildings, structures, etc. I. Orloff, Alexander. II. Shvidkovskiǐ, D. O. (Dmitriǐ Olegovich) III. Title.
NA1196.G6613   1996
720'.947'4530903—dc20   96-17849

For bulk and premium sales and for text adoption procedures, write to Customer Service Manager, Abbeville Press, 137 Varick Street, New York, NY 10013 or call 1-800-ARTBOOK.

PREFACE

Emerging from a long hibernation, Russia is once more turning toward the West. Virtually forsaken for nearly three-quarters of a century, the city envisioned by Peter the Great as Russia's main port and "window to the West" is on the threshold of a rebirth. The former imperial capital is renewing the historical, economic, and cultural ties that have made it the most European of Russian cities.

Six years ago the historical center of St. Petersburg and the palaces in its environs were added to UNESCO's World Cultural Heritage list, confirming the city's reappearance on the world stage, where it is valued at its just worth. This city, the largest urban center on UNESCO's list, is now seeking international support to ensure its preservation for the future.

A "window to the West," the imperial capital became a city of the Enlightenment. Peter the Great's heirs pursued his great enterprise, commissioning some of the most brilliant representatives of the European schools of art and architecture, from the Italian baroque to classicism, from neo-Gothic to Art Nouveau. They transformed the marshy delta of the Neva into that remarkable architectural ensemble so often referred to as the "Venice of the North."

This glorious city soon became the symbol of Russian culture and was greatly admired by the most enlightened personalities of the time. In his *Essay on Morals*, Voltaire marveled at both the vision of Peter the Great and its realization, emphasizing the speed with which the arts and letters had blossomed in St. Petersburg. He saw "Russia's march toward civilization" as one of the major events of his century, and concluded his essay by invoking a European civilization extending from St. Petersburg to Madrid.

All the principal Russian arts—literature, music, theater, ballet—were and remain to this day inextricably linked to St. Petersburg, the true cultural heart of Russia. During the reign of Catherine the Great alone the acquisitions of the imperial collection in the Hermitage exceeded those made by the Louvre over a period of several centuries. These treasures—still held in the Hermitage, which is recognized as one of the world's greatest museums—are so precious that UNESCO has made a commitment to contribute to their preservation.

For the greater part of the twentieth century St. Petersburg was effectively in a state of siege. Damaged by war, subject to vandalism of every sort, disfigured, and neglected, today its cultural patrimony is safeguarded by a mere handful of defenders, who continue their efforts against all odds. Miraculously, the sovereign vision of Peter the Great still prevails. Thanks to restorations and total reconstructions of remarkable quality, the imperial heritage has recovered some of its luster, attesting to the city's continuing vitality and its attachment to its glorious past. Neither war nor revolution has succeeded in severing its cultural roots. Now a new generation of defenders must take up the enterprise so steadfastly carried forward by its predecessors.

St. Petersburg, mistreated but still vital, is now at a crossroads. In this new period of unrest, the turn toward Europe willed by its founder three centuries ago has become rife with hidden perils. Among the younger generation many are unaware of the important role culture plays in maintaining a sense of historical continuity and as a repository of collective memory. Alienated by a dark past, dazzled by the superficial allure of modernity, and seduced by the laws of the marketplace, they are rushing headlong into a world stripped of references. But there is no future without roots to ground identity. History has demonstrated time and again the grave consequences of rupturing cultural continuity. Hence the importance of mobilizing the young, explaining, showing, and making this cultural heritage meaningful and accessible.

Now inscribed on the World Cultural Heritage list, St. Petersburg belongs to the memory of humanity, and its protection has become our collective responsibility. Its cultural integrity must be preserved for future generations. This volume should prove an invaluable tool in instilling awareness of this necessity.

—Federico Mayor
General Director of UNESCO

CONTENTS

Preface by Federico Mayor, General Director of UNESCO   5

ST. PETERSBURG City of Imperial Culture   12

1   PETER THE GREAT A Window to the West   14

The Founding of St. Petersburg 16 ✳ The Initial Plan for St. Petersburg 20 ✳ The Architects of Peter the Great 24 ✳ The Peter-Paul Fortress 34 ✳ The Palaces of Peter the Great 36 ✳ Monuments from the Era of Peter the Great on Vasilievsky Island 40

2   ANNA IVANOVNA AND ELIZABETH PETROVNA
The Dazzle of the Baroque   44

Anna Ivanovna: The Second Birth of the City 48 ✳ Elizabeth Petrovna, or the Blossoming of the Rastrelli Baroque 61 ✳ Smolny Convent 65 ✳ Cathedral of St. Nicholas of the Sea 71 ✳ St. Petersburg Palaces in the Baroque Era 74 ✳ Winter Palace 76

3   CATHERINE II The City of Enlightenment   82

From the Baroque to Classicism 84 ✳ Vallin de la Mothe and the Birth of Classicism in St. Petersburg 91 ✳ Palladianism and Classicism in the Late Eighteenth Century 100 ✳ The Cathedral of the Alexander Nevsky Lavra and the Tauride Palace 102

4   PAUL I The Tormented One   110

The Romantic Castle 112

5   ALEXANDER I AND NICHOLAS I Classical Grandeur   120

St. Petersburg and Its Culture in the First Half of the Nineteenth Century 122 ✳ The Tip of Vasilievsky Island 136 ✳ The Admiralty 140 ✳ General Staff Headquarters and Palace Square 147 ✳ Senate Square and Decembrist Square 150 ✳ St. Isaac's Cathedral 151 ✳ The Beginning of Nevsky Prospekt 156 ✳ Kazan Cathedral 159 ✳ From Kazan Cathedral to Gostiny Dvor 160 ✳ Mikhailovsky Palace 162 ✳ Theater Square 164 ✳ Nevsky Prospekt Beyond the Anichkov Bridge 169 ✳ The Field of Mars and the Work of Vasily Stasov in St. Petersburg 169 ✳ Palaces on Kamenny and Elagin Islands 172

6 ALEXANDER II AND ALEXANDER III
Retrospection and Nationalism 176

A Rapidly Evolving City 178

7 NICHOLAS II The Rise and Fall of Art Nouveau 190

The Great Upheaval 192

8 TSARSKOE SELO 204

The Mystique of Tsarskoe Selo 206 ✳ The Triumph of the Baroque 207 ✳ Catherine
the Great's Chinese Caprice 218 ✳ The Return to Antiquity 220 ✳ Rooms from the
Era of Catherine the Great 222 ✳ The Meaning of the Park 229 ✳ Classicism and
Romanticism 234 ✳ A City of Parks and Salons 234

9 ORANIENBAUM 242

The Palace of Vicissitudes 244 ✳ The Menshikov Palace 253 ✳ Peterstadt, or the
Dream of Peter III 259 ✳ Catherine the Great's Personal Dacha 262 ✳ The Chinese
Palace 264 ✳ The Sliding Hill Pavilion 266

10 GATCHINA 268

The Masters of Gatchina 270 ✳ The Palace at Gatchina 271 ✳ The Park at Gatchina 276

11 PAVLOVSK 282

Pavlovsk and Its Domain 284 ✳ The First Years at Pavlovsk 289 ✳ The Exterior of
the Palace 290 ✳ The Interiors of the Palace 292 ✳ The Conception and History
of the Park 293 ✳ The Park Around the Palace 293 ✳ The Vale of the Slavyanka 294
✳ Daily Life and Festive Occasions at Pavlovsk 299

12 PETERHOF 306

The History of Peterhof and Its Personalities 310 ✳ The Great Palace 325 ✳ Waterfalls and
Fountains 331 ✳ Monplaisir 338 ✳ Marly and the Hermitage 341 ✳ The Cottage 344

Notes 354
Index 356

ST. PETERSBURG

CITY OF IMPERIAL CULTURE

RUSSIA WAS A PART OF EUROPE FOR TWO CENTURIES AND FOURTEEN YEARS: from 1703, the year St. Petersburg was founded, to 1917, the year of the Bolshevik victory. Before the eighteenth century, however, Russia had quite another historical destiny. It maintained closer ties with the Asian steppes and Byzantium than with Europe. The country was open to the south, the north, and the east rather than to the west. After the Revolution of 1917, Russia in many respects reverted to its past, to the time before the reforms of Peter the Great. Thus the years of communism were an anomaly, and perhaps the greatest, strangest, and most absurd error in the history of humanity, but one from which Russia is now extricating herself. Her 214 European years remain firmly inscribed in her history. They were sometimes troubled, it is true, but by and large they were happy, triumphant, and victorious. St. Petersburg is their principal witness and monument. It is the city of imperial culture, the capital city, the city of the court: Rome and Versailles rolled into one and set within a cityscape resembling a Baltic Amsterdam or a Finnish Venice—the "Palmyra of the North," as the poets dubbed it. This allusion to antiquity is a fitting one, for St. Petersburg has always been a classical city, whether the brand of classicism in question was romantic or decadent, marked by the baroque or by the Enlightenment. This characteristic is indelibly engraved on its architecture.

In this volume we trace the evolution of St. Petersburg over the course of these two centuries. One after the other, all the periods of life in St. Petersburg will be examined through the lens of its

OPPOSITE
Peter the Great by
Jean-Marc Nattier,
1717.

RIGHT
Perspective view of the
Kronstadt naval yards,
c. 1720, watercolor by
Johann Friedrich
Braunstein.

FAR RIGHT
The Fontanka near the
Summer Garden and
the Grotto, etching by
Kachalov, 1753.

historical monuments. We have divided its architectural history by reigns. In organizing the illustrations, however, we have often adhered to geographic criteria to facilitate a unified presentation of architectural ensembles. In the Russia of the eighteenth and nineteenth centuries, as in France, each change of ruler was accompanied by a change of style. This is almost a law of stylistic evolution, and it was the basic premise of Igor Grabar's important history of Russian art, which dates from the early twentieth century. We have decided to follow his approach, which is consistent with historical reality.

St. Petersburg of the eighteenth and nineteenth centuries cannot be thought of without its environs, just as one could not imagine London without its parks or Paris without Versailles. The great events in the history of Russian architecture of the period often took place at Tsarskoe Selo, Oranienbaum, Gatchina, Pavlovsk, and Peterhof—outlying estates that, along with the city proper, constituted an immense, unique, and superb domain saturated with historical monuments.

These monuments are so numerous and so diverse that we can describe each of them only briefly. But we have attempted to restore these architectural achievements to their proper role in Russian imperial history.

1

PETER THE GREAT

A WINDOW TO THE WEST

This great shadow of Tsar Peter pursues you ceaselessly in Petersburg; it perches on all the monuments and wanders along all the embankments and through all the squares. A great monarch never abandons his people and his state.

—Paul de Julvécourt
Autour du monde, Paris, 1834

OPPOSITE
*The Peter-Paul Fortress
seen from the Neva.*

THE FOUNDING OF ST. PETERSBURG. St. Petersburg was founded on May 27, 1703. Prince Vladimir Odoyevsky, one of the best-known Russian Romantic writers of the early nineteenth century, described the establishment of the city by Peter the Great: "Construction of the city had begun, but the marsh swallowed all the stone; a great many had already been piled on, block after block, but all had disappeared and nothing remained on the surface but swamp. Meanwhile, the tsar . . . took a turn around the site: he looked and saw that this was still not his city. 'You don't know how to do anything,' he told his people, and with these words he began to lift block after block and assemble them in mid-air. In this manner he constructed the entire city, and when it was complete he let it fall to earth."[1]

There is a grain of truth in this fantastic legend, which derives from an ancient Eastern fairy tale but is now part of the mythology of St. Petersburg. The new imperial capital of Russia sprang up at the country's northwestern extremity so unexpectedly and became a great city with such dizzying speed that it made sense to say that it had "fallen from the sky" onto the narrow, swampy islands at the delta of the Neva River.

The history of the site prior to the city's founding has long since been established by historians. The earliest Russian chronicler, Nestor, writes that in his time the route linking the Varangians to the Greeks went from Scandinavia to Byzantium by way of the Neva, Lake Ladoga, and the rivers of Russia.[2] In the ninth, tenth, and eleventh centuries this was one of the vital communication corridors of Europe. It was along this route that the structure of the Russian state evolved, and this same passage provided Russia with a tentative link to the West. St. Petersburg might well have been established then, but this did not happen. In truth, we are not even sure that the site of the future city existed at the time, for the delta of the Neva changed form quickly and the islands did not assume their present form until relatively recently. It is known that in the ninth century the Normans settled in a village situated a hundred kilometers from Lake Ladoga, before proceeding farther

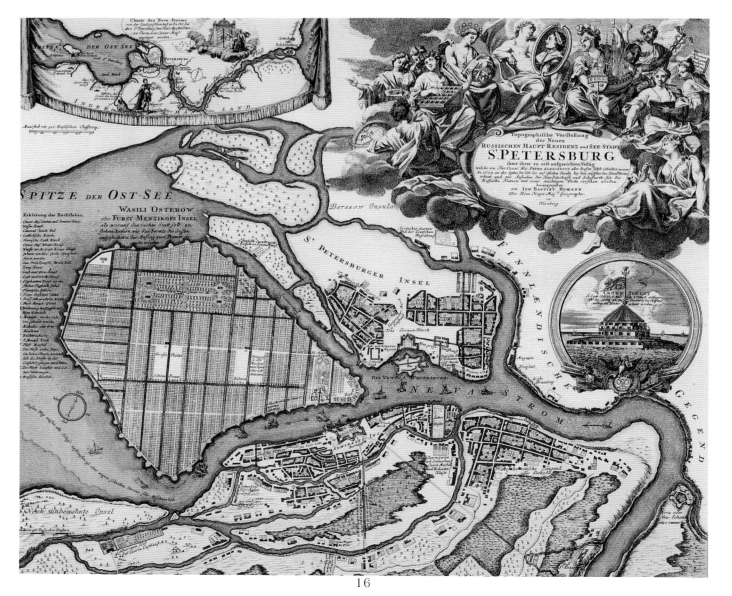

LEFT
*Map of St. Petersburg
in 1717.*

OPPOSITE
AERIAL VIEW OF
THE PETER-PAUL
FORTRESS.
*Across the canal, the
Kronverk fortifications.*

THE PETER-PAUL
FORTRESS.
FAR LEFT *St. Peter
Gate by Domenico
Tressini, 1717–18.*
LEFT *The Neva Gate
leading to the landing
pier, by Nikolai Lvov,
1782–89.*

to the south, deep into Russia as far as Novgorod and Kiev.

In the mid-thirteenth century the Tatar invasion cut off the river route between Scandinavia and Byzantium, but this did not lessen the determination of the Scandinavians and the Russians to establish themselves in the Neva delta. Throughout the medieval period the area belonged to the mercantile republic of Great Novgorod. The Swedes tried to conquer it but failed. Grand Prince Alexander Yaroslavich defeated the Swedish army there in 1240, which merited him a prominent place in Russian history as Alexander Nevsky, which means Alexander of the Neva. All the grand princes and tsars of Moscow were descended from him. The fortress of Landskron ("crown of the earth") was built there in 1300 by an Italian would-be engineer traveling with the Swedish armies; the Russians soon destroyed it, but at the beginning of the seventeenth century the Swedes erected a new fortress on roughly the same spot, which they called Nienshantz ("fortification on the Neva").

According to the terms of the peace of 1617, the northeastern seaboard of the Baltic Sea reverted to Sweden. She retained control until the beginning of the eighteenth century and the Northern War, in which Russia, Sweden, Poland, Denmark, Saxony, and some of the other German principalities took part. This conflict completely transformed the balance of power in the region, to Russia's advantage. Hitherto the prehistory of St. Petersburg was one of scarcely populated and impoverished territorial frontiers. Now all that changed.

The Northern War began badly for Russia. Peter the Great's troops invaded Sweden by way of the southern Baltic coast but were cruelly defeated by young Charles XII, who then proceeded to conquer Poland, chasing from the Polish throne the Russian-allied Augustus the Strong, elector of Saxony, and installing in his place Stanisław Leszczyński, the future father-in-law of Louis XV. In the meantime Peter the Great reorganized the Russian army on the European model. Profiting from the absence of Charles XII from the Baltic Sea, he went on the offensive. In the middle of 1702 his troops headed toward the Neva, and on May 1 the Russians took the fortress of Nienshantz and occupied the current site of St. Petersburg. Three weeks later Peter founded a fortress there that he called, after his patron saint, the city of Saint Peter—or, in Dutch transcribed into Cyrillic, "Sankt-Piterburkh."

The August 1703 issue of the leading Russian periodical, the *Record*, reported that "his majesty the tsar has ordered the construction of a city and a fortress on the banks of the sea, so that henceforth all goods destined

THE PETER-PAUL
FORTRESS.
*The Cathedral of
Peter and Paul, built
by Tressini between
1712 and 1733. To the
left, the "boathouse,"
built in 1762 to contain
the legendary small
boat that the young
Peter 1 himself built
using the remains of
an old vessel.*

[for the Baltic ports] . . . will arrive here, including goods from Persia and China."³ This statement makes it perfectly clear that the city was conceived from the start as a crossroads linking Europe and Asia, as a point of intersection between Eastern and Western commerce. The tsar had understood that the creation of such a center was vital for Russia. But was he being realistic?

The terrain on which St. Petersburg rose was a marshy coastal plain covered with stunted vegetation and divided into many islands by the branches of the Neva. It was also subject to periodic flooding. There were many places where the ground was too unstable to support construction. Consequently it was necessary to drain the swamp and reinforce the soil with thousands, perhaps even millions, of piles (they have never been counted). The resulting difficulties would have struck a prudent man as insurmountable, but Peter the Great was not known for being reasonable; his fiery temperament, his obstinacy, and his thirst for action sometimes brought him to the brink of madness. And the lives of ordinary people mattered very little to him in any case. In the popular imagination he soon took on a divine quality, and even now he remains the principal character in the mythology of St. Petersburg.

What vision of Russia's future lay behind such an extraordinary undertaking? The city in which Peter had been raised—sprawling, ancient, luxurious, picturesque, and sluggish Moscow, the quintessence of medieval Russian culture and national character—could not be rebuilt. In any event, the tsar wanted to live in a city by the sea, which fascinated him. Moscow was the home of an assimilated Byzantine culture modified to suit Russia's needs. Peter the Great dreamed of establishing a model of Western life in his country, and above all in his capital city. When he committed himself to this idea he had not yet visited the West. He knew its way of life only second-hand, via books and hearsay. Nonetheless he had developed an unbridled passion for the sea and for this other way of life.

History decreed Peter the Great's arrival on the scene at a moment when ancient traditions were dying out, when necessity dictated the choice of a new culture. Russia had already lived through one such situation. In the tenth century Grand Prince Vladimir found himself confronted with a similar choice: he rejected Catholic, Islamic, and Jewish culture in favor of the Orthodox world of Byzantium. Peter the Great, faced with analogous circumstances, opted for the Western model and abandoned Moscow. In 1704 he began to refer to the city he had founded as his "capital," and in 1712 St. Petersburg's status as Russia's premier city became official.

THE INITIAL PLAN FOR ST. PETERSBURG. The structure of the city was determined by nature. Before emptying into the Gulf of Finland the Neva subdivides into several branches, creating numerous islands. There were more than a hundred in the eighteenth century, but their number decreased over time as many canals were filled in. Today there are forty-four. The principal riverbed divides into two branches that embrace vast Vasilievsky Island, which faces the sea to the west. To the north are several smaller islands (Elagin, Kamenny, Krestovsky, and so forth), while upstream, on the right bank of the Neva, is Zayachy Island, on which the Peter-Paul Fortress was built. Behind this is large Gorodskoy Island. The left bank of the Neva, on which the Admiralty was constructed, is subdivided by the Moika and Fontanka rivers, which run virtually parallel to each other after separating from the main riverbed, still joined together, at the level of the Summer Garden, thereby defining another large island, sometimes called Admiralty Island.

In the early eighteenth century the construction of such a gigantic city on virgin terrain, and according to a regular plan, was an extraordinary undertaking not only in Russia but in all Europe. It had no equivalent in Western urbanism of this period. The first plan for St. Petersburg was based on military considerations, for at the time the outcome of the war with Sweden was still unknown. During the summer of 1703 the hexagonal Peter-Paul Fortress was built on Zayachy Island, on the right bank of the Neva. A village with rectilinear streets and a central square was laid out nearby. Its structures included the wooden Trinity Cathedral, a *gostiny dvor* (merchants' court), and housing for bureaucrats and artisans. The city itself was protected by the Peter-Paul Fortress. The defensive fortifications on Kotlin Island in the Bay of Finland, now the Kronstadt Fortress, precluded hostile access by water. Everything was done in keeping with contemporary European military requirements. The tsar monitored the progress of the construction and himself provided some of the plans, which were based on models in Dutch, French, and German treatises on military construction.

A fundamental question determining the very existence of St. Petersburg, just after construction of the fortress, was the creation of a fleet and the building of the city's maritime facilities. On the other bank of the Neva, across from Zayachy Island, construction began in the fall of 1704 on the Admiralty, the main dockyard of the young Russian Baltic fleet. After the unexpected attack of the Swedes in 1705 it was reinforced by bastions. Artisan communities began to spring up under its protection along the Neva.

SUMMER PALACE.
Façade facing the Fontanka.

SUMMER PALACE.
LEFT *Relief. Several such reliefs representing marine allegories were designed and placed on the façade by the architect Andreas Schlüter in 1714.* OPPOSITE *The Green Salon.*

But Peter was possessed by the idea of building his capital on an island open to the sea. In 1709 the idea was born of "constructing the capital on Kotlin Island," in the Gulf of Finland some twelve miles (twenty kilometers) from the river. The long, narrow island was crisscrossed by a network of canals and short streets perpendicular to one another, and there was a long canal running through the center that provided an important axis. The land was parceled for construction into lots of identical dimensions, which reinforced the systematic rhythms of the street plan. The conception suggested that all the tsar's subjects were of equal stature in relation to this all-powerful plan. On January 16, 1712, Peter issued an ukase stipulating that a thousand noble families, a thousand merchant families, and a thousand artisan families were to emigrate from old Russian cities to the new capital, and he specified that only the best candidates could settle there. This document is perhaps the most telling indication of the kind of city he envisioned.

In 1715 the tsar ordered the architect Domenico Tressini to devise a master plan for Vasilievsky Island. Again a site near the sea had been selected. The banks of the island were shored up. The ground was subdivided by a network of perpendicular canals paralleled by streets. They were laid out straight as a ruler and were even called "lines," an appellation that they retain to this day. In the matter of residential architecture, all inhabitants were obliged to follow official guidelines; this was

to be a city of strict architectural conformity. Four models were developed, three for the "inferior classes," the "prosperous classes," and the "notables," respectively, as well as a fourth "for construction along the rivers, where buildings are to be more sumptuous." These designs were engraved and distributed to everyone who received a lot and intended to build on it. Even today Vasilievsky Island retains the broad outlines of the plan dating from this period.

For Peter the Great, such regular urban planning was not so much an aesthetic principle as a means of social organization. The tsar had imposed a "table of ranks" that obliged all nobles to serve the state and subdivided the "first order" into fourteen categories according to their relative status in the bureaucratic, civil, and military hierarchies. This system made it possible for an obscure individual to enter the "table of ranks" at the bottom and, after a successful career, enter the nobility. Strictly defined prerogatives were allotted to each category, determining all aspects of life in the new city: building sites, the number of horses permitted, the place assigned each functionary's wife in church, and so forth. There were also ukases concerning dress and coiffure, and decreeing attendance at public functions, one of which involved the communal consumption of strong beverages. These measures applied to all inhabitants of St. Petersburg—soldiers, merchants, courtiers—but the closer one was to the monarch the more rigorous they

became. If the tsar organized a masquerade, it was incumbent upon everyone to amuse themselves; pregnant women were expected to drink as much as anyone else, which could result in miscarriage or death. Arriving late at one of the daily meetings with the tsar was extremely dangerous; the guilty party was obliged to make amends by drinking more than a liter of vodka in a single gulp from the "great eagle goblet." The beginnings of this infinitely beautiful city were frightening, and they anticipate much of the history of modern Russia.

But Russia would not be Russia if all government decisions were indeed implemented, even under so cruel an emperor. Peter the Great kept a close watch over the construction of the new city, but it evolved more in accordance with the exigencies of daily life than with the monarch's will.

On the tsar's death in 1725, the city consisted of several parts that were not yet well integrated with one another. The Peter-Paul Fortress was completed, and the quarters situated to the north continued to develop. Vasilievsky Island was not destined to become the center of the city. Plans had called for the construction of 3,500 houses, yet by 1725 there were only 500, despite the establishment of the administrative center on the eastern tip of the island, a complex that included the building that housed the Twelve Colleges (as the ministries were called during Peter the Great's time), the Kunstkamera (the first Russian museum), and Menshikov Palace, the residence of the governor of the city.

The true heart of St. Petersburg, the area in which most of the population lived, was the Admiralty quarter on the left bank of the Neva. Inhabitants were drawn there by the presence of several industrial enterprises: the Admiralty naval yards and the rope- and oaryards, where everything needed to outfit the fleet was produced. Peter the Great's first Winter Palace was also built there, as were the later ones, including the palace complex that stands today. Upstream the Summer Garden was laid out, beside what was then the Summer Palace. Somewhat farther from the Neva in this quarter, the first suburban residences began to appear on the banks of the Fontanka River in the first quarter of the eighteenth century.

On this same left bank of the Neva two streets that were to become major arteries in St. Petersburg soon took shape. One of them proceeded from the Admiralty toward the palaces along the sea: Peterhof, Strelna, Oranienbaum. This was the future Voznesensky Prospekt. The other linked the Alexander Nevsky Lavra, founded by the emperor, with the center of the city. This was to become the celebrated Nevsky Prospekt. Between these two avenues a population of artisans settled on the remaining large undeveloped tracts, developing them in ways that were sometimes regular and sometimes not. Such was the first St. Petersburg in the era of Peter the Great. The city had been laid out on an enormous scale, but that was all. Construction was everywhere under way but little had been completed.

THE ARCHITECTS OF PETER THE GREAT. In the early years of the twentieth century the preeminent historian of Russian art, Igor Grabar, wrote: "On the day its founder died, the architectural aspect of Petersburg was entirely the work of foreign architects. . . . At that time there was not a single Russian master capable of shaping the city's style. . . . The Italians, Germans, French, and Dutch all arrived in Petersburg at the same time. . . . Quite often a design was drawn up by an Italian, began to rise under the supervision of a German, was continued by a Frenchman, another Italian, and then another German, only to be taken over by a Dutchman. One can easily imagine just how architecturally unified was the result of this unorthodox collective approach."[4] Even so, "architectural unity" of a kind indeed emerged under Peter the Great, and the St. Petersburg style was born.

The first architect to appear on the scene was Domenico Tressini. He arrived in St. Petersburg from Denmark but had been born in Switzerland, in the canton of Ticino. Trained in Lugano, he was imbued with Italian artistic traditions, but like many of his compatriots he had worked in northern Europe, and by the time he

SUMMER PALACE.
LEFT *A mirror hanging on the wall like a painting. Mirrors were considered more important works of art than paintings in this period.*
OPPOSITE *Painted wall panel in the Green Salon.*

SUMMER PALACE.
*Tapestry in the
tsarina's bedroom.*

SUMMER PALACE.
Bedroom of
Peter the Great.

SUMMER PALACE.
LEFT *Built at the junction of the Fontanka and the Neva by Domenico Tressini beginning in 1710, it was enlarged by Andreas Schlüter in 1714.*

BELOW *Watercolor depicting the Summer Palace of Peter the Great and its gardens, artist unknown.*

SUMMER GARDEN.
*Sculpture of Cupid and
Psyche, 17th century.*

SUMMER GARDEN.
Coffeehouse, built by
Carlo Rossi in 1826.

Nonetheless, in his designs Schlüter managed to achieve a convincing blend of the new Russian architecture with the northern German baroque idiom. The other architects who came from Germany—Georg Johann Mattarnovy, Johann Christian Ferster, Johann Braunstein—were to work in the same style. Indeed, the last two men were students of Schlüter. Braunstein built a good deal in Russia, and his role in the diffusion of his master's style was considerable. After Schlüter's death in 1715, another Prussian architect arrived on the scene: Theodor Schwertfeger, who worked in the sumptuous baroque style of southern Germany. Nikolaus Härbel came from Basel and Gottfried Schädel from Hamburg, but after Schlüter's death all the Germans were placed under the direction of a Frenchman. In early June, when the tsar was abroad taking the waters at Pirmont, he was introduced to the French architect Jean-Baptiste-Alexandre Leblond. He made such an impression on the Russian monarch that Peter characterized him in a letter to one of his favorites as a "true wonder," and he decided that the architect had been sent to him by Providence.

Leblond arrived in St. Petersburg on August 7, 1716; the governor of the city gathered all the architects together and announced that the Frenchman had been named architect general. From the start Leblond was critical of everything that had been done in the city, and he soon drew up a new master plan. It was a grand and complex design inscribed within immense fortifications tracing an ellipse. He designated Vasilievsky Island as the heart of the city and proposed the construction of an imperial palace at its center, from which were to radiate, along diagonals proceeding from the corners of a rectangle, four main streets, each of them terminating in a square dominated by a cathedral. Leblond's ideal plan was among the most magnificent and elaborate of the early eighteenth century. It was not realized, however, partly because Peter the Great had always envisioned St. Petersburg along much simpler lines and partly because the plan struck him from the beginning as too costly. So the French architect was dispatched to the suburban palaces and charged with making sure that these "kept up" with Versailles. Leblond died of smallpox in February 1719, but not before leaving his mark on quite a few projects in St. Petersburg's environs.

Shortly before Leblond's death, the tsar's foreign agents invited two Italians to St. Petersburg. Nicolò Michetti was recruited in Rome; he had studied with the celebrated architect Carlo Fontana as well as with Andrea Pozzo, the famous master of perspective decors. When he came to St. Petersburg, Michetti brought with

SUMMER GARDEN.
Peter the Great populated his garden with sculpture. Pictured is an allegory of the Peace of Niesdtadt, which marked the definitive victory of Russia over Sweden in 1721.

went to Russia he had assimilated both the German and Danish variants of the Italian baroque style. A group of Italian masters arrived at the same time as Tressini: Giovanni Mario Fontana, Galeazzo Quadro, Carlo Ferrara, and Domenico Ruto. They had little or no artistic freedom. For example, the architects were ordered to work "in the Prussian manner," using timber-frame construction, which was completely at odds with Italian practice. But the emperor was well versed in German and Dutch building methods, so he stipulated that they be used.

Tressini remained the dominant architectural presence in St. Petersburg until 1713, when Andreas Schlüter, the celebrated "Baudirektor" of the king of Prussia, arrived from Berlin. Peter the Great was delighted to have lured this eminent figure and gave him lodgings in his own palace, so that he would always be close at hand. This arrangement was short-lived, however. The emperor's way of life proved too much for the architect, in terms of both work and play. "Schlüter was a man of sickly constitution, and there he was constantly beset by administrative duties, which soon brought about his death, after having spent only one year in Petersburg."[5]

GATE OF THE
SUMMER GARDEN
ON THE FRENCH
EMBANKMENT.
*Executed by Georg
Velten between 1770
and 1784, it was
celebrated throughout
Europe for its beauty.*

33

him the "picturesque" Roman baroque of the late seventeenth and early eighteenth centuries. Gaetano Chiaveri, born in Rome, arrived in the same period. His subsequent work in Dresden won him a reputation as one of the finest Saxon baroque architects. The Dutch architects Stephan Van Switten and François de Waal arrived later, in 1720, despite the emperor's passion for Amsterdam, but Dutch engineers had long worked for the sovereign. One of them, Hermann von Bolius, had been recruited to work in Russia as early as 1711.

These architects brought with them all varieties of the baroque—Roman, Bavarian, north German, Swedish, and Danish—as well as French and Dutch versions of seventeenth-century classicism, and these were blended with elements drawn from the stylistic spectrum extending from late Mannerism to the rococo.

The collaborative nature of the enterprise obliged these masters trained in different national traditions to devise a common artistic language, to elaborate a synthetic "St. Petersburg" style drawing upon all these sources.

T HE PETER-PAUL FORTRESS. The Peter-Paul Fortress was the first foothold in St. Petersburg, and it still dominates the city. Its granite silhouette rises assertively over the Neva, lifting the gilded tip of its spire toward the sky.

The fortress is a repository of troubling memories associated with its founder. During the first emperor's lifetime it was the principal state prison, and it continued to serve this function until the Revolution. Tsarevich Alexis, Peter the Great's only legitimate heir, was put to death here by torture. (Disliked by his father, he had fled abroad but had been lured back to Russia under false pretenses.) It was also in the fortress that the celebrated Princess Tarakanova, who pretended to be the first emperor's granddaughter, met her end. The Decembrists, who masterminded the aristocratic revolt of 1825, were imprisoned in its cells as well, and they were succeeded by revolutionaries of every stripe.

The Peter-Paul Fortress was originally made of earth. In 1706, three years after it was created, a decision was taken to rebuild it in stone. The emperor himself produced the first design. The fortress then consisted of six bastions connected by fortified walls. Tressini oversaw the work with the assistance of his student Zemtsov. The walls are nearly sixty-six feet (twenty meters) thick and were not completed until the 1730s, after a quarter century of work and well after the death of Peter the Great. Much of the credit for seeing the project through to completion must go to Field Marshal Münich, a remarkable military engineer.

Between 1714 and 1718 Tressini built the fortress's principal entrance, the St. Peter Gate, which was de-

LEFT

KUNSTKAMERA.
Neva façade. The first
Russian museum,
founded by Peter the
Great, was begun by
Georg Johann
Mattarnovy in 1718,
completed by Mikhail
Zemtsov in 1734, and
completely restored in
1948. The tower con-
tains an observatory.

OPPOSITE

MENSHIKOV PALACE.
Neva façade. The
palace was built
by Giovanni Mario
Fontana in 1710. All
the architects in
St. Petersburg at the
time worked on it.
Three levels of pilasters
establish a rhythm
across the façade.
Freestanding sculpture
once terminated the
attic story.

signed as a baroque triumphal arch. It is decorated with a relief by Konrad Osner celebrating Peter the Great's victory over Charles XII. Disguised as a biblical allegory, the relief is entitled *The Apostle Peter Casting out Simon the Magician*, Simon of course being a surrogate for the king of Sweden.

In 1712 Tressini turned his attention to the Cathedral of Peter and Paul, which was completed in 1733. It is a rectangular basilica with three naves, and its interior is reminiscent of northern baroque models. There is no evidence here of the synthetic, logical approach to space characteristic of the Italian tradition. The spire plays an important role in the design, for it recalls the Russian penchant for high, multistoried bell towers.

It was Peter the Great's intention that this structure become the symbol of the new city. Initially it rose 348 feet (106 meters) into the air, and before Peter's death its height was increased by another thirty-three feet. In 1756 the spire was struck by lightning and destroyed. The rest of the cathedral was damaged as well, but everything was restored. In its interior a remarkable iconostasis made of carved and gilded wood was installed, a work created in 1722–27 by the Ukrainian master Ivan Zarudny, known for his work in Moscow. Early-eighteenth-century panels illustrating New Testament themes were also preserved. During the eighteenth and nineteenth centuries the cathedral served as burial

site for the imperial family; all the emperors were interred here, as were all the members of their family who died in St. Petersburg.

Two mid-eighteenth-century constructions should be singled out: the residence of the *Oberkommandant* and the *gauptvakhta*, or engineers house. The Neva Gate, which faces the river, was erected by the celebrated neo-classical architect Nikolai Lvov in 1784–87. A mint, originally built during Peter the Great's time, was reconstructed between 1798 and 1806.

Behind the fortress, on the opposite bank of the canal separating it from Zayachy Island, is another fortification, the Kronverk, which was rebuilt and refurbished many times. The current building resulted from a complete reconstruction in 1850–60, when it was given a neo-Gothic character and became an artillery arsenal. Shortly thereafter, in 1872, it was transformed into the Artillery Museum.

THE PALACES OF PETER THE GREAT. The residences of the first emperor of Russia were not particularly luxurious. They were consistent with his relatively modest way of life. A foreigner who visited St. Petersburg in 1713 left the following description of a typical day for Peter the Great: "His Majesty rises very early . . . meeting with his secret council at

MENSHIKOV PALACE.
*Salon on the main floor
as refurbished in the
mid-eighteenth century.*

three in the morning. He then goes to the naval yards, where he oversees the construction of ships and sometimes works on them himself. . . . At nine o'clock he does woodwork, at which he need cede nothing to any master in the matter of skill. . . . At eleven o'clock he eats, but he doesn't like to linger at table, and having napped after lunch as is the Russian custom, he returns to observe some construction site. . . . In the evening he goes out to pay social calls or take supper. . . . The tsar has no taste for games or hunting. . . . His greatest pleasure is to be on the water. Water is his true element. . . . Once, when the Neva was almost frozen over and only a hundred feet of unfrozen water remained, he sailed back and forth on it ceaselessly in a little boat."[6]

In light of these singular preferences, it is not surprising that all of Peter's palaces were built on the banks of the Neva and that they were not large. The earliest of them, in fact, is not a palace at all. This is "Peter's little house," which was built on the right bank of the Neva in 1703. A modest wooden structure, it conformed to the tastes of the tsar, who preferred small rooms and low ceilings. The entry, in the center of the building, accesses a vestibule, onto which open a study, a dining room, and a bedroom. The walls were originally decorated with a vegetal motif painted on canvas against a black ground. On the exterior, the log walls were protected by planks and painted to resemble bricks.

On the other side of the Neva, the first Winter Palace was built in 1711. Eight years later Georg Johann Mattarnovy designed another palace, which in 1721 was erected on the Neva embankment, on the site now occupied by the theater of the Hermitage. Neither of these structures survives, but archaeologists have recently uncovered the lower portion of the second Winter Palace in the basement of the theater, and it can now be visited. As far as one can tell, the architectural style of this building resembled that of the Summer Palace upstream on the Neva.

Peter the Great's palace in the Summer Garden was built between 1710 and 1714 on the banks of the Neva. A small, rectangular structure of two stories with discreet decors attributed to Tressini, it is a typical example of the first St. Petersburg style, having a pronounced European flavor that distinguishes it from older Russian palaces. The work was already completed when the monarch ordered the façades to be decorated with twenty-nine reliefs after designs by Schlüter. Cast as allegories, these compositions celebrated Russia's victories in the Northern War. They introduced a triumphal note into the building's otherwise unostentatious design. The rooms in the Summer Palace, which have been completely restored, give the visitor a good idea of the imperial family's

daily routine in the first quarter of the eighteenth century. The walls were covered with fabric, the parquet floors were laid in geometric patterns, the stoves were decorated with Delft tiles, and the superb doors were made of oak. The decor of the study is more elaborate, featuring wooden pilasters on high pedestals, inset painted compositions, panels of grotesques between the pilasters, and circular medallions.

Peter the Great was especially proud of the Summer Garden. He designed it himself in 1704, and for the rest of his life he was involved in all decisions concerning its plantings, sculpture, grottos, pavilions, and fountains. It was his idea to introduce trees and flowers from all parts of the empire as well as from abroad. He had cedars imported from northern Russia, cold-resistant apple trees from Sweden, flowers from Holland, and linden trees and white lilies from Estonia. In 1720 the emperor boasted to foreign visitors that if he lived for another three years his garden would be more beautiful than those at Versailles, a remark that makes clear the extent to which he envisioned them in the French style.

In the second half of the eighteenth century, when Russia developed a passion for landscaped parks, the clipping of the trees in the Summer Garden was discontinued. In the nineteenth century, when the gardens had been converted from a court enclave into a public park, the site was renowned for its long, shady walks. By that time the leafy walkways obscured the Summer Palace and the grotto rebuilt by Carlo Rossi in 1826, and the baroque gallery on the Neva embankment had disappeared. The famous fence rose between 1771 and 1784 after designs by Georg Velten, who worked in the classical first St. Petersburg style. Made of cast iron and selectively gilded, it is held in place by thirty-six round columns of polished red granite. It is undoubtedly the most beautiful park fence in all of Russia. In 1855 a monument commemorating the renowned Russian fabulist Ivan Krylov was erected in the garden by Pyotr Klodt.

MONUMENTS FROM THE ERA OF PETER THE GREAT ON VASILIEVSKY ISLAND. Aside from the city plan, which in many respects adheres to the one developed by Tressini, the most significant monuments in the city dating from the era of Peter the Great are preserved on Vasilievsky Island.

The city center as well as the principal governmental buildings were supposed to be located here. The Twelve Colleges was begun in 1722, again after designs by Tressini. This was a composite of twelve buildings intended for the twelve principal administrative services of the empire, aligned in a row and linked by a long corridor. In its center was the assembly hall of the Russian Senate. The façade was designed in 1724 by Theodor Schwertfeger. The windows of its three floors are surrounded by decorative frames. Intervening pilasters establish a steady rhythm, while projecting frontispieces and individual hipped roofs articulate each of the component parts. Unfortunately, the composition is rather boring, notable only for its considerable length. In 1819 it became the home of St. Petersburg University.

The nearby Kunstkamera is much more curious. It was built to house the collections and library of Peter the Great, an anatomical theater, and the first observatory in Russia. The basic design was devised by Mattarnovy in 1718, but construction continued until 1734 under the direction, successively, of Herbel, Chiaveri, and Zemtsov.

MENSHIKOV PALACE. *Bedroom of Menshikov's niece Varvara Arsenieva.*

MENSHIKOV PALACE.
The apartment of
Varvara Arsenieva,
west wall. The cabinet
dates from the early
eighteenth century;
the Delft vase, from the
first quarter of the
eighteenth century.

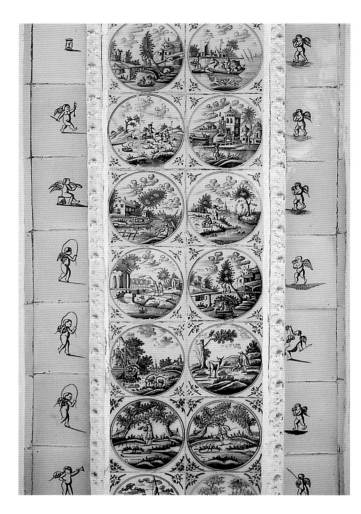

found on the same embankment as the Kunstkamera: the residence of Prince Alexander Menshikov, Peter's favorite and governor of the city. Menshikov Palace, like all of the more ostentatious structures of the period, is situated on the bank of the Neva. An elaborate landing pier was built at the front, while behind the palace, which consists of three blocks of three floors each, a large, regular garden was laid out and enclosed within a high fence supported by turrets. Like the emperor's Summer Garden, it boasted fountains, sculpture, a grotto, and an orangery. This palace was much grander and far more sumptuous than Peter's own modest residence, so it was here that he received foreign ambassadors.

Between 1720 and 1727 the main building was enlarged by the addition of two blocks extending along the Neva on either side. In 1727 the small palace of Peter II, Peter the Great's young grandson and heir, was built on the same property. Menshikov hoped to retain his enormous influence through this arrangement, but to no avail, for eventually he was removed from power. In fact, Peter II and his court abandoned the new capital and returned to Moscow.

The building, as defined by the last campaign of restoration work, combines all the characteristics of the St. Petersburg style of the first quarter of the eighteenth century. Fontana began the construction in 1710, and he was succeeded by Schädel. The Italian and the German were representatives of the two major architectural traditions that influenced palace architecture in St. Petersburg during this period. Inside, the vestibule with its ceremonial staircase and the Walnut Study with a ceiling of Russian workmanship depicting Peter the Great in Triumph are all that remain of the original decor. The other rooms are re-creations.

MENSHIKOV PALACE. Detail of the Delft tiles in Varvara Arsenieva's bedroom. Each tile bears a different image.

Rebuilt in the mid-eighteenth century, after a fire, by Savva Chevakinsky, it consists of two identical blocks linked by a five-story tower in the center. The relatively complex volumes and rich decoration make the Kunstkamera the most baroque edifice in St. Petersburg to have survived from the era of Peter the Great.

Of all the palaces accessible to visitors during Peter's time, the largest and most luxurious is to be

MENSHIKOV PALACE. *Varvara Arsenieva's bedroom. Executed between 1716 and 1720, the ceiling consists of Delft tiles set into a network of moldings characteristic of the first quarter of the eighteenth century. The tiles bear images relating to the sea: fish, dolphins, whales, walruses, and seahorses. Such imagery was popular in seventeenth-century Russian interior decoration.*

2

ANNA IVANOVNA AND ELIZABETH PETROVNA

THE DAZZLE OF THE BAROQUE

*St. Petersburg has been increasingly embellished by the successors of Peter the Great,
especially Elizabeth and Catherine II. Beautiful brick houses rising from granite bases
display all the riches of architecture both ancient and modern; magnificent palaces and
superb residences have sprung up everywhere. The Neva embankments and those of the
Moika, Catherine, Saint Nicholas, and Fontanka canals, all arrayed in granite and
featuring sidewalks for pedestrians, create an ensemble that should make St. Petersburg
renowned as one of the most beautiful cities in the universe.*

—Abbé Georgel,
Voyage à Saint–Pétersbourg en 1799–1800, Paris, 1818

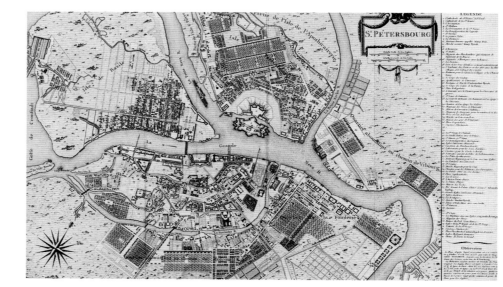

LEFT
*St. Petersburg during
the reign of Elizabeth
Petrovna, print by
P. F. Tardieu, after
the famous plan by
Mikhail Makhaev,
1786.*

OPPOSITE
SUMMER PALACE
OF ELIZABETH
PETROVNA.
*Northern façade, oil
painting by Grekov.*

CATHEDRAL OF
ST. NICHOLAS OF
THE SEA, KNOWN
AS NIKOLSKY
CATHEDRAL.
*View from the
Catherine Canal.*

47

ANNA IVANOVNA: THE SECOND BIRTH OF THE CITY. One of the most remarkable baroque structures ever built in St. Petersburg lasted no more than three months, disappearing with the spring thaw. This was the famous Ice Palace, constructed during the winter of 1740. Power was then in the hands of Empress Anna Ivanovna, the niece of Peter the Great. She loved entertainments on a grand scale. Not that she neglected her obligations to the state, but both these responsibilities and the exigencies of daily life made her nervous, and as a result she needed constant diversions. She always kept jesters nearby, including simple women capable of chattering ceaselessly for days at a time who had been specially recruited in the various cities of the empire, as well as persons of distinction who, whether suited to the jester role or not, had to fulfill it. For the tsarina's amusement, one of the jesters, the elderly Prince Golitsyn, was married off to a Kalmyk woman, the object of particular curiosity because her people had only recently been integrated into Russian territory. A house was built and furnished for the newlyweds between the imperial palace and the Admiralty. Since the winter that year had been particularly harsh, the entire structure was built of ice.

"The purest ice was cut, it was decorated with architectural ornaments, all was done with compass and ruler, the blocks of ice were placed one atop another by levers, and each row was sprayed with water that immediately froze and acted as cement."[1] Such is the description of the construction of the Ice Palace left by Georg Kraft, a member of the St. Petersburg Academy of Sciences, who witnessed it.

The structure was more than fifty-two feet (sixteen meters) long and, in accordance with Russian baroque taste, profusely decorated. It was ringed below by a balustrade, and its roofline was crowned by a series of statues on columns. The windows were framed, and the exterior walls were adorned with pilasters tinted to resemble marble. Inside, visitors could view a bedroom and bed of ice, an ice vanity, an ice fireplace outfitted with ice logs, a dining room with a clock whose works were made entirely of ice, and just beside it a cabinet filled to the brim with ice dishes. At night, when candles were lit, the Ice Palace glowed from within. Outside, next to the palace, stood ice cannons of such solidity that they could be, and occasionally were, fired, to general amusement. Near the cannons were some dolphins and an elephant made of ice that served as fountains by day and torches by night. What's more, Kraft reports that the elephant could "cry out like a living elephant, thanks to the sound produced by a man hidden inside and equipped with a horn."[2]

Most astonishing of all was the wedding itself. Men and women representing all the many peoples of the

CATHEDRAL OF ST. NICHOLAS OF THE SEA. *Built between 1753 and 1761 by Savva Chevakinsky, a follower of Rastrelli. In many respects it resembles the Smolny Convent cathedral (see page 103), notably in its monumental composition, profusion of decorative detailing, and blue-and-white color scheme. It also incorporates features from traditional Orthodox churches, above all a central Greek-cross plan topped by five cupolas.*

THE CATHEDRAL
OF ST. NICHOLAS
OF THE SEA.
*Freestanding bell
tower. View from the
Catherine Canal.*

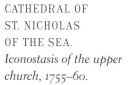

CATHEDRAL OF
ST. NICHOLAS
OF THE SEA.
*Iconostasis of the upper
church, 1755–60.*

CATHEDRAL OF
ST. NICHOLAS
OF THE SEA.
Interior view of the
upper church.

THE LION BRIDGE.
*Like the Bank Bridge,
it was intended for
pedestrians and was
built in 1825–26.*

the contrary, members of the old aristocracy, especially the Dolgorukov princes, who had strong ties with Moscow, helped the new sovereign rid himself of Menshikov. After coming to the old capital for the coronation of the new emperor, the court lobbied to remain there. The entertainments characteristic of Moscow court life, and much favored by previous tsars, were resumed, including falconry, wolf hunting, and bear stalking, all of which thrilled the young monarch. He fell ill during one of these expeditions, however, and shortly after returning to Moscow he died, before attaining his majority. The question of succession arose once again, and along with it that of the fate of the new capital.

Power fell into the hands of the High Privy Council, which was dominated by members of the old Muscovite aristocracy opposed to radical reforms. They were determined to prevent any direct descendant of Peter the Great—above all his daughter Elizabeth—from ascending the throne. As a result the crown fell to Anna Ivanovna, the daughter of Peter the Great's brother Ivan. She was compelled to sign a sort of constitution granting the old aristocracy unlimited influence. The Moscow faction seemed to have gained the upper hand. But the members of the High Privy Council had neglected to take into account the class of bureaucrats and government officials who had become imbued with the "St. Petersburg spirit." With their support Anna Ivanovna managed to crush those who had tried to impose limits on imperial power. If the system of government and the way of life established by the first emperor, Peter the Great, were to be reinstituted, it would be necessary to assemble a new group of advisers and establish a base of operations far from the advocates of the old system. Accordingly, Anna Ivanovna opted for a return to St. Petersburg, which was a symbol of both reform and orientation toward the West, and the new city once again became the capital of the Russian empire.

The circumstances confronting the new government were difficult. The economy had been ruined by precipitous innovations as well as by the enormous sums spent on reforming the army, creating the fleet, and constructing St. Petersburg. Peter the Great had married Anna to the Duke of Kurland, and after his death she had governed this small Baltic state. When she ascended the Russian throne, she brought with her from Kurland many Germans, including Ernst Johann Biron, her favorite. At that time Russian cultural ties to Germany were particularly strong: of the 288 Russian students in the country's only cadet corps, 51 studied French while 237 studied German; during Anna Ivanovna's reign, no advancement in rank was possible without a knowledge of German.

Russian empire were brought to St. Petersburg and dressed in their national costumes. They took part in the celebration and the procession escorting the couple to the Ice Palace, where they were to spend their wedding night. Legend has it that the union was a happy one, but that is difficult to believe. It is more certain that the festivities were organized by the master of the hunt, Artemi Volynsky, and that Empress Anna Ivanovna was greatly pleased. It would seem that such success should have advanced Volynsky's career and distanced other favorites from the throne. But the success of the Ice Palace incited such jealousy among the other courtiers that Volynsky was accused of conspiracy, and after being interrogated under torture, put to death. The architect Pyotr Eropkin, the true author of St. Petersburg's "second birth," perished along with him.

But we interrupted our account of the history of the city at the moment when, after the successive deaths of Peter the Great and his widow, Empress Catherine I, Peter II ascended the throne. In 1728 the court and all governmental agencies returned to Moscow. The new capital city, founded a mere quarter century earlier, was on the verge of death. Unlike his illustrious grandfather, Peter II did not surround himself with personalities such as Menshikov who were deeply committed to reform. On

THE CATHERINE
CANAL. *Winter.*

THE MARIINSKY
THEATER.
*Founded in 1783 and
devoted exclusively to
the musical arts since
1803, it has been rebuilt
several times. The cur-
rent building consists of
several remodelings of
the theater erected by
Kavos in 1859. These
refurbishment cam-
paigns, which in the
aggregate amounted to
a total reconstruction,
were overseen by
V. A. Schröter between
1883 and 1896. During
the Soviet era, the
Mariinsky was renamed
the Kirov Theater.*

Any attempt to characterize this period must begin with an assertion that the evolutionary process begun by Peter the Great continued without interruption. The German functionaries occupying the highest government posts succeeded in imposing order—not without brutality, yet with efficiency and logic—on the complex mosaic of reform initiatives that were Peter the Great's legacy. Rationalism and perfectionism were the watchwords of Russian government in the 1730s, and the same could be said of Russian architecture during this decade.

It was under Anna Ivanovna that Russian architects began to establish a presence along with the foreign masters who had held sway under Peter the Great. This was in large part due to Peter's decision in 1716 to send young people abroad to study the "various arts." Among them were eight who were instructed to study architecture; four were sent to Holland and four to Italy. These architects began to make their mark during Anna Ivanovna's reign. Of those who had studied in Antwerp, the best known is Ivan Korobov. He began as architect of the Admiralty and was placed in charge of all the naval constructions in the city. The main building of the Admiralty, featuring a tower and spire that became the major landmark on the city skyline, was his work. Its construction continued into the nineteenth century, when it was replaced by the building that stands today, the work of Adrian Zakharov, whose design retained the general massing and overall conception of the original structure.

Another architect whose reputation acquired luster in the 1730s was Mikhail Zemtsov, who, after studying with Domenico Tressini, had worked with Nicolò Michetti. Pyotr Eropkin, one of the young men sent to Rome, was more imbued with the Italian architectural tradition than was Zemtsov. He spent seven years in Italy, where he received rigorous training as an architect and engineer, and he produced the first Russian translation of Andrea Palladio's *Four Books of Architecture*. After returning to Russia his career advanced rapidly, and by the middle of 1737 he was already in charge of urbanism in St. Petersburg. It was at this moment that a special commission was formed to survey the existing layout of the city and draw up a new master plan. Eropkin's studio developed plans for each of the city's quarters; after being revised in collaboration with Zemtsov, Korobov, and Tressini the younger, these plans were submitted to the empress for her approval.

The results were extraordinarily successful. It was decided once and for all that the focal point of the city should be neither the Peter-Paul Fortress nor Vasilievsky Island but rather the Admiralty quarter. The most important development entailed by this decision was the famous crow's-foot configuration of streets leading to the building. Three main avenues—Nevsky, Gorokhovaya, and Voznesensky—were oriented such that the spire of the Admiralty served as their endpoint. The commission stipulated that "nothing would be allowed to impede the

LEFT
New Holland as depicted by the contemporary architect Fabritzky.

OPPOSITE
NEW HOLLAND ARCH.
Conceived by the Frenchman Jean-Baptiste Vallin de la Mothe in 1765, this magnificent entryway led to a lumberyard serving the shipyards that had been established by Savva Chevakinsky on a triangular island accessible by canal.

TOP
VORONTSOV PALACE.
Lithograph by
H. Avnatomov after a
drawing by Joseph
Charlemagne, 1858.

BOTTOM
STROGANOV PALACE
AND THE POLICE
BRIDGE.
Lithograph by
Jacottet after a
drawing by Joseph
Charlemagne, 1855.

STROGANOV PALACE.
*Façade on the Moika.
As the urban fabric
grew denser it became
necessary to build
palaces without gardens
and flush with the
street. Between 1751
and 1754 Rastrelli built
such a "block palace"
for Count Stroganov.
It features a rusticated
ground floor and
particularly elegant
window treatments.
Their alternating
rectangular and
circular forms combine
with the monumental
pilasters to create a
compelling rhythm
across the façade.*

view of the Admiralty spire." Even today this effect is one of the most striking features of St. Petersburg's urban landscape. Special care was taken with the disposition of the embankments. The most opulent residences with gardens continued to rise along them, notably in the Admiralty quarter along the Palace Embankment of the Neva and along the banks of the Moika and the Fontanka. A network of streets was developed to link the main avenues of the Admiralty quarter. The Eropkin plan called for the development of a large residential neighborhood in this part of the city. Known as Kolomna, it still retains the basic street configuration laid out by the commission. Vasilievsky Island was left as it had been envisioned by Tressini, but new plans were drawn up for all the other quarters of the city.

These plans were unusually skillful in the way they integrated the city's principal buildings into an urban conception of remarkable clarity and equilibrium, without ever losing touch with reality. Eropkin incorporated existing structures and streets into his scheme with great ingenuity, managing as well to showcase the picturesque quality of the rivers and canals. Today, in the late twentieth century, the influence of this exceptional master can still be felt in most parts of the city. Under Eropkin's direction St. Petersburg became one of the masterpieces of baroque urbanism. Especially notable in this regard are his preferences for distant perspectives, grandiose geometric constructions, and diverse juxtapositions of regular elements, which, like decorative motifs, are integrated into a harmonious whole. It was in this period—during the reign of Anna Ivanovna, and thanks to the efforts of Eropkin—that the unique beauty of St. Petersburg was born, a beauty that continued to blossom in subsequent years, during the reign of Elizabeth Petrovna.

ELIZABETH PETROVNA, OR THE BLOSSOMING OF THE RASTRELLI BAROQUE. Anna Ivanovna died childless in October 1740. But she had taken care to designate a successor: Ivan VI, the son of her niece Anna Leopoldovna. He was four

STROGANOV PALACE.
The Mineralogy Room.

STROGANOV PALACE.
*Arabesque Room
(detail). The interior
decor of this palace was
completely refurbished
by Andrei Voronikhin
between 1790 and
1800, after his return
from Paris.*

years old at the time of her death, but she had also designated a regent: Ernst Biron, who had been her faithful lover for many years. Biron was rapidly overthrown by Anna Leopoldovna, who declared herself regent and her husband, Prince Brunswick, commander in chief. But their rule did not last long. On the night of November 24, 1741, a large woman wearing a cuirass and accompanied by guards entered the queen regent's bedroom, proclaiming "Up, little sister!" and ordered her arrest. She was none other than Elizabeth, the daughter of Peter the Great. Crowned Empress Elizabeth I, she was to reign for twenty years, until 1761. As for the unfortunate child-emperor Ivan VI, he was detained in the fortress and eventually killed by the guards during an escape attempt.

The era of Elizabeth Petrovna was a happy one for Russia. During her reign the reforms began to bear fruit, the Russian army was successful in battle, and the empire gained a solid footing in European politics. Ties with the German states grew stronger, and an alliance was successfully negotiated with France and the Holy Roman Empire against Frederick the Great of Prussia. Within Russia's borders transformations continued at a moderate pace. Overall, it is fair to say that life became more civilized. The cruelty of the reign of Anna Ivanovna gradually disappeared under Elizabeth's influence. She adored masquerades, was extremely pious, and loved liturgical chanting. She remained faithful her entire life to a single favorite, Aleksei Razumovsky, whom she named a count. A handsome Ukrainian, he was blessed with a fine voice and a calm disposition. Capital punishment was all but discontinued, and life in St. Petersburg became calmer and more luxurious. In the matter of art and architecture, her reign saw the further blossoming of the baroque.

In his unsurpassed survey, Igor Grabar wrote of the architecture of this period: "Under Peter the Great Petersburg was a kind of city of architectural experiment. Artists of every stripe flocked there: great ones, middling ones, and quite a few nonentities. To be sure, each of them transformed what had been done before . . . but most of them either died relatively quickly or left Petersburg forever. Is it possible to develop an authoritative style of any kind under such conditions? Petersburg had received little more than the debris of the Italian baroque; German baroque forms had made a stronger impact, but a strong hand was still lacking . . . an artist of giant stature who could shoulder all the problems and who had the ability to leave his mark on the Petersburg of his day. Such a man in fact appeared . . . and it was only then that the city acquired its idiosyncratic baroque character. That man was Rastrelli."[3]

The architect Bartolomeo Francesco Rastrelli was the son of an Italian sculptor who was invited to Russia in 1716 from Paris, where he had enjoyed a certain success. With the help of the papal nuncio he had managed to acquire the title of pontifical count. The future architect grew up in Paris and subsequently accompanied his father to St. Petersburg. From there, thanks to a stipend provided by the tsar, he was sent to study abroad, probably in Germany. Soon after his return to Russia he began to execute important commissions for the court: first in Moscow, where he built out of wood the enormous Annenhof Imperial Palace; then in the Baltic states, where he erected the magnificent palace of the Dukes of Kurland in Jelgava, or Mitau (still standing); and finally in St. Petersburg, where Anna Ivanovna appointed him chief architect. Beginning in 1741 he was the favorite architect of Empress Elizabeth Petrovna, and he was responsible for all major projects undertaken in the capital and its environs until her death.

Rastrelli's buildings perfectly express the buoyant mood of Russian culture in the mid-eighteenth century. They are characterized by a picturesque opulence suffused with optimism, an idiosyncratic solemnity, a certain majesty, and a taste for monumentality. In Russia the baroque assumed forms at odds with intense mysticism and tortured virtuosity, and Rastrelli's art is marked by élan, unforced fantasy, organic conception, and strength. His works are notable above all for the richness and profusion of their decorative detailing and their brilliant use of color. Boris Vipper, a celebrated historian of Russian art, wrote an especially successful description of Rastrelli's approach to interior decoration: "His interiors, sumptuous and crackling with life, are full of movement, sparkle, and vibration. The reflections in their many mirrors, the carved and gilded moldings, the ceiling paintings and arabesque parquet floors, the cartouches and shells, the delicious rosettes and airborne cupids: everything glitters and shimmers, creating a dazzling frame for the crowd of elaborately dressed courtiers."[4]

Rastrelli had an astonishing gift for expressing the artistic originality of the milieu in which he found himself. This Italian, who had spent his youth in Paris, was sensitive to the particularities of Russian taste. Having worked in both Moscow and Kiev, he was familiar with the monuments of old Russian architecture and capable of absorbing the lessons they had to teach, especially with regard to ornament, massing, and the use of color. It was in his work that the new Russian architecture found its true voice.

The general development of culture in St. Petersburg under Elizabeth Petrovna's reign proved favorable to Rastrelli's success. Prints executed by Mikhail Makhaev in 1753 depict a vast metropolis of extraordinary beauty opening onto distant landscapes, a city full of water, greenery, and palaces adorned with gilded sculpture. Yachts and smaller craft, both sail- and oar-driven, circulate on its rivers and canals past the façades and the openwork galleries that served as landing piers.

The St. Petersburg of this period was characterized by perfection, consistent detailing, and the prevalence of baroque architecture. Very possibly the city appeared more prosperous, more regular, and more European in Makhaev's prints than it was in reality. Neither the small artisan dwellings nor the many remaining empty tracts and marshes attracted contemporary artists, and the same could be said of "military" St. Petersburg and the dreary barracks complexes beyond the Fontanka River. What is important to note here, however, is the city's

PALACE SQUARE. Aerial view. To the right, the Winter Palace, known as the Hermitage Museum. To the left, General Staff Headquarters.

THE WINTER PALACE.
Façade facing the Admiralty. In the foreground, a corner of the Admiralty.

considerable extent, its expansion and increasing grandeur, the result of a half-century of rapid development, as well as the luxury of its extraordinary "fabric" of baroque decorative elements. Within this fabric, Rastrelli's colossal constructions—the Winter Palace; the Vorontsov, Shuvalov, Bestuzhev-Ryumin, and Stroganov palaces; and the Smolny Convent—figured very much like flowers or enormous jewels, and they were complemented by the work of his contemporary and competitor, the Russian Savva Chevakinsky, who was every bit as gifted as he, as is demonstrated by the famous Cathedral of St. Nicholas of the Sea.

SMOLNY CONVENT. The Smolny convent is perhaps the most impressive of all St. Petersburg baroque buildings still standing today. Empress Elizabeth Petrovna loved the pomp and ritual of religious services, and she would often sing the hymns and recite the prayers along with the choir. On stipulated weeks and days the empress and her court fasted scrupulously; only her favorite Razumovsky was granted permission to eat fish. The chancellor of the empire, Count Bestuzhev-Ryumin, was obliged to petition His Grace the Orthodox Patriarch of Constantinople to obtain authorization to moderate his fasting and not eat mushrooms, which were the empress's sole nourishment during the great weeks of fasting. Her religious sentiments were not a matter of posturing: she rigorously observed the obligations of her faith, and she often dreamed that in her old age she would abdicate and enter a convent, becoming its prioress. For this reason Rastrelli built a convent complex on the site of some old warehouses erected during the reign of Peter the Great to store tar for the fleet.

The people began to refer to the complex as the Smolny, or "Tar," convent, and the appellation stuck, even though its official name was the Convent of the New Maidens and the Resurrection. This double dedication was meant to pay homage to two famous convents of old Russia that Elizabeth liked to visit: that of the Resurrection, near Moscow, usually called the New Jerusalem, and the Novodevichi, or New Maidens, Convent in Moscow. These names also evoke the emergent "Petersburg mythology" of the baroque period. The theme of the New Jerusalem was linked with the idea of

THE WINTER PALACE. LEFT *West façade in 1840, watercolor by Vasily Sadovnikov.* OPPOSITE *Façade facing the Neva. This, the fourth palace to bear the name, was designed by Rastrelli for Empress Elizabeth Petrovna and was built between 1754 and 1762. The profusion and variety of its decorative detailing, especially in the window treatments, make it one of the most celebrated examples of St. Petersburg baroque architecture. The palace boasts more than two thousand of these elaborate windows, which are unified by a steady progression of monumental Corinthian columns across the façade.*

the rebirth of the Orthodox faith and the uniqueness of its truth among Christian teachings. The Novodevichi Convent had ties to Muscovite tradition: the women in the tsar's family entered this convent at the end of their lives, in accordance with established tsarist rituals. And, as already discussed, the name Smolny harked back to the period of Peter the Great. All these connections influenced the architecture of the new complex.

Rastrelli completed his design in 1744, and the cornerstone was laid four years later. Except for its interior decors, the cathedral was basically complete in 1764, as were the other buildings. The last structures to be added were completed by the architect Vasily Stasov in 1832. The convent was situated in a quarter far from the city center, nestled in a bend of the Neva. Its placement at the entry to the city by a water route, its richness, and its solemnity all conspired to make it function as an emblem of the capital. The ensemble's configuration is rigorously centered. Around the five-domed cathedral, which has a Greek-cross plan inscribed within a square, is an enormous courtyard, also in the shape of a cross, bordered by the convent proper. Four small chapels, each with its own cupola, punctuate the corners, and a turreted stone wall encloses the whole. In front of the main façade, facing the city, an oblong square was laid out along a central axis, which is accentuated by the service buildings that flank the entrance to the square. The regularity of the ensemble is altogether characteristic of St. Petersburg baroque architecture. The skillful accumulation of masses along the diagonals leading to the five-domed cathedral is especially spectacular, achieving a rare blend of monumentality and dynamism. It is this last quality, in fact, that most distinguishes Rastrelli's baroque idiom from the Italian version, making his work closer in spirit to the Austrian and Bavarian baroque.

The references in Rastrelli's buildings to the architecture of old Russia are of exceptional interest to the art historian. Empress Elizabeth Petrovna had instructed him to seek inspiration in traditional Russian Orthodox churches, drawing his attention to two buildings in particular: the Cathedral of the Assumption in the Kremlin, in Moscow, and the Bell Tower of Ivan the Great immediately beside it. In his model for the freestanding Smolny bell tower, the upper part is an almost exact replica of the belfry in Moscow. His design for the cathedral incorporated many features characteristic of Russian churches, notably the Greek-cross plan and the use of

THE WINTER PALACE.
LEFT *The Ambassador's Staircase, also known as the Jordan Staircase because the reigning sovereign descended it each year on Epiphany on his way to bless the waters of the Neva in ritual observance of Christ's baptism. Initially built to designs by Rastrelli, it has since been reconstructed, but in a way that retained its Rastrellian character.*

BELOW *The Little Throne Room, or Peter's Memorial Hall. Decorated by Auguste Ricard de Montferrand in homage to Peter the Great in 1833, it was faithfully reconstructed after the fire of 1837. Above the throne, the work of English goldsmith Nicholas Clausen, is a portrait of Peter the Great accompanied by Minerva, executed after the tsar's death by the Italian G. Amiconi.*

five cupolas, with the central one much larger than the others, as in the Novodevichi Convent in Moscow. Finally, Rastrelli used the vivid, high-contrast approach to color—white details against a colored background—typical of Muscovite churches of the late Middle Ages, but in this case the walls were painted not red but turquoise blue, the empress's favorite color.

In the nineteenth and early twentieth centuries the Smolny Convent was widely regarded as the most perfect creation of the baroque master. When Giacomo Quarenghi, one of Catherine II's finest architects, passed by the complex, he tipped his hat and proclaimed, "Now that's what I call a church!" The only structure to challenge its status in St. Petersburg is the Cathedral of St. Nicholas of the Sea.

CATHEDRAL OF ST. NICHOLAS OF THE SEA. The cathedral was begun in 1753, when the baroque was in full flower, and was completed in 1761, at a moment when the style suddenly fell out of favor in the capital. It was designed by one of the most gifted Russian masters of the mid-eighteenth century, Savva Chevakinsky. He studied at the St. Petersburg Naval Academy as well as with Korobov, the architect of the Admiralty. When Korobov died, Chevakinsky succeeded him in his post, thus assuming responsibility for building the Cathedral of St. Nicholas, which was commissioned by the Navy. Ever since then this building has popularly been known as the Cathedral of St. Nicholas of the Sea.

In many respects this church resembles the Smolny Convent cathedral. Its composition, too, is monumental and overloaded, and it features an equal abundance of decorative detailing and a vivid color scheme. It is also characterized by references to traditional Russian Orthodox churches, most notably a Greek-cross plan and five cupolas. It is distinguished from Rastrelli's church by its quieter massing and the somewhat ponderous majesty of its volumes, but these differences do not deprive it of charm. Its façades have a secular character, resembling those of a palace. The arrangement of the approach to it lacks the sophisticated spatial organization and elegant dynamism of the Smolny complex, but by way of compensation it has more natural light and a greater feeling of intimacy.

All this becomes evident inside the cathedral, which houses two churches, an upper one and a lower one. The space on the ground floor seems somber and compact, but when one arrives in the upper church via

THE LITTLE
HERMITAGE.
*Roof garden onto
which the Pavilion
Hall opens.*

71

THE LITTLE HERMITAGE. RIGHT *The Pavilion Hall. It was built by A. Stakenschneider between 1850 and 1858 to replace rooms in which Catherine II had displayed the finest works of art in her collection. The architect modeled the decor after the description of an Oriental salon in Alexander Pushkin's poem "The Fountain of Bakhchisarai."* OPPOSITE *The Pavilion Hall, detail of the semi-dome.*

THE HERMITAGE
THEATER.
*Built between 1783
and 1787 by Giacomo
Quarenghi on the site
of the old Winter Palace
of Peter the Great, the
theater was designed
after the antique model
of the amphitheater,
with its rising semi-
circle of benches for
the audience. The
decor was inspired by
Palladio's Teatro
Olimpico in Vicenza.*

OPPOSITE
THE NEW HERMITAGE.
Grand Staircase.

one of the long lateral staircases, one is surrounded by volumes flooded with light originating from the cupolas and intensified by the sparkling gold decor. The iconostasis, which dates from the mid-eighteenth century and was executed by Russian sculptors after Chevakinsky's designs, is exceptionally well preserved. Although the delicate proportions of the gilded Corinthian colonnade are neoclassical, the opulent garlands are still baroque in feeling. Many of the icons were painted in the mid-eighteenth century by the Kolokolnikov brothers.

In front of the cathedral's western façade the architect placed a slender three-story belfry culminating in a gilded spire.

ST. PETERSBURG PALACES IN THE BAROQUE ERA. While Moscow was celebrated in the mid-eighteenth century for its "forty times forty" churches (making a total of 1,600), baroque St. Petersburg was renowned as the "city of palaces." New ones rose each year of Empress Elizabeth Petrovna's reign.

Between 1746 and 1757 Rastrelli built a palace on the bank of the Fontanka for the chancellor of the Russian empire, Count Mikhail Vorontsov. This building was something of a breakthrough in private baroque architecture in Russia. Its façades are not so much decorated planes as sculpted surfaces, for here the master began to make extensive use of carved moldings. The contrast between the smooth, austere walls and the opulent projecting frontispiece is especially striking. Rastrelli established lively rhythms by alternating columns and pilasters, and the façade was also notable for its rich play of light and shadow. A garden was laid out between the façade and the river.

Between 1751 and 1754 Rastrelli built the palace of Baron Sergei Stroganov, the black sheep of one of Russia's richest families. (Starting during the reign of Ivan the Terrible the Stroganovs owned most of the country's salt mines.) Rastrelli seized the occasion to introduce even greater sculptural solemnity into his architecture. As the urban fabric in the capital grew denser, it became necessary to build palaces flush with the street and without gardens. Accordingly, Rastrelli devised a block-palace surrounding a square courtyard and featuring a rusticated ground floor, richly rhythmed façades, unusually refined window treatments, a sophisticated interplay between straight and circular lines, and powerful columns articulating the frontispieces. The interiors were

realized by the classicizing architect Andrei Voronikhin in the 1780s.

Rastrelli was not the only architect producing important work in this period. The large residence of the Sheremetev family, which still stands, was erected on the banks of the Fontanka on the site of a villa that had belonged to one of Peter the Great's greatest Russian generals, Field Marshal Boris Sheremetev. The design was primarily the work of Chevakinsky, but the famous serf architect of the Sheremetevs, Fedor Argunov, also contributed to it. Between 1753 and 1755 the same Chevakinsky built a palace at the corner of Malaya Sadovaya for Elizabeth Petrovna's favorite Count Ivan Shuvalov, and its austere design signaled the transition from the baroque to the neoclassical age. It was remodeled between 1816 and 1819, and again between 1846 and 1852, but its basic eighteenth-century configuration remains intact. Members of the aristocracy were not the only ones to build palaces. The Stegelman house, built for a wealthy merchant on the banks of the Moika between 1750 and 1753 after a design by Rastrelli, still exists. And then there is the Grabbe residence on Gorokhovaya Street, which gives some idea

of what an ordinary mid-eighteenth-century house in St. Petersburg was like. The monumentality of these buildings, as well as their solemn elegance and picturesque detailing, contribute to the city's festive, celebratory air.

WINTER PALACE. Of all the palaces of this period, the most significant was unquestionably the principal residence of the empress in St. Petersburg, the Winter Palace. We have already mentioned the two earlier Winter Palaces from the era of Peter the Great, neither of which survives.

Between 1732 and 1735 Rastrelli built a Winter Palace for Empress Anna Ivanovna on the Palace Embankment. It was completely renovated under his direction between 1754 and 1762, and the result was the fourth Winter Palace, the one that stands today. It was begun under Elizabeth Petrovna and completed shortly after her death. The monumental forms of this block-palace are typical of Russian baroque architecture.

A courtyard was placed in the center and four structures linked by passages were erected around its periphery. The ground floor serves as a base for the two upper floors, which are united by a colossal Corinthian order. The changing rhythm of the columns, the variety of the decorative detailing, the richness of the sculpture and vases surmounting the cornice, the varied window treatments incorporating angel and lion heads, and the capricious little pediments, some of which have broken and/or semicircular gables, combine to create a unique decorative scheme. It must be admitted that the result of all this ornamental abundance—heightened still further by the use of white columns, turquoise walls, and gilded details —borders on the garish.

Three of the façades of this grandiose palace face onto the Neva, Palace Square, and the Admiralty, respectively. The fourth façade is contiguous to the buildings of the Hermitage. The palace is so immense that the full extent of its grandeur can be grasped only across the Neva, from the Peter-Paul Fortress and from Vasilievsky Island. It clearly dominates Palace Square. Its architecture is most attractive when viewed from nearby, for then the façades take on movement, and the relief of the columns, cornices, sculptures, and frontispieces is most apparent.

The Winter Palace was Rastrelli's last building, and most of its interiors date from after 1762. Catherine II's finest architects—Georg Velten, Jean-Baptiste Vallin de la Mothe, and Antonio Rinaldi—worked there in the 1760s and 1770s. In the 1780s and 1790s Giacomo Quarenghi designed the "Neva enfilade," including the

LEFT
THE NEW HERMITAGE.
Designed by Leo von Klenze, the architect of the Neue Pinakothek in Munich, to house the royal collections after the fire of 1837, it was inaugurated in 1852. Its construction was overseen by Vasily Stasov and Nikolai Efimov. The public entrance is accessed by a monumental portico supported by six granite atlantes carved by Alexander Terebenev.

OPPOSITE
THE HERMITAGE.
The Winter Canal. Bordered by the New Hermitage (left) and the theater (right), it was dug in 1718 to link the Neva to the Moika. It is spanned by a bridge designed by Georg Velten, built in 1770 as part of a campaign to recast the banks of the Neva. In 1787 it was enlarged by the addition of a gallery linking the palace to the theater.

PALACE SQUARE. *View of the General Staff Arch. Built by Carlo Rossi between 1819 and 1828, the "square" is in fact an enormous semicircular open area facing the Winter Palace. The monumental triumphal arch is decorated in the Roman manner with military trophies and victories bearing laurel crowns, and is surmounted by a large group featuring a chariot pulled by six horses and bearing a winged figure of Glory.*

Great Throne Room, which came to be known as the Hall of St. George. In the nineteenth century Carlo Rossi built the War Gallery, while Alexander Bryulov oversaw decoration of the Alexander Room. Auguste Ricard de Montferrand decorated the Hall of the Field Marshals, the Little Throne Room, or Peter's Memorial Hall, and the Hall of the Coats of Arms. After the disastrous fire of 1837 the palace was rebuilt under the direction of Vasily Stasov and Bryulov. The library of Nicholas II (designed by A. Krasovsky), the Gold Salon (designed by Vladimir Schreiber), and the Red Bedroom (designed by Harald Bossay) date from the end of the nineteenth century and the beginning of the twentieth. These decors were executed in a style discussed below.

If one considers all of the buildings erected in St. Petersburg in the mid-eighteenth century, it becomes clear that a new style was being born at the very moment when the most flamboyant baroque idiom was in full flower. The baroque structures of the 1760s are not marked by decline or lassitude. On the contrary, Rastrelli was completing his principal works just as the rococo made a brief appearance and Russian classicism began to assert itself.

OPPOSITE
GENERAL STAFF
ARCH.
Aligned with the main entrance to the Winter Palace, the arch was designed to link the square to a small curved street that leads to Nevsky Prospekt. The architect widened the arc of the segment negotiating the actual bend in the street so as not to interfere with the impression created from the square that all the openings are parallel to the façade facing the square.

LEFT
PALACE SQUARE
WITH THE
ALEXANDER COLUMN.
Erected by Auguste Ricard de Montferrand between 1829 and 1834, lithograph by Jacottet after a drawing by Joseph Charlemagne.

3

CATHERINE II

THE CITY OF ENLIGHTENMENT

As your Imperial Majesty maintains that Moscow cannot become the seat of the court until a hundred years have passed, in the meantime would it not be possible to increase the population of Petersburg, to make it more lively, more vigorous, and more commercial by connecting its multitude of isolated palaces with private houses?

—Denis Diderot
Memoirs for Catherine II, 1773

OPPOSITE
SEMENOV BRIDGE
OVER THE FONTANKA.
At the end of the eighteenth century, public squares were laid out at either end of the bridge along Gorokhovaya Street. In the first third of the nineteenth century buildings in a classical style were constructed on the lots along the embankments, some of them after identical designs.

FROM THE BAROQUE TO CLASSICISM. Empress Elizabeth Petrovna died on Christmas day, 1761, and the era of baroque architecture in St. Petersburg died with her. Such close ties between the destiny of a monarch and artistic developments were characteristic of eighteenth-century Russia. To a certain extent they can be attributed to the rapidity and abruptness of the changes the country was then undergoing. Russia's campaign to strengthen its ties to Europe was moving forward, but not smoothly. It proceeded without harmony, by fits and starts, according to rhythms established by radical political reforms, plots, and would-be revolutions.

The heir to the throne was Elizabeth's nephew, who was crowned Peter III. He was a sickly creature of limited intelligence and eccentric temperament. What little we know about his artistic taste, above all as reflected in the country palace at Oranienbaum, suggests that he was partial to the rococo, but his personal habits were anything but refined.

In his notes, Prince Shcherbatov recounts the most famous anecdote about Peter III's reign. One day he wanted to retreat with a lady of the court. He told his official favorite that he would be working all night with his secretary on important new legislation. The secretary was locked in a room, given a Great Dane as a companion, and ordered to draft some sort of ukase. The result was the decree declaring the "liberty of the nobility," which abolished the obligation of nobles to serve the state. The following morning Peter III signed it, an act that completely transformed the status of the nobility, its way of life, and consequently the appearance of St. Petersburg.

Peter III was not always so easily manipulated by his courtiers. His crudity, the extravagance of his political maneuvers, which often did damage to Russia's foreign interests, and above all his contempt for religion and for Russian traditions prompted the formation of a coalition determined to overthrow him. As their standard-bearer, the conspirators settled upon his wife, whom his late aunt had summoned from Germany: Princess Anhalt-Zerbst, known in Russia as Catherine II or Catherine the Great. Her sharp intelligence and spirited personality won her many admirers, and her consummate political skills were largely responsible for the success of the plot to place her on the throne and her husband in his grave. Such maneuvers were contingent upon obtaining the support of the palace guards, and Catherine proved adept at this. Her long reign, which lasted from 1762 to 1796, ushered in a new era for Russia, one of the most triumphant in its history. There were many military victories. The Turks were driven from the northern shore of the Black Sea, and much of Ukraine, Belarus, and Lithuania were annexed by the empire under the terms of the partition of Poland jointly concluded by Austria, Prussia, and Russia. The domestic reforms initiated under her rule in the fields of legislation, administrative reorganization, commercial and urban development,

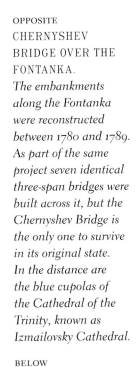

OPPOSITE
CHERNYSHEV
BRIDGE OVER THE
FONTANKA.
*The embankments
along the Fontanka
were reconstructed
between 1780 and 1789.
As part of the same
project seven identical
three-span bridges were
built across it, but the
Chernyshev Bridge is
the only one to survive
in its original state.
In the distance are
the blue cupolas of
the Cathedral of the
Trinity, known as
Izmailovsky Cathedral.*

BELOW
THE FONTANKA.
*Anonymous nineteenth-
century painting.*

TOP
THE MOIKA.
In the background is a glimpse of Nevsky Prospekt and the Stroganov Palace.

BOTTOM
View of the Catherine Canal with the Bank Bridge in the far distance.

agriculture, and the church were even more successful. All these measures were introduced only after careful study; they were often inspired by the latest European ideas, and in implementing them Catherine was some-times in advance of the countries in which they had first been formulated, such as France and Germany.

It was Catherine's ambition to transform Russia into an ideal nation of the Enlightenment. This grand enter-prise was to encompass both politics and the fine arts, for in the second half of the eighteenth century government artistic patronage was seen as an essential complement to political and economic reform. When it came to artistic matters, Catherine's advisers were of an exceptionally high caliber. Among them was Denis Diderot, with whom she corresponded. Indeed, having heard that he was in fi-nancial difficulties, Catherine generously purchased his library on the express condition that he retain use of it until his death. When visiting St. Petersburg in May 1773, Diderot told her: "The court lays down the law for the city, the city lays down the law for the provinces. The city, if it is to serve as lawgiver, must be quite populous and quite distinguishable from provincial towns. This prox-imity of people establishes connections among them, connections that soften and civilize them; it is from such workshops as these that all the fine arts will emerge as in-digenous and durable."[1] Ideas like these played an impor-tant role in shaping St. Petersburg's evolution in the second half of the eighteenth century.

Shortly after ascending the throne Catherine II established a "commission to oversee stone construction in St. Petersburg and Moscow," but it quickly assumed responsibility for all the cities in Russia. One of the com-mission's first acts was to impose Vitruvian notions of architectural harmony on the entire city. To cite one of its official pronouncements: "Three rules must be hon-ored in the construction of houses: solidity, utility, and beauty. The qualities of a city as a whole will correspond to those of its individual residences." For this reason it was stipulated that "streets [be] wide and straight. . . . The façades of all houses on a given street . . . must align with one another."[2] Rephrasing the words of Diderot, which Catherine had quoted to them, the members of the committee declared that "the capacities of society will increase as the city grows denser and its inhabitants become closer to one another."[3] In other words, a deci-sion was taken to transform the vast spaces typical of the Russian baroque city into urban landscapes that were more compact and architecturally unified.

Andrei Kvasov, one of Catherine's urbanists, wrote of the necessity "to make the city more regular" and called for the drafting of a master plan that would remain in force "forever." It was believed at the time that a plan

capable of determining the city's future "forever" could indeed be devised, if only reason played a sufficient role in its development. It could almost be said that Russian urban planning in this period was imagined along lines consistent with the classical theater: Enlightenment Russia attempted to build cities gathered into a single entity (unity of place), in accordance with precise struc-tural indications (unity of action), as a result of which they would remain for eternity (unity of time). This ideal was operative in the planning of St. Petersburg.

It was decided to establish boundaries that would prevent the city from growing too large. Laid down with great precision, they coincided with the Fontanka to the south, while to the north they encompassed the Peter-Paul Fortress, the adjacent neighborhoods, and the east-ern half of Vasilievsky Island. All areas not contained within these boundaries were designated as suburbs. Two solutions were considered: either the city plan would be completely recast or the extant buildings would be re-tained and the areas between them built up around newly laid-out squares. It was the second option that won out, largely because it was the less expensive of the two. As a result, the basic configuration of Peter the Great's city survived and was incorporated into the urban fabric.

The city center was still defined as the area on the left bank of the Neva around the Admiralty and the three ave-nues radiating from it. Many new squares were envisioned,

THE BRIDGE OF THE IMPERIAL STABLES.
View of the Moika.

CHESME CHURCH.
*Built by Georg Velten
between 1777 and 1780
adjacent to the nearby
palace (begun in 1770),
it was intended to
celebrate Aleksei
Orlov's victory over the
Turks in the Bay of
Chesme in 1770. It is
one of the earliest
examples of neo-Gothic
architecture in Russia.*

ACADEMY OF
FINE ARTS.
*Façade on the Neva.
Begun in 1764, it was
designed by Jean-
Baptiste Vallin de la
Mothe; his project was
an expanded reworking
of an earlier design by
Jacques-François
Blondel and originally
intended for Moscow.*

ACADEMY OF
FINE ARTS.
*Façade on the Neva.
Begun in 1764, it was
designed by Jean-
Baptiste Vallin de la
Mothe; his project was
an expanded reworking
of an earlier design by
Jacques-François
Blondel and originally
intended for Moscow.*

however, notably where principal streets crossed the Fontanka. In the 1770s and 1780s the Neva embankments were rebuilt to designs by Georg Velten. This project was the point of departure for the subsequent reconstruction in granite of the embankments along the Fontanka and Moika rivers as well as the canals, an undertaking that considerably altered the city's appearance. What had previously been little more than overgrown, marshy shorelines punctuated by landing piers were transformed into powerful stone monoliths whose assertive and solemn horizontals created the foundation for the development of St. Petersburg's major architectural ensembles. Their crisply revetted surfaces effectively established the antique ideal on the banks of the Neva.

At the beginning of the new reign Bartolomeo Rastrelli was still alive. His students were quite active, and the resulting baroque residences were so overloaded with sculpture and decoration that, in the words of the empress, they resembled "cuffs of Alençon lace." But architects with quite different tastes were already making their mark. Antonio Rinaldi, a student of the Neapolitan master Luigi Vanvitelli, had been recruited in Italy as early as 1752. He worked in Ukraine before becoming the personal architect of Peter III and then of Catherine, building sumptuous structures on their country estates—Oranienbaum, Gatchina, Tsarskoe Selo—beginning in the early 1760s. He did not begin to work in the capital until somewhat later, because French architectural taste still held sway there owing to the activity of another master from abroad, Jean-Baptiste-Michel Vallin de la Mothe.

VALLIN DE LA MOTHE AND THE BIRTH OF CLASSICISM IN ST. PETERSBURG. In 1759 Vallin de la Mothe was invited to teach architecture at the St. Petersburg Academy of Fine Arts, which had been established two years earlier at the instigation of Count Ivan Shuvalov. Shuvalov had commissioned Jacques-François Blondel to design the academy building for Moscow, and when it was decided in 1757 to shift the site to St. Petersburg, an effort was made to adapt the Parisian's design to fit the new circumstances. Nothing was done, however, until Catherine's accession, and then the matter took a new turn. The enlightened empress, sensing an opportunity to signal the depth of her commitment to the sciences and the arts, made known her desire to house the Academy of Fine Arts in a grandiose structure. Blondel's design, however, was on a relatively small scale. It was at this point that Vallin de la Mothe became the man of the hour; not only had he just arrived in Russia, but he was a student of Blondel. In collaboration with the Russian architect Alexander Kokorinov, he was engaged to design an enormous edifice on the Vasilievsky Island embankment of the Neva using the architectural vocabulary of his former master. The result was intended to serve as an example of classical architecture for the academy students.

Construction began in 1764, and the structure was completed in 1788. In plan it is a large rectangle 460 feet (140 meters) long and 410 feet (125 meters) deep, with a round courtyard in the center and four smaller rectangular courts in the corners. In addition to a series of exhibition

galleries, it contains drawing and painting studios, a chapel, and amphitheaters. Originally, the space now occupied by the vestibule was filled by a passage leading to the round central court. There are significant differences between the realized building and Blondel's design. Vallin de la Mothe and Kokorinov used a more contemporary classical idiom marked by greater geometric rigor and simplicity of massing, qualities that are especially apparent in the plan. Overall, their design is more severe in feeling, a shift reflected in the use of the Doric order instead of the Corinthian one originally proposed by Blondel. Finally, the realization itself is more sober than either of the designs. The columns on the lateral frontispieces and the central portico were retained, but pilasters were used across the rest of the façade. The academy's construction was overseen by Kokorinov and completed after his death by Velten. Many of the interiors were remodeled in the nineteenth century.

The complex known as New Holland, built by Vallin de la Mothe in the Admiralty quarter, is no less spectacular. It was an immense repository of lumber for use in shipbuilding. The site had been designated as early as the 1730s for reasons of convenience (the wood could be transported by water). In 1763–65 Savva Chevakinsky devised a new plan that was implemented, although the

ACADEMY OF FINE ARTS.
LEFT *Dome of the vestibule; paintings by Shchebuev.*
BELOW *Decor of a staircase in one of the lateral structures.*

ACADEMY OF
FINE ARTS.
*Vestibule and
main staircase.*

THE MARBLE PALACE.
*Façade on the Neva.
Begun by Antonio
Rinaldi in 1768 for
Grigori Orlov, one of
Catherine II's favorites,
it was completed in
1785, after the death
of the patron. The
austere granite facing
of the sub-basement
and the ground floor
are in marked contrast
with the refined
marble treatment of
the upper stories.*

façades were designed by Vallin de la Mothe. The design consisted of long buildings with rounded corners articulated by powerful coupled columns, and a triumphal arch spanning the canal that enters the complex. The sobriety and audacity of its volumes prefigures the extravagance of Claude-Nicolas Ledoux's city gates in Paris.

Other important structures by Vallin de la Mothe can be found on Nevsky Prospekt, including Gostiny Dvor, erected between 1759 and 1785, and the Catholic church of St. Catherine, built in 1763. Between 1764 and 1775 he built, beside the Winter Palace, the Little Hermitage, with its large Ionic colonnade and its high sub-basement.

Another great classicist was Georg Velten, the son of one of Peter the Great's head cooks. Born in St. Petersburg, he studied in Germany, in both Stuttgart and Berlin. After returning to Russia he worked with Rastrelli, but his first independent projects were in an early classical idiom stripped of baroque features. His works of the 1770s include the Large Hermitage, built beside Vallin de la Mothe's Little Hermitage; the Alexander Institute, which housed a school next to the Smolny Convent; two Lutheran churches of St. Catherine on Vasilievsky Island; and St. Anne's, an Armenian church on Nevsky Prospekt. All of them display Velten's idiosyncratic use of the classical vocabulary, which was touched by genius. The same could be said of his design for the Summer Garden fence, built in 1783–84.

One of Velten's most curious constructions was originally situated outside the city but now falls within its limits: the Chesme Palace, the first neo-Gothic building in

Russia. Its design dates from 1770. Ten years later Velten designed and built a church beside it. Despite the classical plan and restrained composition of the palace, it is undoubtedly one of the first indigenous manifestations of the taste for things medieval that reached St. Petersburg via England. Not only was it designed to resemble a toy castle, but a fictional genealogy was invented to go along with it. As a marsh full of frogs was allegedly situated on the property, it was baptized La Grenouillère and given a green frog as its emblem. Catherine the Great even commissioned Wedgwood to make a table service bearing this emblem and views of English castles. Inside the palace a collection of portraits and medallions of crowned heads, both living and dead, was assembled to bring history to life. Thus the European sovereigns took on the appearance of a chivalric society. Catherine the Great herself wrote a tale about it:

> The old sentinel making his turn around Chesme Palace heard noise inside. . . . The portraits and medallions were conversing among themselves. . . .
>
> *Louis XVI:* I seek to do good.
>
> *His queen:* I kiss you, majesty, for these marvelous words, and I will honor them by giving a ball this very evening. . . .
>
> *Empress Maria-Theresa (the queen's mother):* Antoinette so loves society that I fear for the health of her soul. . . .
>
> *Joseph II:* But she is so beautiful, so lovable, so young.[4]

THE MARBLE PALACE.
The main staircase by
Antonio Rinaldi.

THE MARBLE PALACE.
*The Large Marble
Salon.*

THE MARBLE PALACE.
*Two details of the decor
of the Large Marble
Salon, designed by
Antonio Rinaldi.
The reliefs are the work
of F. Shubin and
M. Kozlovsky.*

This playful imaginary dialogue wonderfully captures the spirit that prevailed at the beginning of Catherine the Great's reign. But nobility entailed obligations as well as prerogatives. St. Petersburg was to become progressively more severe and majestic as the second half of the eighteenth century advanced; exoticism and the rococo were to penetrate the classical façades with increasing rarity. Even such architects partial to unbridled fantasy as Antonio Rinaldi, who was responsible for most of the chinoiserie on the outskirts of St. Petersburg, put on a serious face in the city. In 1766 Rinaldi designed the Marble Palace for Count Orlov. Erected on the Palace Embankment in 1781, its impressive façade, which incorporates Corinthian pilasters of pink marble, is as cold as it is elegant. A baroque plasticity and dynamism are indeed present in the Cathedral of Prince Vladimir, built by Rinaldi between 1766 and 1789, but even here one senses the restraining chill of classical rationalism.

However, it was a sculptural event that did most to give a new direction to urban planning in St. Petersburg: the celebrated *Bronze Horseman*, an equestrian monument honoring Peter the Great and erected by Etienne Falconet on Senate Square. For more than two centuries now it has served as the symbol of St. Petersburg. In his poem of the same title, Alexander Pushkin wrote:

*And high above those rails, as if
Of altitude and darkness blended,
There rode in bronze, one arm extended,
The idol on its granite cliff.
[...]
Oh, Destiny's great potentate!
Was it not thus, a towering idol
Hard by the chasm, with iron bridle
You reared up Russia to her fate?*[5]

It is not a matter of chance that, of the many proposed inscriptions for it, the shortest was chosen: *To Peter the First/Catherine the Second.* The message was clear: Catherine was the true heir of Peter the Great, the city's founder. "My monument will be simple," Falconet wrote to Diderot in Paris: "a charge up a steep rock—that's the subject Peter the Great has given me."[6]

The sculptor arrived in Russia in 1766 and remained there until 1778, when the casting of the equestrian group was completed. The emperor's head was the work of Marie-Anne Collot. Installation of the monument was a heroic undertaking. The transport of the gigantic granite rock that was to serve as its base—dubbed the *tonnerre-pierre*, a pun on the French words for "thunder," "ton," and "rock," as well as on the French version of the subject's name—was the talk of all Europe. This whole

THE MARBLE PALACE.
Ceiling of the Baroque
Salon in one of
the wings. Both the
paintings and the decor
date from the mid-
nineteenth century.

formidable venture was overseen by Georg Velten. The *Bronze Horseman* was inaugurated with great ceremony in 1782, in the presence of Catherine the Great.

PALLADIANISM AND CLASSICISM IN THE LATE EIGHTEENTH CENTURY. The reign of Catherine the Great falls into two nearly equal parts: the first fifteen years, from 1762 until the end of the 1770s, and most of the following two decades, which ended with her death in 1796. Catherine wrote to the philosopher Friedrich Grimm in 1779: "There is an illness, it is the passion for drafting laws, and the empress of Russia has come down with it on two occasions: the first time she decreed only principles, this time everything that's for the best has taken hold of her."7 Twice she not only defined her political principles but also modified her intentions with regard to architecture. She wanted to continue to build as much as possible: "The fury to build rages in us now more than ever. . . . It is a veritable sickness, something like intoxication and perhaps also like a habit."8 But the French classicism that had prevailed in previous years no longer satisfied her. The latest developments in French architecture, as exemplified by the designs of Ledoux and Etienne-Louis Boullée, struck her as incomprehensible and overly complicated. "I want two Italians," she wrote, "for we have Frenchmen who know too much and build wretched houses . . . all because they are too clever."9 She indeed invited two Italians to St. Petersburg, Giacomo Quarenghi and Giacomo Trombara, but she also recruited the Scot Charles Cameron, who claimed to have been raised in Rome. At this same time a few Russian architects were becoming fashionable, above all Nikolai Lvov, who had translated Palladio's *Four Books of Architecture* into Russian. The work of all these architects was characterized by two features typical of the classicism of the 1780s and 1790s: Palladianism and a penchant for meticulous imitation of ancient monuments.

Quarenghi played a key role in the formation of St. Petersburg classicism. In addition to building numerous private residences and major public buildings, he was a conspicuous figure in the daily life of the capital. A contemporary recalled that Quarenghi was often seen making his way through the streets from one construction site to another, and that he was easy to recognize: "Everyone knew him by the enormous bluish bulb that nature had stuck on his face where his nose should have been."10 His nose was indeed extraordinary.

Quarenghi was born in the northern Italian province of Bergamo. He studied in Rome with the celebrated painter Raphael Mengs and then traveled widely. In 1780 he arrived in Russia and by 1783 came under the empress's protection. From then on he received numerous important commissions. Quarenghi built the Hermitage Theater, which enlarged still further the imperial residence on the Palace Embankment. The auditorium was modeled after an ancient amphitheater via Palladio's Teatro Olimpico in Vicenza, and the façade was laden with Palladian motifs. In the words of Igor Grabar, Quarenghi here "achieved an architectural style that was irreproachably severe but no less picturesque than that of Rastrelli." Simultaneously he was building the Academy of Sciences on the Vasilievsky Island embankment across the Neva. Even more restrained than the Hermitage Theater, this building consists of a long rectangle stripped of all decoration but with a heavy Ionic portico supporting a tall, empty pediment. It displays, however, a mastery of proportion typical of Quarenghi's best work, and the same could be said of the Roman solemnity of the building's interiors.

In our view, this architect's finest building in St. Petersburg is the Currency Bank on Sadovaya Street, built between 1783 and 1788. In its center is a three-story Palladian villa with a Corinthian portico and sculptures punctuating the three points of its pediment. Its dimensions are relatively modest, resembling those of a medium-size country house. This structure is surrounded by a two-story building shaped like an immense horseshoe, through which threads a long, curved corridor. Its façade is articulated by pilasters of equal size. A columned passage connected the villa to the horseshoe-shaped structure, as though tensing a bow. The courtyard was closed off by a remarkable fence and gate. In its general conception as well as its detailing, it is one of the most perfect examples of eighteenth-century classical architecture in St. Petersburg.

Quarenghi worked in the capital over an extended period. In 1784 he began building the Stock Exchange on the tip of Vasilievsky Island, but this structure was not completed in accordance with his design. Catherine's death did not interrupt his activity. In 1798 Paul I commissioned him to design the Church of the Maltese Order, and he subsequently worked on the Horse Guards Manège (1800–4), the Imperial Cabinet building, or Chancellery (1805–6), and colonnade of the Anichkov Palace (1805–6), and finally, next to the Smolny Convent, the institute for the education of the daughters of the poor nobility (1806–8). His last structure in St. Petersburg was the Narva Triumphal Gate, erected on the occasion of the return of the Russian armies from France in 1814, at the end of the Napoleonic wars. The result of this remarkable career is that there are very few quarters of the city that do not boast at least one example of his severe classical style, characterized by Palladian proportions and meticulously observed Roman orders.

THE MARBLE PALACE.
Detail of the neo-Gothic decor in a salon in one of the wings.

SMOLNY CONVENT.
LEFT *General view.
Built by Bartolomeo
Rastrelli between 1748
and 1754 (except for
the interiors, completed
by Vasily Stasov in
1835), the complex is
rigorously central in
conception. The
enormous courtyard is
in the shape of a Greek
cross, like the plan of
the cathedral itself.
Four domed chapels
punctuate the corners
of the complex. In front
of the main façade,
which faces the city,
an oblong square was
laid out along the
central axis.*
OPPOSITE *The five-
domed cathedral, built
in accordance with a
Greek-cross plan.*

The second admirer of Palladio in the late eighteenth century was Nikolai Lvov. A man of many accomplishments (musician, engineer, poet, translator), Lvov's stylistic range was more varied than that of Quarenghi. If his first building in St. Petersburg, the Main Post Office, was canonically Palladian, the churches he built on noble estates—on the outskirts of the city at the time but now within its limits—reveal his taste for the play of purely geometric forms influenced both by Palladian models and by more experimental approaches to classical syntax. The most interesting of these churches is St. Catherine's, constructed in the 1780s on the property of the Counts Vorontsov at Murino. Here the architect juxtaposed a cylindrical sanctuary (a rotunda surrounded by an Ionic colonnade) and a tall, pyramidal bell tower. The people nicknamed it Kulich and Paskha after traditional Russian Easter dishes of the same name, for the building's forms recall the high, round shape of the former (a cake) and the pyramidal shape usually given the latter (a cheese paste with raisins).

THE CATHEDRAL OF THE ALEXANDER NEVSKY LAVRA AND THE TAURIDE PALACE. These two buildings were designed by Ivan Starov, one of the most important masters of Catherine's reign. After a stint at the Academy of Fine

Arts, Starov studied with Charles de Wailly in Paris and then visited Rome. He subsequently produced much work for Prince Potemkin, the empress's famous lover.

In 1775 Starov was commissioned to design a cathedral for the oldest monastery in St. Petersburg, the Alexander Nevsky Lavra, founded in 1710 by Peter the Great on the reputed site of Alexander Nevsky's victory over the Swedes. A first design for the complex was drafted in 1717 by Domenico Tressini. It featured a centrally placed cathedral surrounded by the monks' cells. Only the latter were actually built, the northern part in the 1720s and the southern part in the 1740s. Between 1717 and 1722 the Church of the Annunciation was built in one of the wings. Theodor Schwertfeger began to build the principal cathedral in the late 1710s, but technical problems made it necessary to demolish the building. Between 1755 and 1767 structures were built to house the administrative offices.

A new phase began in 1776, when Starov started to construct the large Cathedral of the Trinity. A Latin cross in plan, it also featured two towers and a mighty cupola, and its architectural volumes were remarkable for their severity. Starov also reworked the entrance to the monastery. The road leading to it from the Admiralty was none other than Nevsky Prospekt, laid out under Peter the Great and one of the city's main arteries. As its culmination the architect designed a circular square surrounded

ALEXANDER NEVSKY
LAVRA.
FAR LEFT *Cathedral of
the Trinity: drum and
pendentives of the dome
with royal entry below.*
LEFT *Cathedral of the
Trinity: exterior view
of the dome. Built
between 1774 and 1780
by Ivan Starov, it has a
Latin-cross plan and a
dome over the crossing
of the transept.*
OPPOSITE *Cathedral of
the Annunciation. Built
by Domenico Tressini
between 1717 and 1725,
it houses the tomb of
Field Marshal Suvorov,
who died in 1800.*

by a low fence, and between 1783 and 1785 he erected gates marking the main entrance to the monastery.

In the eighteenth and nineteenth centuries the Alexander Nevsky Lavra acquired a new symbolic significance. The ashes of Alexander Nevsky were moved there in 1723, and the tomb of Field Marshal Suvorov was placed inside the Cathedral of the Annunciation. Close to the gates a necropolis was laid out that eventually was to contain the funerary monuments of many illustrious representatives of Russian culture, including Lomonosov, Dostoevsky, Tchaikovsky, Mussorgsky, and Rimsky-Korsakov, as well as many architects who had worked in the city.

The other exceptional building erected by Starov in St. Petersburg is the Tauride Palace, constructed between 1783 and 1789 for Prince Potemkin, famous not only as the empress's favorite but also for his political accomplishments, particularly in southern Russia. After the Russian annexation of ancient Taurida (the Crimea), for which he had paved the way, Potemkin was awarded the title of Tauride Prince along with the palace of the same name, which Catherine ordered specially built for him.

The Tauride Palace is without doubt the most significant of all Russian classical buildings, and it perfectly exemplifies the pervasive ambition to revive the language of Roman imperial architecture. Located near the bank of the Neva, it originally dominated the river, to which it was connected by a canal. Today the river view of the palace is blocked and the main entrance is through a walled courtyard whose detailing is remarkably restrained. The central building, which is quite deep, is entered through an austere Doric portico. The lateral structures, which are square in plan, are connected to the main building by sumptuous galleries. On April 28, 1791, shortly before his death, Potemkin, the Tauride Prince, gave a party in honor of Catherine the Great, the most famous such festivity of the period. An account of the event by one of the guests provides a vivid description of the palace's interior decor: "Past the main entrance we found ourselves in a low vestibule whose doors opened onto an octagonal salon with tribunes and a dome resembling a temple of some sort. . . . The cornice bore an inscription in goldletters: *To Catherine the Great.* This room was called the Pantheon. Beyond was the grandiose Large Gallery. Entering it, we saw a long, oval room, or more precisely a plaza, that could comfortably accommodate 5,000 people. It would seem that through Herculean efforts all of nature had been brought into it."[11] Thirty-six white columns of an Ionic order resembling that of the Erechtheum separated the gallery

TAURIDE PALACE.
RIGHT *The octagonal
room; views of the entry
wall and of the dome.
The design of this room
was inspired by the
Pantheon in Rome.*
OPPOSITE *General view.
Built between 1783
and 1789 for Marshal
Potemkin, who after
conquering the Crimea
was named the
Tauride Prince, it
is the prime example
of St. Petersburg
palace architecture
inspired by classical
Roman models.*

from the no less grandiose Winter Garden. Here "spring reigns everywhere, and art competes with the charms of nature. The soul is awash in pleasure!" added our observer. A landscape garden was created around the palace by the English master William Gould, a student of the great eighteenth-century British garden designer Lancelot Brown. The sumptuousness of the entertainment given by Potemkin has become legendary, above all because of the costume worn by the master of the house. He dressed for the occasion in a scarlet caftan and a cape of black lace. There were so many diamonds in his hat that he could not wear it; it was carried behind him by an aide-de-camp.

During the last years of her reign Catherine continued to build, and on an increasingly grandiose scale. She asked Starov to design a new palace for her upstream on the Neva. It was intended to surpass all previous palaces and realize the fantastic dreams of the visionary architects of the late eighteenth century by reviving the splendor and majesty of ancient architecture. Catherine christened the new palace Pella, after the capital of ancient Macedonia, and this evocation of the city where the ancestors of Alexander the Great had lived was not fortuitous. She was in the evening of her life, and she was thinking of her favorite grandson, Alexander, suggesting a parallel between them. She was not alone in making such comparisons. Claude-Nicolas Ledoux dedicated his book to the "Alexander of the North." In the eyes of the empress, Grand Duke Alexander was the rightful heir to a throne from which she wished to distance her own son Paul, Alexander's father. But history turned out otherwise. Catherine the Great died on November 5, 1796. Alexander did not dare seize the throne, and Paul I became emperor.

TAURIDE PALACE.
This monumental room lined by thirty-six Ionic columns of white marble is perpendicular to the palace's main axis.

4

PAUL I

THE TORMENTED ONE

We lack extensive and accurate information concerning construction of the imperial castle of St. Michael. None of the information we repeatedly tried to obtain from local sources was provided. . . . This imperial residence is much less celebrated for the beauty and good taste of its architecture than for the frightful catastrophe to which Paul I fell victim.

—Percier and Fontaine
Résidences de Souverains . . . , Paris, 1833

MIKHAILOVSKY CASTLE. ALSO KNOWN AS THE ENGINEER'S CASTLE. *General view. Begun shortly after the death of Catherine II in 1796, its design was commissioned by Paul I from his personal architect, Vincenzo Brenna. Square in plan with an octagonal court in the center, it is a genuine fortified citadel that was once surrounded by moats. Two large obelisks decorated with military trophies adorn the principal stone portico, and the relief on its pediment is an allegory of the Glory of Russia. In the distance are the Field of Mars, the Marble Palace, and, across the Neva, the Peter-Paul Fortress.*

LEFT
The Field of Mars,
*painting by De Mayr,
eighteenth century.*

OPPOSITE
MIKHAILOVSKY
CASTLE.
*View from the
Fontanka.*

T HE ROMANTIC CASTLE. Countess Varvara Golovina recounted the following episode: "The accession of the new emperor incited terror in all hearts. Possessed of everything necessary to be a great sovereign, and one of the most charming men in all the empire, he managed only to inspire fear and alienate people. Paul had an impetuous soul. . . . His character, irascible from birth, grew increasingly bitter. He became suspicious, stern, and exacting even about trifles. . . . His singularity was such that people steered clear of him as best they could. But . . . there was no telling what would happen in his fits of temper. One's post, or deportation, or even life itself might be at stake."[1] These lines convey something of the bleak atmosphere that prevailed in St. Petersburg during the four years of Paul I's reign. It seemed to contemporaries that "all the glorious things accomplished during the thirty-four years of Catherine's reign were collapsing, and that Paul was possessed by a single passion: to debase his mother."[2] In any case, the architectural projects of Catherine's last years were interrupted, and some buildings on the verge of completion were even destroyed. Many of the architects who had worked for the empress now found themselves without employment.

Paul's favorite architect was an Italian of Florentine origin, Vincenzo Brenna. He had studied in Rome and Paris, and he also worked in Poland before arriving in Russia at the end of 1783, to design the residences of the heir to the throne at Pavlovsk and Gatchina. Brenna knew how to please the grand duke, and his career—like that of most who had grown close to Paul prior to his accession—flourished during the brief reign of the emperor, who showered him with honors. It was he whom Paul commissioned to build his new imperial palace in St. Petersburg, which came to be known as the Mikhailovsky Castle.

Paul I wasted no time, and the ukase ordering the palace's construction was issued less than a month after Catherine the Great's death. The foundation stone was laid, with great ceremony, a mere two months later, in February 1797. The work proceeded at a feverish pace without interruption, both day and night, when torches were used. Completed in 1800, the enormous edifice is situated close to the junction of the Moika and the Fontanka, on the site of the Summer Palace of Empress Elizabeth Petrovna. The Summer Garden, where Peter the Great's small Summer Palace was located, was to serve as its park.

The castle is quirky and strange, rather like Paul's personality. Classicism was the dominant style in this period, after all, and this building seems decidedly odd when compared with the palaces designed by Starov and Quarenghi. A sketch of the plan by the emperor himself survives, and it is possible that the famous Moscow architect Vasily Bazhenov, who had grown close to the emperor through their common Masonic ties, also contributed to

MIKHAILOVSKY CASTLE. *Northern façade facing the Summer Garden. A monumental stairway leads to a Doric colonnade surmounted by a balcony. Note the attic decor, which consists of alternating reliefs and term atlantes.*

MIKHAILOVSKY
CASTLE.
Main staircase.

its design. The definitive conception, however, is unquestionably the work of Vincenzo Brenna. In any case, the result has something of the closed off, impregnable quality of a real castle. In plan it is a gigantic square with rounded corners suggestive of small towers. At its center is an octagonal court onto which most of the rooms face.

From the exterior the castle makes a somber and monolithic impression. The approach to it was laid out along a rectilinear axis defined by two symmetrical rows of long, low buildings housing the stables, then two rather large octagonal pavilions facing each other, and finally an open square with an equestrian statue of Peter the Great by Bartolomeo Rastrelli the elder, the architect's father, which bears the inscription "To the great-grandfather from the great-grandson." This dedication was of more than passing interest to Paul I, for his veins ran with the blood of Peter the Great, while his mother Catherine's had not.

The composition of the main façade is organized around a heavy stone portico with a set-back attic and decorated with two obelisks; it provides the only entrance to the central court. The ground floor consists of a heavy, monumental sub-basement faced with diamond-pointed rustication. The façade facing the Summer Garden is somewhat lighter and more agreeable in feeling, featuring a large central balcony on the second-floor level. The Mikhailovsky Castle is full of arresting architectural detailing, such as trophies and medallions bearing the emperor's monogram in sumptuous frames. There is something about the building that is in tune with the nascent Romantic sensibility.

Of the many concerns that tormented Paul I, fear of death must be counted the principal one. He was aware of the many plots and coups d'état that had been the downfall of his predecessors. That is why Mikhailovsky Castle was conceived as a secure, almost impregnable building, and it also explains the original presence of surrounding moats. The bridges over them were movable and were raised at night. The guards were subject to a rigorous disciplinary regimen. But all these measures proved insufficient to save the emperor. On the night of March 2, 1801, his courtiers, who had come to despise him, managed to penetrate the castle and murder him. Given this circumstance, his son Alexander I certainly could not live there, and the castle was turned over to the engineer corps, which housed administrative and staff offices there. Hence the building's second name: the Engineer's Castle.

MIKHAILOVSKY
CASTLE.
*The iconostasis in
the church.*

MIKHAILOVSKY
CASTLE.
*View from the Summer
Garden and its canal.*

5

ALEXANDER I AND NICHOLAS I

CLASSICAL GRANDEUR

The prophecy of Peter the Great, carved from the sea in blocks of granite, has been fulfilled over the last century before the eyes of the universe. When one considers that such phrases, which would be exaggerated in any other context, are here but an accurate expression of reality, one pauses respectfully and says to oneself: God is here! This is the first time that pride has seemed touching to me: whenever the power of the human soul manifests itself as completely as it does here, then there is indeed reason to marvel.

—Marquis de Custine
La Russie en 1839, Paris, 1843

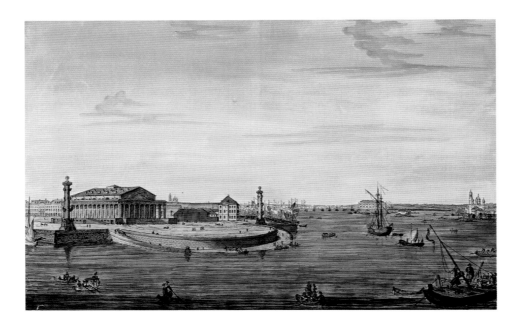

THE STOCK EXCHANGE.
LEFT *Drawn and engraved by I. Ivanov in 1814.*
OPPOSITE *Aerial view. The building was commissioned from Thomas de Thomon by Alexander I in 1805. Cast in the form of a Greek temple, it was completed in 1810. It is situated on the tip of Vasilievsky Island and framed by two immense rostral columns in the Roman style.*

ST. PETERSBURG AND ITS CULTURE IN THE FIRST HALF OF THE NINETEENTH CENTURY. The nineteenth century began with the accession of Catherine the Great's grandson, the young emperor Alexander I. This event prompted exceptional excitement throughout the country and especially in the capital. In the words of one contemporary, "Catherine lives again in this marvelous young man. The child of her heart, her cherished grandson, announces in a decree that he will bring her era back to us. We shall see how well he keeps his word. But no: even in Catherine's time we did not experience the feeling of well-being that took hold throughout Russia during the first six months of Alexander's reign. Love governed it, and both liberty and order were renewed under it . . . everyone sensed a [new] moral tenor . . . glances became kinder, actions bolder, breathing freer."[1]

Indeed, the early reign of Alexander I, from 1801 to the Napoleonic invasion, was an exceptionally happy period marked by an unprecedented degree of liberalism. The young emperor wanted to pursue the reforms begun by Catherine the Great, and the secretary of state, Mikhail Speransky, working with his political allies, introduced sweeping legislative reforms. The country's finances were placed on a more solid footing, there was much commercial development, and ties with Europe were strengthened.

Russia made a concerted effort to establish itself on the European political stage, notably by joining most of the alliances directed against revolutionary France. When Napoleon was named first consul after his return from Egypt, however, the situation changed. Paul I had concluded an alliance with him against England, but Alexander I again declared war on France. After the defeat of the allied Russian and Austrian armies at Austerlitz and the rapid fall of Prussia, the armies of Napoleon and Alexander met once again in Poland. Although they put up a good fight, the Russian armies were obliged to retreat after the defeat at Friedland. In the small border town of Tilsit, Russia and France signed a peace accord that was to transform the country's foreign policy as well as its cultural orientation. The alliance with Napoleon was brought to an end by the War of 1812 and the French occupation of Moscow. A harsh winter, the immensity of the country, the talents of Field Marshal Kutuzov, and the stoicism of the Russian soldiers all conspired to bury the Grande Armée in the snows of central Russia. After Napoleon's final defeat some of the Russian forces found themselves in France. Many officers and nobles then discovered French culture with their own eyes, and on returning home they brought with them a whole new outlook and the latest French fashions.

Alexander Pushkin had the following to say about this matter: "Meanwhile the war had ended gloriously. Our regiments returned from abroad, and the people went out to meet them. The bands played the songs of the conquered: 'Vive Henri-Quatre,' Tyrolese waltzes and airs from 'Joconde.' . . . The soldiers chatted gaily among themselves, constantly using French and German words in their speech. Unforgettable time! Time of glory and enthusiasm! . . . The women, the Russian women, were then incomparable. Their usual coldness disappeared. Their enthusiasm was truly intoxicating, when welcoming the conquerors they cried 'Hurrah!'"[2] All Russian culture was pervaded by a feeling of triumph during this period. Classicism reigned not only in architecture but also in the realms of fashion and interior decoration.

"Modes of dress preserved by sculptures on the banks of the Aegean and the Tiber are taken up on the Seine and thence imitated on the Neva. If not for the full-dress uniforms and the tailcoats the balls would have resembled antique reliefs and Etruscan vases. And truly the result was quite striking: on the young women everything was so clean, simple, and fresh. . . . Alabaster vases carved with mythological images, censers, and tripod tables appeared everywhere . . . long sofas where one's arms rested on eagles, griffins, and sphinxes. Gilded, painted,

Allegorical statue of the Dnepr, one of Russia's great rivers, at the foot of one of the rostral columns.

RIGHT
STOCK EXCHANGE.
The Doric colonnade.

FOLLOWING PAGES
UNIVERSITY
EMBANKMENT.
*View of the Academy
of Sciences, built by
Quarenghi between
1783 and 1789, and
the Kunstkamera, the
first museum in
St. Petersburg, founded
by Peter the Great,
begun by Georg Johann
Mattarnovy in 1718 and
completed by Mikhail
Zemtsov in 1734.
In the background, the
Peter-Paul Fortress.*

BELOW

LANDING PIER OF THE ACADEMY OF FINE ARTS. *Built in 1830 to a design by Konstantin Ton, it is decorated with two sphinxes dating from the reign of Amenophis III and discovered during excavations in Thebes. They were purchased by the Russian ambassador and transported to St. Petersburg in 1832.*

RIGHT

View of the English Embankment and St. Isaac's Cathedral.

SENATE SQUARE,
WITH THE
EQUESTRIAN
STATUE OF
PETER THE GREAT.
*Colored print by
Ludwig after a
composition by
B. Patersen, 1799.*

and lacquered wood was forgotten. . . . Mahogany entered general use and began to be decorated with gilt bronze figures . . . lyres, and Medusa, lion, and ram heads. None of this had reached us prior to 1805, and to my mind nothing better in this genre could be imagined."[3] Such are the words of Filipp Vigel, one of the finest Russian memoirists of the first half of the nineteenth century. The Empire style, which was introduced into Russia about 1805, remained fashionable there until the 1840s, and it completely transformed the appearance of the city.

Of the pleiad of architects active in the capital before the War of 1812, we have already encountered Giacomo Quarenghi, who remained faithful to the tenets of Palladianism despite the advent of new tendencies. Three other architects were adept practitioners of the new style. Andrei Voronikhin—probably the illegitimate son of one of the wealthiest of all Russian nobles, Count Stroganov—was educated alongside the count's legitimate son and heir. For a long time they both lived in Paris, where Voronikhin developed a passion for architecture. He was recalled to Russia in 1790 as a means of protecting him from revolutionary ideas, but it was late-eighteenth-century Prix de Rome entries that most influenced his design for the Kazan Cathedral. Like many of his contemporaries he was subsequently attracted to the model of ancient Greece, and even to its more archaic monuments, as evidenced by his use of the baseless Greek Doric order in his Academy of Mines. His final

THE BRONZE
HORSEMAN.
Catherine II commissioned a monument to the glory of Peter the Great from the French sculptor Etienne Falconet. Falconet arrived in St. Petersburg in 1766 and spent more than ten years completing the work. The head is by his student Marie-Anne Collot. The rock came from Lakhta, on the outskirts of St. Petersburg. The monument was inaugurated in 1782 by Catherine the Great in the sculptor's absence; he had returned to France four years earlier.

THE SENATE.
Façade facing the Neva with, in the background, the dome of St. Isaac's Cathedral. Built between 1829 and 1833 by Carlo Rossi, the Senate is linked to the Synod building on the right by a structure with an inset monumental pediment surmounted by a horizontal relief.

works, however, are more consistent with the decorative Roman idiom of the Empire style. This developmental trajectory is typical for the period. Like Voronikhin, Adrian Zakharov began his studies at the St. Petersburg Academy of Fine Arts, where he was awarded the gold medal. He, too, went off to Paris, where he worked in the studio of Jean-François-Thérèse Chalgrin until 1786. However, his principal work, the Admiralty, is closer in spirit to designs by Boullée.

As for Thomas de Thomon, here is what Vigel has to say: "Monsieur Thomon . . . was a man not without talent, as is demonstrated by the Stock Exchange that he built. He was also known to be a rabid monarchist and an ardent Catholic."[4] Thomon, originally from Nancy, resided in Italy for an extended period. He arrived in Russia in 1799 as part of the entourage of the comte d'Artois, and his drawings soon attracted attention in St. Petersburg. His work reflects tendencies pervasive at the French Academy in Rome at the time, blending archaeological precision with the romantic spirit that was beginning to inflect the Empire style.

Giacomo Quarenghi died in 1817 at a very advanced age. Adrian Zakharov died much younger in 1811, Thomas de Thomon in 1819, and Andrei Voronikhin in 1814. Other architects began to give St. Petersburg a very different character, and in tandem with this development the prevailing approach to urbanism changed. At the end of the eighteenth century and the beginning of the nineteenth, St. Petersburg was basically evolving one isolated and monumental building at a time. Mikhailovsky Castle, the Stock Exchange, Kazan Cathedral, and the Admiralty were all conceived as entities sufficient unto themselves. After the War of 1812, however, planners once again began to think more organically. Beginning in the second half of Alexander I's reign, all new buildings were conceived in light of their function within the entirety of the urban fabric, in accordance with a decree stipulating that "the regularity, beauty, and propriety of each building [be] adapted to the city as a whole." This pronouncement was a key determinant of the triumph of Alexandrian classicism, which gave the city an exceptionally unified character.

A new agency, the Committee for Buildings and Waterways, was created to oversee urban planning. The

era."[7] His gifts were many and various: he could design an intimate, poetic country house like the one for Emperor Alexander I on Elagin Island, but he was also capable of imagining a complete reconstruction of the city center. He was responsible for the Mikhailovsky Palace complex (now the Russian Museum) as well as the square in front of it. He transformed Palace Square and Senate Square, and he built Theater Square and Theater Street—now called Architect Rossi Street—from scratch. All in all, he took part in the remodeling of twelve squares and thirteen streets in St. Petersburg. Stylistically his work is in the tradition of Adrian Zakharov, favoring austere but grandiose and even triumphal classical conceptions richly ornamented with architectural and sculptural detailing. He was largely responsible for the rigor and coherence that is such a striking feature of the city.

Rossi's contemporaries tried to equal the grandiose scale of his projects. Vasily Stasov was one of the first Russian noblemen to pursue an architectural career. According to Filipp Vigel, he was "the exact opposite" of Rossi: "Gloom could be read in his eyes. He was not a bad man but he was always morose."[8] This characterization comes as a surprise, because Stasov's designs, even for such large buildings as the Court Stables on the Moika and the Pavlovsk Regiment Barracks on the Field of Mars, are less solemn and reserved than Rossi's work. Stasov's brand of classicism is much softer than his colleague's, and much freer.

The other architects working in the city during the first half of the nineteenth century could be divided into two categories, according to whether they preferred Greek or Roman models. Igor Grabar called the first tendency "Hellenism" and the second one "Latinism." Such classification schemes are always arbitrary to some degree, but this one is useful and contains more than a grain of truth.

In 1817 Andrei Mikhailov II designed the new Academy of Fine Arts building, using the Greek Doric order for its powerful and severe portico. Giovanni Lucchini complemented the heavy archaic columns of Thomon's Stock Exchange on Vasilievsky Island with the elegant Ionic orders on the façades of the nearby custom houses he built between 1825 and 1832. By contrast, the Summer Theater, built by Smaragd Shustov in 1827 on Kamenny Island, was modeled after a Roman temple, and David Vichonti's designs, notably the Catholic church of St. Stanislav, also were notably "Latin" in feeling.

The Russian empire of Alexander I and Nicholas I was the stylistic beneficiary of the empire of Napoleon I. This lineage is especially apparent in the work of one of

architects Carlo Rossi, Vasily Stasov, Andrei Mikhailov II, and William Guestier were appointed to it, and it was headed by Augustin Béthencourt (Betankur y Molina), who came to Russia from Spain. The committee determined that it would be indispensable "to regularize old squares and lay out new ones." This would entail "the construction of public buildings and other structures suitable for these sites and consistent with industrial needs, the public good, and aesthetic pleasure."[5] In other words, it deemed necessary a complete reorganization of the capital, from its center to its most distant islands. Carlo Rossi, an architect of Italian origins born in Russia who had studied with Vincenzo Brenna, aptly summed up the essence of St. Petersburg urbanism in the period while characterizing one of his own designs for the city: "The dimensions of my proposed design exceed those adopted by the Romans in their constructions. We must not fear comparison with them in the matter of magnificence. This word should be understood to mean not an abundance of decoration but rather grandeur of form, nobility of proportion, and stability of materials."[6] Although he was a master of detail and composition, Rossi was most interested in large-scale projects. He once wrote that he had set out "to surpass everything constructed by the Europeans of our

ST. ISAAC'S CATHEDRAL.
LEFT *Aerial view.*
OPPOSITE *Built by the French architect Auguste Ricard de Montferrand between 1818 and 1848, it is the largest church in St. Petersburg. It has a Greek-cross plan and each of its façades features an immense columned portico of Finnish granite topped by a sculpted pediment. The design of the dome was inspired by Western models.*

ST. ISAAC'S
CATHEDRAL.
*Exterior view of the
ribbed dome.*

ST. ISAAC'S
CATHEDRAL.
*Interior of the dome,
decorated with a
painting by Karl
Bryulov representing
the Virgin surrounded
by saints. Paintings of
the twelve apostles
adorn the drum, and
the four evangelists are
depicted on the
pendentives.*

ST. ISAAC'S
CATHEDRAL.
*Mosaic panel from the
iconostasis representing
St. Alexander Nevsky.*

pletely unnoticed by our great architects but whose success soon occasioned their disappointment and envy. One morning I encountered at Béthencourt's house [as president of the Committee of Buildings and Waterways at the time, Béthencourt oversaw all the construction projects in St. Petersburg] a light-haired Frenchman about thirty years old dressed in the latest fashion, who had come with a letter of recommendation from his friend the clockmaker Bréguet. When he left I asked who he was—Montferrand."[9] Auguste Ricard de Montferrand soon made it clear that he was a virago of energy: "He drafted twenty-four designs . . . in every style current at the time: Chinese, Indian, Gothic, Byzantine, Renaissance, and of course Greek."[10] All of these designs were for the same project, a great urban cathedral. The album containing them was submitted to Alexander I. He was taken with it, and Montferrand was commissioned to design the new St. Isaac's Cathedral, which was completed in 1857. It is not only the largest church in St. Petersburg but also the last important classical monument of the first half of the nineteenth century.

Such were the principal actors in the history of St. Petersburg's architecture in the years 1815–20. All were more or less conversant with recent European developments, to which Russia was especially attentive in this period. But it should not be forgotten that their work and careers were largely determined by internal developments, by the evolution of Russia's own culture and history.

In the second half of Alexander I's reign the prevailing mood in St. Petersburg took a reactionary turn. The emperor clung to the principles of the Holy Alliance, masterminded by him in the wake of the last French revolutions, which had revived anxieties about insurrection. Centralized power was consolidated, a martial mentality was encouraged, mysticism was embraced (the tsar himself began to consult mediums), and the bureaucracy grew. Part of the Russian aristocracy—especially educated officers who had come into contact with the West during the Napoleonic wars—were extremely dissatisfied with this new orientation, and more generally with Russia's backwardness in certain areas, above all the institution of serfdom. A strong liberal opposition began to coalesce in St. Petersburg in the form of secret societies. This was the period of the Decembrists, but it was also the "golden age" of Russian culture. During the first half of the nineteenth century the Russian language—its vocabulary, poetry, and prose idiom—acquired its "classic" form. The work of Alexander Pushkin played a crucial role in all of these developments, and in a very real sense St. Petersburg became the city of Pushkin in those years. His poetry came to be associated with memories of his

the last great masters of St. Petersburg classicism in the first half of the nineteenth century, Alexander Bryulov. After leaving the St. Petersburg Academy of Fine Arts Bryulov pursued his studies together with his brother, the painter Karl Bryulov, in Munich, Rome, Naples, Paris, and finally London. This itinerary reflects a set of interests shared by many Russian artists in this period. It attests to Russia's close ties to Germany; to the necessity of studying antiquity, starting in Rome and according special attention to Pompeii, a site of exceptional interest to architects in those years; and, finally, to the need to shape and refine the traveler's taste by absorbing the latest developments in French and English architecture. Perhaps better than most, Bryulov knew how to achieve a satisfying blend of European and indigenous elements. His designs are notable for their rational compositions and spare detailing, as can be seen in his General Staff Headquarters building on Palace Square as well as in the Peter and Paul Lutheran Church on Nevsky Prospekt. His work is not unlike that of Leo von Klenze, whom he had met in Munich and who was subsequently invited to St. Petersburg to design the New Hermitage.

"I don't remember whether it was in June or July of that year [1816]," wrote our memoirist Filipp Vigel, "that a man arrived from Paris whose appearance went com-

ST. ISAAC'S
CATHEDRAL.
A partial view of the
iconostasis, with
the royal doors open
to reveal the stained-
glass window of
Christ in the choir.

MARIINSKY PALACE. *Erected between 1839 and 1844 by Andrei Stakenschneider, it revives a traditional classical formula: powerful central frontispiece with a colossal Corinthian order supported by a portico and surmounted by an attic, and two projecting side wings terminating in pedimented porticos.*

friends and associates, the Russian nobles whose uprising on the death of Alexander I in December 1825 initiated a new period in Russia's history.

Nicholas I, the second son of Paul I, reigned from 1825 to 1855, and the Russia over which he presided continued to be reactionary. Pushkin lived until 1837. Gogol was still writing, and Turgenev, Tolstoy, and Dostoevsky were beginning to express themselves. The emperor may have regarded literature with suspicion, but he had the greatest esteem for military men and engineers, a category in which he placed architects. Bureaucracy flourished and strict order seemed to reign. But in reality problems were brewing, and the momentum initiated by Catherine the Great's reform measures was finally slowing down. The end of Nicholas I's reign was marked by Russia's bitter defeat in the Crimean War and the fall of Sevastopol to Franco-English forces. Such was the sad finale of a period that had begun so triumphantly with the victory over Napoleon.

Yet one witness remains to speak in its favor: its architecture.

THE TIP OF VASILIEVSKY ISLAND. The place where the exceptionally wide Neva flows by the Peter-Paul Fortress and divides in two is among the most beautiful in St. Petersburg. The promontory on

the eastern side of Vasilievsky Island dominates an unusually expansive view.

The Stock Exchange, begun by Quarenghi during the reign of Catherine the Great, was demolished under Alexander I in 1801 to make way for a new building designed by Thomas de Thomon. A lavish ceremony was organized to mark the laying of its foundation stone. A large amphitheater was devised on the promontory to accommodate the invited guests, who were presented with a temporary decor representing the new building to scale, surmounted by an eagle grasping in its claws a cornucopia and the flag of the Russian merchant fleet. Construction began soon thereafter, and the building was completed by 1810, but it was inaugurated only in 1816, after conclusion of the Napoleonic Wars.

Built on a granite platform with monumental stairways and ramps, it is in the form of an enormous ancient temple surrounded by a Doric colonnade: fourteen columns on the long sides and ten on the shorter ones. While unfluted, they were clearly modeled after the columns of the Temple of Paestum. Thomon introduced one eccentric touch, a slight necklike narrowing just below the echinuses and crowning abacuses. Above these columns is a Doric frieze bare of reliefs. The order of the Stock Exchange building is its most notable feature. Thomon wished to return to the archaic classical period, which he held dear as the moment when the classical vocabulary was still fresh. The emperor Alexander had understood this as well. Thomon's architecture creates a strong impression; there is something oddly moving about it, something that links it to the European romantic sensibility.

Behind this "Greek" colonnade, however, one encounters Rome. The walls are decorated with arches, and the frames of the doors are Roman. The part of the building that rises above the colonnade is pierced by enormous thermal windows, and inside, the vault of the Stock Exchange's great hall is reminiscent of the ceilings of Roman baths. The sculpture, consisting of various maritime allegories, is meant to edify. On the attic level of the short façades, in front of the thermal windows, are figural groups depicting Neptune surrounded by water nymphs and Navigation encountering Mercury. Since 1940 the Naval Museum has been housed here, and the huge space now contains more than a thousand models of ships.

The architect also designed an environment for the building. He laid out a square in front of it featuring a granite semicircular terrace projecting into the Neva, and on each side of it he placed immense rostral columns with gray granite sculptures at their feet and culminating in cast-iron tripods. These were lit on solemn occasions, giving Thomon's romantic urban tableau added life.

Between 1826 and 1828, depots for merchandise being assessed by the St. Petersburg customs office were built on either side of the Exchange. Buildings had existed on the site to serve this purpose since the reign of Peter the Great, and subsequently they had been rebuilt several times. The great flood of 1824, one of the worst catastrophes in the city's history, destroyed them again, and the following year new structures were commissioned from Giovanni Lucchini. He devised a design of remarkable restraint, calling for symmetrical buildings in a compatible architectural idiom rather than in one that competed with or softened the impact of Thomon's structure. He aligned the short façades of the buildings with the tip of the island, and gave greater prominence to the façades facing the embankment, ornamenting them with blind Doric colonnades answering those of the Exchange proper.

The Customs House, built by the same architect between 1825 and 1832, currently houses the Academy of

ADMIRALTY SQUARE.
Print by Ferdinand Perrot, 1840.

Sciences Institute of Russian Literature. Here the manuscripts of Russia's most celebrated authors are preserved, including those of Pushkin. Indeed, the building is generally known as Pushkin House.

Beyond the southern depot is the University Embankment of Vasilievsky Island, which is lined with important buildings that have already been discussed: the Kunstkamera, the Academy of Sciences, the short façade of the Twelve Colleges, the Menshikov Palace, the Academy of Fine Arts, and the landing pier designed by Konstantin Ton. The two sphinxes on either side of it came from the ancient Egyptian city of Thebes and are often invoked in St. Petersburg poetry of the early twentieth century. Continuing along the embankment one encounters the old Naval Academy with its Ionic colonnade, erected by the architect Fedor Volkov in 1798. Further along is a church in the neo-Russian style that once belonged to the "representation" of the Pechersky Monastery in Kiev, the oldest such institution in Russia.

Beyond the church are some eighteenth-century houses, and finally one of the most famous of all Russian classical buildings: the Academy of Mines, erected by Andrei Voronikhin between 1806 and 1811. The stairs leading to its portico are flanked by vigorous sculptural groups that immediately set a dramatic tone. Executed after

THE ADMIRALTY.
LEFT *East Pavilion.
The two wings of the
Admiralty culminate
in symmetrical
projecting pavilions
featuring arches
flanked by colossal
Doric colonnades.*
BELOW *Watercolor
from the collection
entitled* Panorama of
St. Petersburg between
1817 and 1820 *by
Angelo Toselli.*

THE ADMIRALTY:
VIEW OF THE SPIRE.
*Alexander 1 com-
missioned Adrian
Zakharov, who had
studied with Chalgrin
in Paris, to redesign the
Admiralty, established
by Peter the Great in
1704, stipulating that
he was to adhere to
the massive existing
U-shaped foundations.
Work began in 1806
and the new building
was completed in 1823,
after the architect's
death. The central
portal, which takes the
form of a triumphal
arch, culminates in an
aerial peripteral temple
surmounted by twenty-
four statues and a
gilded spire.*

KAZAN CATHEDRAL.
LEFT *Northern façade.
Commissioned by
Paul I, the cathedral
was built to a Latin-
cross plan with an
eastern apse by the
Russian architect
Andrei Voronikhin
between 1801 and 1811.
The emperor had
stipulated the inclusion
of a Bernini-like
colonnade facing
Nevsky Prospekt that
would define a
monumental public
square. Another
colonnade was planned
for the southern façade,
but it was never built.*
BELOW *View from
Nevsky Prospekt,
c. 1800. Watercolor by
B. Patersen.*

models by the Russian sculptors V. Demut-Malinovsky and S. Pimenov, they represent *The Rape of Persephone* and *Hercules Suffocating Antaeus.* The building's reliefs treat subjects more appropriate for a mining school: *Venus Fetching Mars's Armor from Vulcan* and *Apollo Fetching His Chariot from Vulcan.* Voronikhin's design is a hymn to Greece. Its portico, which dominates the building to an almost overwhelming degree, features a true Greek Doric order with deeply fluted columns, and a wide triglyph frieze makes the empty pediment seem especially heavy. Voronikhin, too, was touched by the "passion for Paestum" that played such an important role in early-nineteenth-century Russian architecture.

THE ADMIRALTY. Osip Mandelstam, the great twentieth-century Russian poet who perished in Stalin's labor camps, found words in his poem "The Admiralty" that wonderfully evoke the building of its title: "and through the dark green a frigate or acropolis / gleams far away, brother of water and sky."[11] This enormous complex is one of the most conspicuous examples of classical architecture in St. Petersburg. It is visible everywhere, and does indeed seem to sail above the city like a frigate. Its architect, Adrian Zakharov, was in charge of all the maritime constructions in the city, and his many designs capture the romantic image of a

KAZAN
CATHEDRAL.
*Interior view of
the colonnade.*

THE TOWER OF
THE DUMA
(CITY COUNCIL).
Built by G. Ferrari
between 1799 and 1804.

GOSTINY DVOR, OR MERCHANTS' COURT. RIGHT *This monumental edifice, built by Vallin de la Mothe between 1761 and 1785, occupies an entire block and consists of two stories surrounding a central court. The impressive façade with its colossal order and double colonnade was part of a plan to beautify Nevsky Prospekt.* BELOW *View of Gostiny Dvor and the Duma on Nevsky Prospekt. Anonymous watercolor.*

"capital of the sea." He had always envisioned a center in which the "nautical theme" of the city would find its truest urban expression, and the Admiralty, a "maritime Acropolis," was meant to serve this purpose.

Founded under Peter the Great, in the baroque era it had become a key landmark for the entire left bank of the Neva. The three main arteries of the city—Nevsky Prospekt, Gorokhovaya Street, and Voznesensky Prospekt—culminated at the original tower designed by Ivan Korobov, so to all intents and purposes this meant that Zakharov could not move the tower with its golden spire. He retained the basic configuration of the earlier building, which was to enclose on three sides the large area then open to the Neva where the shipbuilding yards were located. The presence of the naval yards in the center of the city as envisioned by Peter the Great had become difficult to justify, but in Zakharov's time there was still no question of doing away with them. Hence the architect found his task all the more challenging, for he was obliged to incorporate the existing foundations. Even so, he resolved to do more than effect a partial reconstruction of the façades, as had been pro-

posed by Quarenghi and Charles Cameron. And in this decision lay his genius.

Arguing that the extant structures had been weakened by a series of fires, especially that of 1783, and stressing the importance of the Admiralty as an emblem of the city, Zakharov convinced the emperor to authorize a complete reconstruction. His design was approved on May 23, 1806, and construction of his grandiose masterpiece began soon thereafter. He did not live to see it, however, for it was completed only in 1823, twelve years after his death.

When Zakharov studied with Jean-François-Thérèse Chalgrin in Paris, designs on such a gigantic scale were commonplace on paper, but none were realized. In St. Petersburg, however, the mad, utopian dreams of an entire generation of European classicists were to assume concrete form.

The central tower, with its glittering spire, is the focus of the design. It is supported by a powerful triumphal arch suggestive of the famous one Chalgrin designed for the Place d'Etoile in Paris. A heavy Doric cornice crowns the smooth wall above the single arched portal, which is decorated with relief figures of Fame

MIKHAILOVSKY PALACE.
Main façade. Resembling a large Russian country house, the Mikhailovsky Palace was built by Carlo Rossi between 1819 and 1825. The main block has three stories and the usual colossal order unifying the two upper ones. The building projects forward at either end, counterbalancing the central portico with its triangular pediment. Two adjoining low wings with colonnaded façades define a courtyard enclosed by a cast-iron fence with three gates.

MIKHAILOVSKY
PALACE.
Main staircase.

and flanked by immense freestanding groups of caryatids supporting spheres representing the sky and the earth, the work of Feodosy Shchedrin. Rectangular reliefs of crowns and torches are inset into the wall just above them, and another relief by Alexander Terebenev entitled *The Institution of the Russian Fleet* extends along the entire length of the attic level. It depicts Neptune presenting Peter the Great with his trident while nymphs and tritons construct ships for the emperor and acclaim the appearance of new vessels. Atop the four corners of the attic there are seated figures representing Achilles, Ajax, Alexander the Great, and Pyrrhus. This block is surmounted by an inset peripteral temple with eight Ionic columns on each of its fours sides, topped by a smooth frieze with a flat attic. Above the temple are twenty-eight allegorical figures representing the seasons, the elements, and the winds, as well as the goddess Isis, who in Egyptian mythology presided over the waters and the winds, and Urania, the ancient muse of astronomy and guide of helmsmen.

The façades on either side of the tower, each about 650 feet (200 meters) long, terminate in immense pavilions resembling overblown versions of country houses in the Russian classical style. Their main façades have ten-column Doric porticos, and their terminating fronts, perpendicular to the main façade, feature smaller Doric porticos. One of the relief pediments depicts Themis crowning artists in recognition of their work; the other shows her rewarding exploits of the Russian Navy. The façades facing the Neva feature central triumphal arches that originally accommodated a canal linking the interior shipyards to the river. Above the arches are relief figures of Fame blowing trumpets, "capricious jellyfish clutch[ing] in anger" to the wall, while blocky pedestals on either side—again in the words of Mandelstam—support "anchors . . . rusting like abandoned plows."

A few interiors reflecting Zakharov's intentions survive. The most interesting is the main staircase; aligned with the main entrance, it is open the full height of the building and richly ornamented with sculpture. The assembly hall of the Admiralty Council is covered by a painted vault incorporating illusionistic sculpture and stucco work. None of the interiors is as impressive as the building's exterior, however, for Zakha-

MIKHAILOVSKY PALACE. *Salon of the White Columns, designed by Carlo Rossi.*

But Zakharov's great building can be fully appreciated only if viewed from a distance; then its character as the city's "maritime Acropolis" becomes readily apparent.

MIKHAILOVSKY PALACE.
Detail of transition from wall frieze to ceiling cove in a salon.

GENERAL STAFF HEADQUARTERS AND PALACE SQUARE. The Admiralty was still under construction when, in 1819, Carlo Rossi began to rework Palace Square, giving it the aspect familiar to us today. Oddly, not a single plan to develop this choice terrain in the very heart of the city had been proposed in the first half of the eighteenth century. A large meadow extended from the Admiralty to the bank of the Moika, along which arose Meadow Street with its small, undistinguished houses. With the completion of Rastrelli's Winter Palace in 1762, a square began to take shape that was worthy of a capital city. Rastrelli envisioned it as a vast, round square surrounded by a colonnade, with the equestrian statue of Peter the Great by his father, the sculptor Bartolomeo Rastrelli the elder, at its center. This ensemble was to be the ideological center of the city. Although the particulars of this design were abandoned after the death of Elizabeth Petrovna, but the idea of a round square in front of the palace was retained. However, instead of its being centered around a memorial to Peter the Great it was turned into a square for festivities. In 1766 a grandiose circular amphitheater was built for equestrian military exercises. This was a temporary structure, but it maintained the square's circular shape. In 1772 the architect Ivan Starov proposed to build a semicircular colonnade facing the Winter Palace, but Catherine the Great rejected his project, preferring to see a square on the site. In 1779 the St. Petersburg Academy of Fine Arts held a competition for its design, and the first prize was awarded to Georg Velten, whose project was subsequently built. It consisted of a semicircle of houses with identical façades. The empress profited from the occasion to present her current favorite, Alexander Lanskoy, with one of these residences, its interiors decorated by Quarenghi. Unfortunately, Lanskoy died shortly thereafter, much to the empress's chagrin. In 1811 the General Staff of the Russian Army, then being reorganized after the Napoleonic model, rented this house from Lanskoy's heirs and before long occupied all the residences in the complex. At the time, the new Admiralty was rising beside the Winter Palace, and this monumental edifice made the buildings across the square seem unacceptably modest. Accordingly, in 1819 a decision was taken to modify the site radically by constructing new offices for Russia's main government agencies—the General Staff, the Finance Ministry, and the Ministry of Foreign Affairs—

rov had been dead for many years by the time they were decorated.

The architect had intended the main façade to front a square that he had designed, but in 1870 a garden was laid out on the site with rectilinear walks, fountains, and small monuments dedicated to prominent figures of St. Petersburg culture: the composer Mikhail Glinka; the writers Nikolai Gogol, Mikhail Lermontov, and Vasily Zhukovsky; and Nikolai Przhevalsky, the Russian traveler celebrated for his explorations in Central Asia, who is depicted with his faithful camel. These features make the area adjacent to the Admiralty quite intimate and cozy, as is evident to anyone who has walked in the garden among the old women, children, and dogs that now frequent it.

LEFT

MIKHAILOVSKY
PALACE.

*Garden façade. Just as
elaborate as the main
façade, it features a
rusticated portico
supporting a long
Corinthian colonnade
flanked by slightly
projecting porticos with
triangular pediments.*

OPPOSITE

*Pavilion at the
landing pier of the
Mikhailovsky Palace
on the Moika, designed
by Carlo Rossi.*

along its periphery. A special commission was created for this purpose, and Rossi was named the principal architect of the project.

Officially, this body was known as the Commission for the Establishment of a Regular Square in Front of the Winter Palace. The use of *regular* here is crucial, for it signified that the result was to be geometrical and feature a unified façade, and Rossi's design adhered to this stipulation. In essence, he combined Starov's idea that a curved façade should face the palace with Velten's notion that this façade should be unified and continuous. The result was a square of unprecedented scale and majesty. Clearly Rossi had decided to follow his own recommendation that Russian architects not be afraid of surpassing in scale the buildings of Imperial Rome.

There are a few roughly comparable urban complexes, most notably the Royal Crescent in Bath, England, with its two semi-elliptical rows of houses framing a landscaped park. In Rossi's design, however, the curve of the façade is not elliptical but parabolic, and this lends greater dynamism to the whole. The final effect is also radically different because this dynamic thrust is directed not toward sylvan vistas dotted with villas but rather toward the sumptuous and luxurious palace of the Russian emperors.

The ceremonial approach to the Winter Palace begins from Nevsky Prospekt. A short side street opens to

its right and then bends to the left to emerge on an axis with the entrance to the palace right beneath the triumphal General Staff Arch. Grandiose and deep, the arch creates a tunnel-like effect. The span facing the square is flanked by enormous cast-iron warriors and trophies between Corinthian columns, as well as figures of Fame carrying wreaths, and is surmounted by a group representing Victory driving toward the palace in a six-horse chariot.

Rossi imagined a gigantic column in the square's center rather like Trajan's column in Rome. Montferrand fulfilled Rossi's dream between 1830 and 1834, when he built the Alexander Column, so called because it is dedicated to the memory of Alexander I and his victory over Napoleon. This perfectly realized monument is held by some to be Montferrand's finest contribution to the cityscape. It is immense in scale, soaring more than 150 feet (47 meters) high. Transporting and mounting its 600 tons was considered an exceptional feat at the time. The angel perched atop the column was intended to invoke the deceased emperor: those close to him — especially the enraptured women in his entourage — referred to him as an "angel incarnate." But this allusion was understood only within court circles; in the eyes of the people the angel signified God's salvation of Russia from Napoleon and continued protection of her. On the pedestal are personifications of Wisdom and Abundance,

149

which reign in the empire, as well as depictions of Victory and Peace. The old man pouring water from a jug represents the river Niemen, which was crossed by the Grande Armée when it invaded Russia. The young woman personifies another river, the Vistula, crossed by the Russian Army during its pursuit of the retreating French forces. The arms on the monument, exact replicas of ancient examples preserved in the Armory Palace in the Moscow Kremlin, are intended to symbolize the valor of the Russian Army. All the reliefs were executed after designs by D. B. Scotti.

Between 1837 and 1843 Alexander Bryulov replaced the drill hall on the eastern side, built by Vincenzo Brenna in the 1790s, with General Staff Headquarters for the Guard. This was the only addition to the original design. Today's square is an accurate reflection of Rossi's intentions, perhaps the most beautiful square in St. Petersburg.

S ENATE SQUARE AND DECEMBRIST SQUARE. On the other side of the Admiralty is another square whose design is much indebted to Carlo Rossi. Here, facing the lateral part of the Admiralty, stood the mid-eighteenth-century baroque palace of the chancellor of the empire, Alexander Bestuzhev-Ryumin. After his death the residence was purchased by the state, and the Senate—Russia's supreme legislative and judicial body—was installed there. In 1768 the second St. Isaac's Cathedral, designed by Antonio Rinaldi, was begun on the south side of the square. The project was never completed, however, and in the nineteenth century the unfinished structure was demolished and replaced by the building designed by Montferrand. Etienne Falconet's monument to Peter the Great was inaugurated in the square in 1782, and during this period the Senate building was remodeled along classical lines.

Between 1804 and 1807 Quarenghi built the Horse Guards Manège, a long, rectangular structure with rustication over two-thirds of its height and a Doric portico with paired columns in the middle of its southern façade. Overall it adheres to the Doric temple format fashionable in the early nineteenth century, but Quarenghi, ever faithful to the Palladian ethos he had introduced into Russia, treated it rather freely, introducing refinements not found in the work of his younger colleagues Voronikhin and Thomon. Statues of the Dioscuri restraining rearing horses, the work of the Italian P. Triscorni, were placed in front of the building.

View of Nevsky Prospekt near the Anichkov Palace, c. 1895, watercolor by A. K. Beggrov.

ANICHKOV PALACE.
*Remodeled several
times since construction
began in 1741, the
building received its
definitive appearance
as part of Carlo Rossi's
project to refurbish the
surrounding quarter
beginning in 1818.*

Such was the state of Senate Square in 1825. And it was here, on December 14 of that year, that the ill-fated uprising led by the members of the secret societies took place. The rebellious regiments remained at the foot of the monument to Peter the Great all day until they were attacked by government forces, whose artillery annihilated the Decembrists, as the rebels have been called ever since. In 1827, shortly after five of the survivors had been condemned to death and the others exiled, a decision was taken to transform the square's appearance in hopes of erasing memories of the episode. In a sense this project was already under way, for the Admiralty had just been completed and construction of St. Isaac's Cathedral had begun. The next step was to reconstruct the Senate, a move rendered all but unavoidable by the solemn monumentality of the new adjacent buildings.

A competition was held, and entries were submitted by many eminent architects, including Stasov, Shustov, and Mikhailov II. Rossi, however, took first prize. The main façade of his design occupies the entire western side of the square, uniting the Senate building with that of the Synod—the highest ecclesiastical body in nine-teenth-century Russia. As in Palace Square, Rossi placed a triumphal arch in the center of his composition.

Reclining allegories of Justice and Piety crown the façade, which is animated by alternating engaged and freestanding paired Corinthian columns. Rossi's handling of the semicircular colonnade at the corner facing the Neva is especially deft.

The majestic square extends as far as the English Embankment and the Laval residence, a beautiful private house whose classical vocabulary is essentially due to Thomon, who remodeled the building in the first decade of the nineteenth century. The main staircase, which features a sculpted ceiling, was conceived in the spirit of Roman baths, and the painted decors in many of the other rooms are quite charming.

ST. ISAAC'S CATHEDRAL.

When Théophile Gautier visited Russia in 1859, he described St. Isaac's Cathedral in glowing terms: "When the traveler approaches St. Petersburg from the Gulf of Finland, it is the dome of St. Isaac's, resting on the city's

ANICHKOV PALACE.
Winter Garden, 1830s.

silhouette like a golden miter, that first catches his eye. In general aspect . . . it resembles a harmonious synthesis of St. Peter's and the Pantheon of Agrippa in Rome, St. Paul's in London, and Ste. Geneviève and the dome of the Invalides in Paris."[12] Elsewhere in the chapter on St. Isaac's in his *Voyage to Russia* he writes: "Every hour of the day has its mirage. If one looks at St. Isaac's from the Neva embankment in the morning, it is the color of amethyst and burnt topaz amid an aureole of milky and pink splendors. . . . In the evening . . . its windows caught in the rays of the setting sun, it seems illuminated, as if it were burning within. . . . When the twinkling stars and indistinct glow of the Milky Way make all objects seem ghostly, the cathedral's great masses rise majestically and take on a mysterious solemnity."[13]

It is incontestably the most grandiose of all the churches in St. Petersburg. Built to a design by Montferrand over a period of forty years, between 1818 and 1858, it is difficult to classify and holds a special fascination for anyone interested in nineteenth-century architecture. It does not sit easily with the tradition that was flourishing in the capital when it was erected, as exemplified by the neighboring buildings by Zakharov and Rossi; instead it exhibits a very different approach to structure and proportion, architectural detailing, and historical precedent. It would seem logical to associate the design with French

models, but there is nothing comparable in the Parisian architectural world of either the Empire or the Restoration. As Gautier suggests, many of its features bring to mind famous European churches and sanctuaries, from the Pantheon in ancient Rome to its namesake in Paris. The dome resembles Christopher Wren's for St. Paul's in London, and there is something of Paris's Ste. Geneviève in the relation between its severe Corinthian portico and its smooth masonry walls. The overall design is perhaps closest to the Cathedral of St. Nicholas in Potsdam, built at almost exactly the same time by the architect Karl Schinkel. All these analogies are debatable, however, as is the importance of Montferrand's French training. There is another factor that must be taken into account: St. Isaac's belongs to a very special and very limited tradition consisting exclusively of gigantic classical cathedrals, the first of which was St. Peter's in Rome. As much as anything else, it is the building's sheer scale that gives it its distinctive character, that prompted unorthodox design solutions.

What is most striking about St. Isaac's is its grandiosity, and the somber mass of its gray marble, which restrains the sumptuous quality of its classical forms. Forty-eight granite columns, each weighing almost 110 tons, are incorporated into its four gigantic porticos. Their heavy pediments are richly decorated with relief

ANICHKOV PALACE.
Main staircase, 1830s.

ANICHKOV PALACE.
Blue Salon, 1830s.

ANICHKOV PALACE.
*View of the
enfilade, 1830s.*

sculpture representing biblical subjects. The architectural detailing is extremely spare. There are only eight
windows; they are of course immense but provide insufficient light to the interior. Four bell towers with small
gilded domes rise above the sanctuary like classical pavilions. A wide cornice gives the building's horizontal lines
considerable emphasis and power. Above, reigning over
not only the church itself but the whole city, is the
grandiose drum with its twenty-four granite columns.
They are lighter than those in the porticos, weighing
only sixty-four tons each, but even so it must have been
quite difficult to lift these monoliths to their lofty
perches some 160 feet (48 meters) off the ground. Above
a balustrade adorned with twenty-four sculpted figures
rises the elegant gilded dome itself. Legend has it that
many of the gilders died during their work as a consequence of having inhaled the mercury fumes in the gold
amalgam. However that may be, the result is a stunning
edifice that marks the apogee of nineteenth-century St.
Petersburg classicism.

As for the interior, its decor is enriched by the combined effect of marble, porphyry, lazulite, and mala-
chite. It also features many gilt bronzes, some splendid
mosaics, and lavish sculpture. The vaults are decorated
with almost two hundred academic paintings. Of the
many artists who worked on the building, several de-
serve mention here: the sculptors I. Vitali, N. Pimenov,

A. Loganovsky, and Pyotr Karlovich Klodt, and the painters Karl Bryulov, V. Shchebuev, and Alexander Andreevich Ivanov. The art they created for St. Isaac's, the
principal sanctuary of the empire, must be deemed official, but never was the official art that prevailed under
Nicholas I to achieve such force and clarity.

THE BEGINNING OF NEVSKY PROSPEKT.
"There is nothing finer than Nevsky Avenue, not
in St. Petersburg at any rate; for in St. Petersburg
it is everything. And, indeed, is there anything more
gay, more brilliant, more resplendent than this beautiful street of our capital? I am sure that not one of her
anaemic inhabitants, not one of her innumerable Civil
Servants, would exchange Nevsky Avenue for all the treasures in the world. Not only the young man of twenty-
five, the young gallant with the beautiful moustache and
the immaculately cut morning coat, but the man with
white hair sprouting on his chin and a head as smooth as
a billiard ball, yes, even he is enthralled with Nevsky
Avenue. And the ladies . . . Oh, for the ladies Nevsky
Avenue is a thing of even greater delight! But is there anyone who does not feel thrilled and delighted with it?"
So Nikolai Gogol, one of Russia's greatest nineteenth-
century writers, begins his story "Nevsky Prospekt," published in 1835.[14]

BELOSELSKY-
BELOZERSKY PALACE.
RIGHT *Gallery.*
OPPOSITE *One of the
first examples of neo-
baroque architecture, it
was built between 1846
and 1848 to a design
inspired by Rastrelli's
then century-old
Stroganov Palace. Its
architect was Andrei
Stakenschneider, who
made use of many
elements drawn from
the late baroque
vocabulary of the early
eighteenth century,
notably semicircular
pediments, elaborate
window treatments, and
term atlantes.*

By that time Nevsky Prospekt had indeed become the center of St. Petersburg. At its far end Starov had completed his Cathedral of the Trinity of the Alexander Nevsky Lavra, and the other end culminated in the new Admiralty spire. The great artery that stretched between these two complexes was lined with some of the finest classical buildings in St. Petersburg. In the mid-nineteenth century it was a locus of the classical style, and it also boasted a few rare baroque palaces. But in the second half of the century and especially in the early years of the twentieth century its appearance changed radically. It became the preferred address for banks, offices, and department stores. This development altered its scale and destroyed the stylistic unity it had acquired before 1850, but the street nonetheless retained an appealingly ostentatious quality and became more picturesque.

Moving away from the Admiralty, the first residence encountered on the left is an extension of the General Staff Headquarters building, conceived very much in the spirit of Rossi's great work. A few buildings farther down, on the same side, are two classical residences built in the 1760s and refurbished in the 1830s. Across the street from them at number 13 is the Chaplin house, whose design by V. Beretti typifies St. Petersburg residential architecture of the first quarter of the nineteenth century. At the intersection with Bolshaya Morskaya Street is a house with a two-story colonnade and a rounded corner. Built during the reign of Catherine the Great for Chicherin, the city's chief of police, it is one of the finest extant examples of the early Russian classical style, but none of its original interiors survive. Approaching the end of the avenue's narrowest portion, close to the Moika, we come upon a cast-iron bridge. Built between 1806 and 1808 to a design by the Scot William Guestier, this was the first metal span to appear in any Russian city. It was originally known as the Police Bridge or the Green Bridge.

On the far side of the Moika, where the avenue broadens, we encounter, directly opposite each other, the Stroganov Palace—one of Rastrelli's finest baroque exercises—and the Kotomin residence, entirely rebuilt in an austere classical idiom during the Napoleonic Wars by Stasov. The building beyond it, the Dutch Church, which dates from the 1830s, provides a good indication of how classicism was developing. Farther along, still on the left but slightly inset from the street, is Bryulov's Lutheran Church, which reveals the influence of German models on St. Petersburg architects in the 1830s. But what is most significant along this stretch of the avenue is the way the aligned façades of the houses are interrupted from time to time by large public structures, beginning with the Kazan Cathedral on the right.

KAZAN CATHEDRAL. Andrei Voronikhin began construction of the Kazan Cathedral in 1801, and it was completed in 1811, shortly before the Napoleonic invasion. It is characteristic of the architecture along Nevsky Prospekt in the degree to which it acknowledges its conspicuous location. From the exterior it seems gigantic, but the interior is relatively small. The architect was especially attentive to the handling of the space around the building. The church itself has a Latin-cross plan. The façade facing Nevsky Prospekt, which is not the main entrance, is flanked on either side by a huge semicircular colonnade. Supported by two rows of Corinthian columns made of pink Finnish granite, it is topped by a powerful entablature further accentuated by a massive balustrade. This serves as a visual base for the dome with its metal calotte, one of the first of its kind in Europe.

Another semicircular colonnade was envisioned for the opposite side of the cathedral, as were three adjacent squares, one in front of the principal entrance and two adjoining the lateral ones. Only the façade facing Nevsky Prospekt was fully realized, however, a telling indication of the importance accorded the proper embellishment of this street. It was primarily because the other colonnade would not have been visible from the avenue that it

was never built. Thus Kazan Cathedral was left incomplete, but its Nevsky façade assumed even greater prominence when two monuments were erected in front of it commemorating the leaders of the Russian Army in the War of 1812, Field Marshal Kutuzov and Barclay de Tolly. The work of Boris Orlovsky, they were dedicated in 1837.

The cathedral itself boasts some remarkable statuary, including bronze figures in the niches—*St. Vladimir* and *Alexander Nevsky* by S. Pimenov, *St. John the Baptist* by Ivan Martos, and *The Calling of St. Andrew* by Demut-Malinovsky; Old Testament reliefs above the eastern and western entrances—*Moses Striking Water from the Rock* by Martos and *The Brazen Serpent* by I. Prokofiev, respectively; and four New Testament reliefs within the northern portico by F. Gordev.

FROM KAZAN CATHEDRAL TO GOSTINY DVOR. Kazan Cathedral is situated at the intersection of Nevsky Prospekt and the Catherine Canal (known in the Soviet era as the Griboyedov Canal, after the nineteenth-century playwright who wrote *Woe from Wit*). Beyond the Kazan Bridge, on the same side of the avenue as the cathedral, is a four-story tower,

BELOSELSKY-BELOZERSKY PALACE. LEFT *Mantelpiece.* BELOW *Green Salon.*

BELOSELSKY-
BELOZERSKY PALACE.
*View of three overdoors
in the enfilade. The one
in the foreground, of
rococo inspiration, was
executed by the sculptor
J. I. Jensen. The two
others are neobaroque.*

YUSUPOV PALACE. *Moika façade. Vallin de la Mothe added the colossal colonnade in 1760, when the palace belonged to Count Shuvalov. It was sumptuously remodeled in the 1830s by Andrei Mikhailov II for its new owner, Prince Yusupov.*

erected between 1799 and 1804. It presides over the "silver galleries" that once housed jewelry shops, built by Quarenghi between 1784 and 1787, and the headquarters of the City Duma, formerly the city hall, refurbished in an eclectic style and crowned by a clock tower.

In the nineteenth century the most important commercial stretch of Nevsky Prospekt began beyond the city hall. Here the passerby encounters the two-story arcades of the large Gostiny Dvor, or merchants' court, built by Vallin de la Mothe between 1761 and 1785, one of the first classical structures to appear in St. Petersburg. In the 1880s the architect Alexander Benois remodeled the façade facing the prospekt, shortening its columns and thus somewhat spoiling its effect. Before the eighteenth century came to a close, another structure rose next door that housed bedding merchants and became known as the "feather bed gallery." In 1806 the architect Luigi Rusca added a Doric portico to it.

Directly across the avenue is St. Catherine's Catholic Church, also designed by Vallin de la Mothe. Just beyond it is little Mikhailovskaya Street, which leads to one of the quarter's most interesting features, Mikhailovsky Palace Square. It is now known as Arts Square, for it is bordered by the Russian Museum, the Maly Theater (opera and ballet), and the Philharmonic. It is one of the great urban ensembles devised by Carlo Rossi.

MIKHAILOVSKY PALACE. Grand Duke Michael was the youngest of Paul I's four sons. He would accede to the throne only if all of his brothers died before him, an unlikely scenario. As a result he was extremely well liked by everyone in the imperial family and the construction of a palace for him was considered an important matter of state.

Carlo Rossi commenced work on the project in 1817, and as usual he came up with several alternative designs. The definitive one was approved in 1819, and the building was completed in 1825. Rossi was given two directives that might seem mutually incompatible, but he managed to reconcile them successfully. On the one hand he was asked to build a palace with a park resembling an *usadba*, or country house, while on the other he was instructed to conceive his design in a way that would ameliorate the surrounding area of the city.

The resulting structure played a significant role in the evolution of the St. Petersburg cityscape. It rose on the former site of the service buildings and orangery of the Mikhailovsky, or Engineers', Castle, constructed for Paul I, and Rossi was very successful in linking the castle with his new palace. In fact, the entire quarter—which also encompassed the Field of Mars and the Summer Garden—was reconceived as a result of the architect's interventions.

YUSUPOV PALACE.
RIGHT *Main staircase.*
BELOW *Neobaroque
main staircase, rebuilt
by Monighetti between
1859 and 1862.*

On the other side of the palace the simple, rectangular Mikhailovsky Square was laid out, and the original design called for the buildings on its three other sides—private residences as well as the French theater—to be given façades in a single style. But Rossi's conception was subsequently modified. In the early twentieth century the Ethnographic Museum, designed by V. Svinin, replaced the palace's eastern wing. In tandem with the conversion of the palace into a museum of Russian art an exhibition gallery was built to its west in 1914.

T HEATER SQUARE. Leaving Mikhailovsky Palace, the visitor crosses the square, passes by short Mikhailovskaya Street and the Europa Hotel, and emerges once again on Nevsky Prospekt. Opposite, on the other side of the avenue, is the public library. Founded in 1795 and opened to the public in 1814, it was long Russia's principal library. It occupies three buildings. The oldest, featuring a curving Ionic colonnade, was built by the architect E. Sokolov between 1796 and 1801, during the reign of Paul I. The most interesting part of the complex was erected by Rossi fifteen years later and expanded at the end of the nineteenth century. The library occupies an entire city block, one side of which fronts Theater Square (known in the Soviet era as Ostrovsky Square, after the famous nineteenth-century playwright).

YUSUPOV PALACE. LEFT *Detail of the decor of the room with white columns.* BELOW *Room with white columns, designed by Andrei Mikhailov II.*

YUSUPOV PALACE.
*Ceiling of the room
with white columns,
known as the Rotunda.*

Opposite the library is the Anichkov Palace. Construction of this imperial residence began in 1741, when the baroque was in its heyday. At that time the site was still beyond the city limits, in a fashionable aristocratic quarter bordering the Fontanka. The principal block, which consists of three stories, faced the embankment; in front of it was a courtyard surrounded by galleries and lateral structures. Empress Elizabeth Petrovna presented this sumptuous palace to her favorite Alexei Razumovsky and then Catherine the Great acquired it for Prince Potemkin. Later it reverted to the imperial family, becoming the residence of the empress's third grandson, Nicholas. After he became emperor, Nicholas I continued to spend time there, and the Anichkov Palace became famous as the site of lavish balls. In the late eighteenth century it was remodeled by one of the finest of Russian classical architects, Ivan Starov. In 1803 Giacomo Quarenghi separated the building from the banks of the Fontanka by erecting a shopping arcade, which was subsequently converted into private administrative offices for Alexander I. The baroque interiors were also refurbished in the eighteenth century, and again in 1809–10 by Luigi Rusca. In 1817–18 Carlo Rossi completely transformed the building's appearance by significantly reducing the size of the garden and incorporating the land thus freed into Theater Square. Today the Anichkov gardens are still separated from the square by Rossi's fence, the corners of which are marked by pavilions in a lighter, more refined variant of the style used in his buildings on Palace, Senate, and Mikhailovsky squares.

Theater Square takes its name from the Alexandrinsky Theater, one of the largest in St. Petersburg, built by Rossi between 1828 and 1832. To best grasp his conception, the theater should be approached not from Nevsky Prospekt but rather from the embankment of the Fontanka. Here the architect laid out a hexahedral square surrounded by austere façades with a colossal Tuscan order supported by a rusticated and arcaded basement. The corners of all the buildings are especially powerful. Three streets converge at the square, yet the main one is not the center street but the one on the right, leading directly to the theater itself. Once named Theater Street, it has now been rechristened Architect Rossi Street—which is appropriate, since it is one of the architect's most characteristic achievements. Both sides of the street feature identical façades extending its entire length, and the lines of the cornices supported by their engaged colonnades of paired columns align precisely with that of the theater at its end. The resulting perspective view, with its strong horizontals echoing those of the theater itself, is among the most remarkable architectural experiences St. Petersburg has to offer. The theater's main façade, however, faces the square abutting Nevsky Prospekt. Above its inset Corinthian colonnade are two winged Victories in relief, and higher still is a sculptural group representing Apollo in his chariot. In front of the theater is an interesting monument to Catherine the Great. Dedicated in 1873, it was designed by the sculptor Mikhail Mikeshin but executed by Alexander Opekushin and Matvei Chizhov. The high pedestal supporting the figure of the empress is decorated with depictions of well-known court dignitaries and generals associated with her reign: Suvorov, Potemkin, and Princess Dashkova, president of the Academy of Sciences. The conception has a theatrical character well suited to the site.

YUSUPOV PALACE.
Moresque Salon.

NEVSKY PROSPEKT BEYOND THE ANICHKOV BRIDGE. The Anichkov Palace is well known to St. Petersburg's inhabitants, not only because of its architectural interest but also because of the exceptionally beautiful bridge nearby that spans the Fontanka. A bridge has existed on this site since the time of Peter the Great, but the current one dates from 1839–41. It is decorated with four bronze *Horse Tamers* by Pyotr Klodt that must be numbered among the finest achievements of Russian classical sculpture. Each of the groups depicts a naked youth restraining a rearing horse. In one the horse has triumphed and the youth lies on the ground. In two others he is fighting with the horse. And in the fourth he leads the tamed horse behind him. They became famous—not only in St. Petersburg but throughout Europe—even before their installation, and as soon as two of them were finished Nicholas I decided to present them to the king of Prussia, who had them placed in front of the Old Palace in Berlin. Klodt cast two more versions for the Anichkov Bridge, but in 1846 another pair was given to the king of Naples and Klodt found himself obliged to cast two more.

In fact, the Nevsky Prospekt of the classical period terminated at the Anichkov Bridge. Just beyond it is the Beloselsky-Belozersky Palace, built by Andrei Stakenschneider in 1846 in a neobaroque idiom indebted to Rastrelli. Thereafter late-nineteenth-century houses dominate the avenue, but there are a few exceptions, notably the Sukhozamet residence, erected in the 1820s and remodeled in 1830, and the magnificent Yusupov residence, with its splendid Ionic portico on a high, rusticated subbasement. Finally, there is the Nicholas Train Station, now the Moscow Station, built between 1843 and 1851 by Konstantin Ton in a neo-Renaissance style. This building marks the beginning of a new era, one whose architecture would be shaped by different functions and stylistic preferences. The classical age was a thing of the past, but Nevsky Prospekt remained.

THE FIELD OF MARS AND THE WORK OF VASILY STASOV IN ST. PETERSBURG. Like the Champs de Mars in Paris, its St. Petersburg namesake was originally intended for military pa-

rades. Subsequently, however, it became an enormous square surrounded by famous buildings. To the northeast it is bordered by Peter the Great's Summer Palace and the Summer Garden, while its southern limit is defined by the Moika, fronted on the opposite bank by Mikhailovsky Palace and Mikhailovsky Castle. Its northern border parallels the Palace Embankment, from which it is separated by the Marble Palace, built by Antonio Rinaldi during the reign of Catherine the Great; the Saltykov residence, built in the late eighteenth century after a design by Quarenghi; and the Betsky residence, generally attributed to either Vallin de la Mothe or Ivan Starov. Between the outbuildings of the Marble Palace and the Saltykov house Carlo Rossi laid out a small square in which was placed the remarkable monument to General Suvorov, Prince of Italy and Count of Rimini, executed by the sculptor Mikhail Kozlovsky in 1801. It is almost as though all the masters of St. Petersburg classicism wanted to contribute something to the Field of Mars. Even so, at the beginning of the nineteenth century one side of this enormous square was not on a par with the rest of this "harmony of masterpieces." The situation was remedied between 1817 and 1819, when Vasily Stasov built his barracks for the

Pavlovsky Regiment. This is an immense and grandiose structure entirely worthy of its prestigious site, especially since Stasov, unlike his predecessors, chose to make the façade facing the square the principal one.

One should not imagine the Field of Mars in this period without military parades. In St. Petersburg these were important public occasions, grandiose rituals in which the emperor often took part. Paul I participated on a daily basis, and his sons Alexander I and especially Nicholas I also officiated quite regularly. The emperor, who wore his dress uniform and was surrounded by guards marching in impeccable formation, was seen to greater advantage on these occasions than on almost any others. In the first half of the nineteenth century these displays unrolled with flawless precision: every button sparkled and every formation went like clockwork. The considerable strength of Stasov's façade was indispensable to the enormous extent of the square.

Not far from there, at the junction of the Moika and the Catherine Canal, Stasov realized one of his most lyrical works: the Court Stables. This complex of several buildings housed stables, a riding school, depots, administrative offices, and a church. Marked by a timid ele-

CATHEDRAL OF THE TRANSFIGURATION. *Built for the Preobrazhensky Regiment. It was consecrated in 1829, two years after construction began, and it commemorates the Russian victory over the Turkish fleet at Navarino in 1827. The architect, Vasily Stasov, acknowledged this by incorporating cannons seized from the enemy during that engagement into the surrounding fence.*

CATHEDRAL OF
THE TRINITY.
Built between 1827 and
1835 for the Izmailovsky
Regiment by Vasily
Stasov. It has a Greek-
cross plan and features
five painted domes.
It played an important
role in the urban
development of this
quarter of the city.

gance, the design is remarkable for its lightness and clarity, especially when viewed from the small square in front of its church or from the Moika embankment near its low, circular colonnade.

Stasov's other works in St. Petersburg are quite different. He built several barracks, depots, churches, and other buildings of triumphal character for the War Ministry. He was also responsible for the gates erected in 1834 on Moskovsky Prospekt to commemorate the victory over the Turks in 1828. The guard regiments had their own churches, and Stasov built two of them: the Cathedral of the Transfiguration for the Preobrazhensky Regiment and the Cathedral of the Trinity for the Izmailovsky Regiment. Both of them must be numbered among the most important Russian classical sanctuaries. Their immense scale and their incorporation of a traditional Orthodox five-dome schema into austerely classical designs were much imitated in Russian ecclesiastical architecture. The circumstances of their commission led to the inclusion of ingenious martial detailing, notably the use of upright cannons in the fence surrounding the Cathedral of the Transfiguration.

PALACES ON KAMENNY AND ELAGIN ISLANDS.

When St. Petersburgers say, "Let's go to the islands," they usually mean the three islands to the northwest: Kamenny, Krestovsky, and Elagin. Each of them played a special role in the city's history. They are an integral part of St. Petersburg, yet their character sets them very much apart from the bustling quarters full of government offices, barracks, impressive residences, shops, workshops, and industrial enterprises. Things are different on the islands, and in the winter they are almost deserted. At the beginning of the nineteenth century they were favorite places for romantic trysts and solitary walks amid their canals, dachas, and palaces.

> *The columns once again covered with snow*
> *The Elagin bridge and two fires*
> *And the voice of a lovesick woman*
> *And the crunch of sand and the snorting of horses*
> *Two shadows fused in kiss*
> *Flee beneath the sleigh's fur. . . .*

Such is Alexander Blok's evocation of a winter promenade in the islands at the beginning of the century.[15]

In 1704 Peter the Great gave Kamenny Island to Count Gavriil Golovin, the first chancellor of the Russian empire, who built a small *usadba* there. In 1746 his son sold the island to Count Alexander Bestuzhev-Ryumin, Elizabeth Petrovna's chancellor of the empire. He commissioned Rastrelli to build a palace and a park there, and the result was the lightest, most luxurious, and most delicate of all the

ELAGIN PALACE.
Porcelain Study,
designed by
Carlo Rossi.

architect's palaces. Unfortunately the count fell from favor and was exiled to Siberia, and the palace was confiscated for use by the empress during the reign of Peter III. When Catherine II acceded to the throne she gave the island to her son Paul, and a new page was turned in its history.

Vasily Bazhenov, a young architect freshly returned from France, where he had studied with Charles de Wailly, was engaged to rework the complex. It is not entirely clear to what degree the extant buildings reflect his designs, for their construction was overseen by Georg Velten, himself an important architect of the first phase of St. Petersburg classicism. In any event, Rastrelli's earlier baroque structure was demolished and replaced by a simple two-story residence with projecting pavilions on either side, adorned only by a modest hexastyle portico of the Tuscan order. The interior of the garden side of the building featured an enfilade with a large oval salon in the center. The original interiors survive; they are in a classical style with touches of rococo extravagance. The original garden was formal, but in the early nineteenth century it was transformed into a romantic garden by the architect Grigori Pilnikov, who is believed to have worked from drawings by Thomas de Thomon. By that time the palace belonged to Alexander I.

Neighboring Elagin Island takes its name from its late-eighteenth-century owner, Ivan Elagin, who was a favorite of Catherine the Great. The first palace there, probably designed by Quarenghi, was for him. When the widow of Paul I acquired the island in 1817, the palace was completely rebuilt by Carlo Rossi. He worked in tandem with Joseph Bush, a remarkable English garden designer who had long resided in Russia, and the result was one of the imperial family's most elegant *usadbas*.

This palace is of exceptional interest, for it reveals another side of Rossi's artistic personality. His customary clarity and virtuosity are very much in evidence here, but his approach to volume is more playful and exploratory than in his other work. Slender porticos on either side of the two main façades frame two central colonnades, a conventional one on the garden side and an outcurving one on the river façade. The main block is surmounted by a kind of belvedere culminating in a low dome. The main house is complemented by a kitchen, stables, and an orangery, all situated nearby in the garden, as well as by three small pavilions bordering the river, which in conjunction with the palace compose charming *vedute* in the classical tradition.

ELAGIN PALACE.
*Oval Salon. The
engaged Ionic columns
answer those of the
exterior colonnade.*

6

❧

ALEXANDER II
AND ALEXANDER III

RETROSPECTION AND NATIONALISM

I must say that from these façades and porticoes—classical, modern, eclectic, with their columns, pilasters, and plastered heads of mythic animals or people—from their ornaments and caryatids holding up the balconies, from the torsos in the niches of their entrances, I have learned more about the history of our world than I subsequently have from any books.

—Joseph Brodsky
"Less Than One"

THE PALACE
EMBANKMENT.
*Former palace of
Grand Duke Vladimir
Alexandrovich. Built
between 1864 and
1872 by the architect
Alexander Rezanov for
the son of Alexander II,
the palace features a
rusticated sandstone
façade in Florentine
Renaissance style.
A portico with three
arches marks the
center of the façade.*

A RAPIDLY EVOLVING CITY. The second half of the nineteenth century—the period of the reigns of Alexander II and Alexander III, the son and grandson, respectively, of Nicholas I—became increasingly enigmatic with the passage of time. It is said to have been an era that saw the rapid development of capitalism in Russia; the economic system evolved in tandem with a strengthening of the government's autocratic grip. Serfdom was abolished in 1861 and Alexander II was dubbed the Tsar-Liberator. At the same time industrialization was actively taking hold and the Russian bourgeoisie was coming to the fore. The country was developing at a staggering pace. There was ample evidence of this in the spectacular growth of St. Petersburg and the profusion of construction.

It is difficult to grasp the character of St. Petersburg in these years without bearing in mind its "heroes," the figures who haunt the streets of the great Russian novels set in this period. St. Petersburg is the city of Dostoevsky and Tolstoy, of *Crime and Punishment* and *Resurrection*. The whirlwind of their strange, intractable passions whistled through its broad avenues and the muddy recesses of its more distant alleys. Dostoevsky himself found in the architecture of St. Petersburg a reflection of the milieu he describes in his novels. In his *Diary of a Writer* he noted: "Now, now no one really knows how to define the architecture of our time. There's a kind of

incoherence that, by the way, corresponds perfectly to the incoherence of the present moment. It is a multitude of extraordinarily tall (above all, tall) houses, of houses 'to let,' as the curious phrase goes, that are thin-walled and boringly lined up, with façades of astonishing architecture: there's Rastrelli, there's also late rococo, and dogelike balconies [like the balconies of the Palace of the Doges] and windows . . . and without exception five stories. And all that in one and the same façade."[1]

The first Russian architectural review, *The Architect*, wrote in 1872, "Petersburg is acquiring a more and more European appearance."[2] And it was true. In effect, the palette of historical styles of the middle and second half of the nineteenth century paralleled the one that predominated all over Europe at the time. Neobaroque and neo-Renaissance, Louis XV and Napoleon III, Gothic Revival and Greek Revival, eclecticism and "Oriental" styles appeared in St. Petersburg just as they did elsewhere. But in St. Petersburg they were combined in idiosyncratic ways. Classical influence was very strong there, and as a result the historicizing idiom tended to stress classical as opposed to medieval models. The phenomenon first appeared in the middle of the century in the work of the best-known architect of the period, Andrei Stakenschneider. In 1848 he was named architect to the imperial court, and during the next two decades he built new palaces and refurbished older ones. Between 1839

PALACE OF GRAND
DUKE VLADIMIR
ALEXANDROVICH.
Main staircase, refurb-
ished by Maximilian
Mesmakher in 1880.

PALACE OF GRAND
DUKE VLADIMIR
ALEXANDROVICH.
*Two views of the decor
of the Moresque Room.*

and 1844 he had erected the first of his great palaces in the city, the Mariinsky. Its exterior aspect, austere and shorn of detailing, is compensated for by its spectacular interiors. An enfilade of rooms leads via a high-domed rotunda to a square salon adjacent to a winter garden. This garden is no longer extant, for in the beginning of the twentieth century Leonti Benois replaced it with a large assembly room when the palace was transformed into the seat of the Imperial Council.

Stakenschneider's originality becomes evident when the Mariinsky Palace is compared with the other buildings along St. Isaac's Square. The Ministry of State Property, begun by the architect Nikolai Efimov in 1844, the year the Mariinsky Palace was completed, is in a neo-Renaissance style. The Astoria Hotel, built by Fedor Lidval between 1908 and 1912, and the building erected by Peter Behrens for the German embassy between 1911 and 1912 face one another across the northern part of the square. They offer two variants of a brand of neoclassicism that flourished in the era of Art Nouveau. The importance of the classical influence is driven home when one grasps the extent to which it shaped the work of masters as different as Stakenschneider and Behrens.

Between 1853 and 1861 Stakenschneider built the Nikolaevsky Palace for Grand Duke Nikolai Nikolae-

vich, brother of Alexander II, on the square adjacent to the bridge linking the Admiralty quarter with Vasilievsky Island. This building bears witness to the increasing prevalence of Renaissance motifs in the work of this architect. In the 1840s, however, he turned to a neobaroque idiom, embracing Russian baroque models, as evidenced by the Beloselsky-Belozersky Palace on Nevsky Prospekt. As a rule Stakenschneider preferred to use one or another specific style for the façades of his palaces, whereas his interiors combine a broad array of different models. His Pavilion Hall in the Little Hermitage is one of the most typical examples of Russian eclecticism.

The neo-Renaissance style continued to develop throughout the second half of the nineteenth century. The graphic lightness of the façade of the Shuvalov Palace, built on the Fontanka embankment in 1846, was one of the first harbingers of this tendency. It is the work of Efimov, one of the neo-Renaissance style's most refined practitioners. Another gifted architect, Harald Bossay, revealed similar propensities in his Bureau of Departmental Affairs, erected on Liteiny Prospekt in the 1840s, and in his Nechaev-Maltsev residence, which combines neo-Renaissance elements with others derived from the *Rundbogenstil* ("round-arch" or Romanesque style) then fashionable in Germany.

PALACE OF GRAND
DUKE VLADIMIR
ALEXANDROVICH.
*Semi-dome of the
Moresque Room.*

STIEGLIETZ
SCHOOL.
*Large hall of
the pedagogical
museum.
Founded by
the wealthy
financier A. L.
Stieglitz, the
Central School
of Technical
Drawing was
accompanied
by a museum
tracing the
history of art
throughout the
world. The
school was built
by A. I. Krakau
between 1879
and 1881, the
museum by
Maximilian
Mesmakher
between 1885
and 1895.*

KELKHA HOUSE.
*General view
and ceiling detail
of the salon.*

A taste for Florentine palace architecture emerged in the 1860s, with the construction by Alexander Rezanov of the palace of Grand Duke Vladimir Alexandrovich on the Palace Embankment. Its entire façade is covered with powerful rustication. Inside, there are carved wooden ceilings, and the staircase is decorated with carved grotesques. As in most of the St. Petersburg palaces of the period, the interiors draw on the broadest possible range of stylistic models, including a neo-Russian banqueting hall, a rococo ballroom, and a Louis XVI salon. The same neo-Renaissance trend is exemplified by the Kochubei residence on the Boulevard of the Horse Guards and the Stieglitz residence on the English Embankment.

The great period of Renaissance Revival was the 1880s, when the style was widely used by Maximilian Mesmakher, Victor Schröter, Vladimir Schreiber, and many other architects. Two works by Mesmakher must be numbered among the finest from this decade: the palace of Grand Duke Mikhail Mikhailovich on the Admiralty Embankment, with its prolix but harmonious façades, and the Archives of the State Council, opposite the New Hermitage, with its austere decoration but perfectly rational plan. The Pampel house, designed by Schröter, combines neo-Renaissance elements with others typical of St. Petersburg domestic architecture.

This style was also used for railway stations. Both the

Moscow Station, built by Konstantin Ton between 1841 and 1851, and the Baltic Station, built by Georg Krakau between 1855 and 1858, are in a neo-Renaissance idiom. There are also many late-nineteenth-century buildings in the style, but these examples should suffice to indicate the extent of its diffusion in the capital. The neobaroque tendency also calls for discussion. In its initial phase it was nourished by local tradition, drawing on the work of eighteenth-century masters like Rastrelli. Stakenschneider's example of 1846 was emulated by Bossay in the 1850s and by Schröter in the 1860s. But in the course of the 1870s, St. Petersburg baroque was abandoned in favor of its European counterpart.

Eighteenth-century classicism remained the principal source of inspiration, although architects also drew upon Italian and French Renaissance models as well as both Russian and European baroque traditions. It is interesting to note that the classicism of Quarenghi, Zakharov, and Rossi was never pastiched, probably because it was too monumental and too closely associated with the official taste of the preceding era.

In the last years of the nineteenth century the very notion of an architectural ideal underwent a crisis. The belief had become widespread that "everything is at our disposition: the hell of Paris streets and Venetian freshness, the distant aroma of citrus groves and the smoky

KELKHA HOUSE.
Gothic courtyard.

CATHEDRAL OF THE
ASCENSION, OR OF THE
SAVIOR OF THE BLOOD.
*Designed by Alfred Parland,
it was begun in 1883 and completed in 1907. It exemplifies
a Russian nationalist style,*
*incorporating elements
from indigenous churches of
the seventeenth century
(particularly those of the
Volga basin) and from
the Cathedral of St. Basil
the Blessed in Moscow.*

. . . What this style is specifically, and how precisely it is used, we need not discuss. What is important is not the style itself, but the fact that it appeared."[3]

This observation was perfectly applicable to St. Petersburg architecture. In the 1880s a "Russian style" indeed appeared, although it did not achieve anything like general currency. It was in St. Petersburg, however, that the most interesting church in the style was built: the Cathedral of the Ascension, or of the Savior of the Blood. It was erected on the Catherine Canal not far from the Mikhailovsky Palace, on the spot where Alexander II had been assassinated by a terrorist belonging to the revolutionary group known as People's Will. His son Alexander III ordered the edifice to be built in the "pure Russian taste of the seventeenth century," when architecture was in the brilliant "flamboyant" style of the late medieval period. The building's definitive design was devised by the architect Alfred Parland in conjunction with the archimandrite Ignati, the father superior of a nearby monastery who had studied architecture at the St. Petersburg Academy of Fine Arts before becoming a monk. Construction began in 1883 but was completed only in 1907, long after the death of the commissioning emperor. Among its most remarkable features are the mosaics, realized by Alexander Frolov after designs by some of the most important artists of the period, Viktor Vasnetsov, Mikhail Nesterov, and Nikolai Bruni. No other St. Petersburg building in the "Russian style" can compare with this one, but the Russian revivalist idiom was not to be the solution to the architectural crisis in the city.

Recent technical advances suggested other solutions. Metallic architecture was increasingly favored for industrial structures. Bridge designs were growing ever bolder, and metal girders were used for building the Hay Market. The Russian Hall of the Bank of Foreign Trade—a round room built by Schröter in 1887–88—is spectacular. In the end, however, these innovations contributed little to the development of a new architectural language. What was needed was something more in line with the new aesthetic trend then sweeping Europe. As the twentieth century dawned, the capital of Russia was ready to receive Art Nouveau.

With its granite-lined canals and rivers, countless bridges, and immense island parks, the St. Petersburg of this period strikes us as particularly attractive. Running water and gas lamps appeared. There were also the outskirts, whose proliferating factories began to surround the splendid capital, but in this period such development was a welcome sign of prosperity. Even so, the prevailing atmosphere of "retrospection" left no room for concern over impending changes of tragic import.

CATHEDRAL OF THE ASCENSION, OR OF THE SAVIOR OF THE BLOOD.
LEFT *Detail of the complex roof.*
OPPOSITE *The interior is covered with mosaics such as this one, situated in the choir behind the iconostasis.*

masses of Cologne." It was as though all past eras were being mobilized to create a perfect civilization in the present. One had only to select a few elements from the repertory of the past and combine them in attractive ways. Construction in St. Petersburg continued apace, but it was becoming increasingly clear that the game of stylistic mix and match could not continue forever, that another idiom would have to be found. Several solutions to the crisis were advanced. One was a return to indigenous traditions exemplified by Russian medieval models. The idea was not new. Between 1830 and 1850, during the reign of Nicholas I, Konstantin Ton devised an official Russo-Byzantine style of primarily ecclesiastical architecture. It enjoyed a certain success in Moscow at the time but did not catch on in classical St. Petersburg, where such traditional forms appeared only in festival decorations, metalwork, and interior decors.

In 1882 Nikolai Sultanov, one of the first historians to specialize in old Russian architecture, had this to say in a lecture intended for engineers and architects: "Russian style began as a matter of details: it started with trinkets—portrait frames, jewel boxes, book covers . . . iconostases, and then spread to entire rooms and even façades. And now every richly appointed apartment, without fail, includes a room in the Russian style. It is also in this style that most of our dachas are constructed.

7

NICHOLAS II

THE RISE AND FALL OF ART NOUVEAU

In the hour of doubt, when I feel sad and question the destiny of my country, you are my only consolation, my sole support, oh Russian language, great, strong, free, and honest! Without you, how could one fail to despair over what is happening to us? But it is impossible not to believe that such a language was given to a great people!

—Ivan Turgenev
Poems in Prose, June 1882

Apartment house, built by Andrei Belogrud and K. I. Rozenstein in 1914, in a style reminiscent of an English castle.

THE GREAT UPHEAVAL. It is said that in 1917, while the Bolsheviks were storming the Winter Palace during what the Soviets dubbed the Great October Socialist Revolution, business as usual continued in the nearby restaurants on Nevsky Prospekt. The orchestras thundered, the regulars drank their wine, and bets were placed at the gaming tables. This was not a tragicomedy; it was how the beginning of the twentieth century in Russia was fated to end. The period was marked by terrible events and omens of impending catastrophe, but also by an arrogant insouciance, a willful failure to see that things could not continue as they were.

Never had St. Petersburg known so intense an intellectual and artistic life as in this fraught moment. Russian poetry attained an unprecedented beauty. The brilliant symbolism of Alexander Blok, the shimmering limpidity of Ivan Bunin, the feminine strength of Anna Akhmatova, and the romantic exoticism of Nikolai Gumilev enriched it with new rhythms and images. Painters set about defining a twentieth-century idiom: the refined manner of the Mir Iskusstva (World of Art) artists competed for attention with the uncompromising avant-gardism of the Jack of Diamonds and Donkey's Tail groups as well as with the epic canvases of Nicholas Roerich. The birth of

LEFT
The headquarters of Fabergé on Bolshaya Morskaya Street, built by K. K. Schmidt between 1899 and 1902 for the famous jeweler of the tsars. It contained workshops, a salesroom, and living quarters.

BELOW
House of the Emir of Bukhara, built by S. Krichinsky in 1913 on Kamennoostrovsky Prospekt.

*"Modern-style" house
on Petrogradsky Island,
unattributed.*

193

abstract art was but one short step away, and it was taken by the futurists and the constructivists.

The St. Petersburg cityscape did not change so radically. Two opposing tendencies battled for dominance: Art Nouveau, known in Russia as the Modern style, and neoclassicism. Neither was monolithic, for both were subject to endless nuances prompted by the personal preferences of each architect. Art Nouveau appeared in the city at the turn of the century. Neoclassicism gave it serious competition toward the end of the first decade and continued to find adherents during the revolutionary period.

The originality of St. Petersburg Art Nouveau is its relative restraint in comparison with examples in Moscow and even the provinces. Linear decoration was typically flat, and color schemes tended to be pale. Natural stone played an important role, especially in gray Finland granite facings and light ceramic tiles. The interior layout of commercial, private, and public buildings became decidedly rational. Austere geometric volumes discreetly decorated with fluid forms were the prevalent format. Vegetal motifs, stylized figures, majolica panels,

and stained-glass windows seduced architects when Art Nouveau made its appearance in the city, but by the outbreak of World War I elements of the new idiom were most often combined with the established historicist vocabulary. Classical crown moldings and neobaroque garlands were juxtaposed with blooming flowers, vines, and spiderweb balcony railings.

Even so, St. Petersburg Art Nouveau remained a romantic style. This makes itself felt in a certain aestheticism, in the subtle refinement with which symbols accumulate in its decors, and in the pronounced modernity of its architectural forms. This elegance was rendered even more seductive by design solutions made possible by early-twentieth-century technical developments, rich materials, and a perfection of practical details, such as door handles, window clasps, ventilators, and even locks.

The St. Petersburg architects attracted by Art Nouveau included many accomplished masters, notably Alexander Gaugin, Paul Suzor, Ernst Virrich, Nikolai Vasiliev, and Gavriil Baranovsky. The most remarkable of all, however, was Fedor Lidval. He managed to combine

POLOVTSOV HOUSE. *Interior courtyard. It now bears the name of its last owner, Senator Polovtsov, who received it from Prince Gagarin. Built in the eighteenth century for Count Golovkin, it was much remodeled in the late nineteenth century. The street façade was designed by A. Pel for Prince Gagarin in a late classical style.*

POLOVTSOV HOUSE. ABOVE *The Bronze Room. View of the skylight.* RIGHT *The Gilded Room. One of several public rooms devised by Maximilian Mesmakher in a style emulating seventeenth- and eighteenth-century models, it is an example of the St. Petersburg neorococo style.*

originality, practicality, and comfort, and all on a large scale appropriate for a great city.

Neither the first revolution of 1905, suppressed by the imperial authorities, nor Russia's unexpected defeat in the war with Japan that same year, nor the manifest weakness of the government stopped the growth of St. Petersburg. Its population increased by a million during the first seventeen years of the century. As a result the city's dimensions were transformed: the outskirts grew and construction increased in the central quarters. Many structures of the classical period disappeared to make room for multistory buildings. St. Petersburg became a city of banks, apartment buildings, and department stores.

In 1903 the Trinity Bridge was built over the Neva, linking the city's center to the northern islands. Thereafter Kamennoostrovsky Prospekt on Petrogradsky Island became one of the liveliest streets in the capital, and many multistory residences were built along it during the first fifteen years of the century. Lidval built an apartment house belonging to his own family at the start of the avenue, and this was the first Art Nouveau building to rise in St. Petersburg. In its design he eschewed conventional orders, used rustication on the ground floor, animated the façades with oriel windows,

Apartment building on Khramovaya Street, by K. K. Schmidt, 1911–12: detail of the façade.

SAVINA HOUSE.
*Art Nouveau façade.
Built by M. F. Geisler
in 1905.*

KSHESSINSKAYA
HOUSE.
Service entrance.

mir Shchuko. Kamennoostrovsky Prospekt, then, was constituted in the early twentieth century as an artistic whole, an urban ensemble dominated by the spirit of Art Nouveau.

Many avenues in the city were to follow this example, among them Bolshoi, Maly, and Kronverk prospekts. On Kronverk Prospekt, for example, is the famous residence of the ballerina Matilda Kshessinskaya, a structure that is the quintessence of St. Petersburg Art Nouveau; it was built between 1904 and 1906 by Gaugin. Similar transformations began to leave their mark on Nevsky Prospekt. Many of its buildings had been reconstructed in the second half of the nineteenth century. Most of these new structures were banks, hotels, stores, and insurance companies, but their volumes had not disfigured the street, for regulations stipulating building height had been in force since 1844.

At the start of the twentieth century the situation changed. On the corner of Nevsky Prospekt and Malaya Morskaya Street, Marian Peretyatkovich built the grandiose Vavelberg Bank. Neo-Renaissance monumentality is carried to the limit in this design, which contrasts sharply with the nearby Admiralty and General Staff buildings. The headquarters of the famous Mertens fur business, built in 1912 by M. Lyalevich beside the Stroganov Palace, is also immoderately large. Its façade features three gigantic arcades separated by grandiose Corinthian columns four stories high, and originally their bays were entirely glazed. Also situated on Nevsky Prospekt is the Singer Sewing Machine Company (now the bookstore Dom Knigi), with its high corner tower culminating in an egg-shaped cupola. It was built between 1903 and 1907 by Paul Suzor. Noteworthy, too, is the merchant Eliseyev's building, with its famous food emporium and theater, erected opposite the Alexandrinsky Theater by Baranovsky between 1903 and 1907.

These sudden Art Nouveau transformations, along with the return of historicism and the continuing strength of neoclassicism, gave the prerevolutionary decade its distinctive profile in St. Petersburg. The headquarters of the Guards Economic Society was among the most important buildings of the period. Erected between 1908 and 1910 by Virrich, it exploited recent techniques of metal-frame construction. The liberal use of glass and the refined linear ornament of its façade make it a typical example of late Art Nouveau architecture in its local variant, in which the severe and measured rhythms of the classical vocabulary reasserted themselves. In the same period Lidval built the headquarters of the Azovsko-Donskoi Commercial Bank on Bolshaya Morskaya Street. Neoclassicism prevails over Art Nouveau in this design, even if the strict, flat façade surfaces are at odds with

devised a delicate ornamental scheme featuring stylized vegetal motifs, and placed an owl with outspread wings on the gable. Next door is the Witte house, designed by Virrich.

A bit farther along, at the intersection with Bolshaya Ruzheinaya Street, V. Staub oversaw the construction between 1901 and 1906 of a small octagonal square surrounded by houses with picturesque towers, spires, and domes. This is one of the rare instances in the city of a square conceived entirely in the spirit of Art Nouveau. Farther still, on the prospekt's left side, is the enormous building of the First Russian Insurance Company, built between 1911 and 1913 by three architects in the Benois family. Here Art Nouveau motifs are combined with elements of the neoclassical vocabulary. Between 1913 and 1915, at the intersection of the Kamennoostrovsky and Bolshoi Petrogradsky prospekts, Andrei Belogrud built an original house featuring high towers rising from powerful consoles, a beautiful example of Art Nouveau influenced by romantic historicism. The new style is dominant here, despite its combination with neo-Gothic and neobaroque elements. Beyond the Karpovka River is another apartment building built by Fedor Lidval in 1906. It is flanked by two neo-Renaissance apartment buildings on the same monumental scale, built by Vladi-

KSHESSINSKAYA
HOUSE.
*Built on Kronverk
Prospekt between 1904
and 1906 by the archi-
tect Alexander Gaugin
for the famous Russian
ballerina, notorious for
her liaisons with the
men of the imperial
family. The epitome of
St. Petersburg Art
Nouveau architecture,
it features a granite
sub-basement, pale
ceramic tile facing,
striking oriel windows,
and delicate cast-iron
railings and fences.*

traditional classical monumentality. One senses here the influence of the "new rationalism" that was to rejuvenate the classical vocabulary.

The design for the Municipal Hospital of Peter the Great was approved in 1907. Construction began under the direction of the civil engineers L. Ilin, A. Klein, and A. Rozenberg. The buildings were arrayed around a semicircular square and continued on its central axis along a boulevard. As an ensemble it is reminiscent of the architecture of Peter the Great's period, particularly the Twelve Colleges. It is a typical example of what has been called "local Renaissance" architecture, the Russian equivalent of the "local revival" movement so popular at the time in England and the United States.

In 1910 Marian Peretyatkovich built the Russian Bank of Commerce and Industry on Bolshaya Street, and in 1911 Nikolai Vasiliev constructed the Commercial Galleries on Liteiny Prospekt. These buildings embodied diametrically opposed tendencies in St. Petersburg architecture. The Commercial Galleries feature a long, two-story glass façade of remarkable lightness but articulated by massive pylons of unpolished granite. This design epitomized the contradictions of the moment, in which architects tried to combine rational and romantic elements, and it also effectively marked the end of the era of St. Petersburg Art Nouveau. In the solemn bank headquarters an attempt was made to integrate neoclassical and neo-Renaissance elements, and the result is overwhelming in its scale, heaviness, and sumptuousness. It was this style that triumphed on the eve of the Revolution, appearing for example in many residential buildings, such as that of the Emir of Bukhara; educational institutions like the Bestuzhev School; and hospitals such as the Kalmeier Clinic, built between 1911 and 1914. This powerful idiom had once again become the preferred style in the Russian capital.

Surprisingly, in the postrevolutionary era, after the twenty-year heyday of the avant-garde, a style very close to it was taken up under Stalin in both Leningrad—as St. Petersburg had been renamed—and, to an even greater extent, Moscow. The neoclassical tradition continued to have its admirers.

It was a more refined neoclassicism that presided over the last prerevolutionary years. The finest example

KSHESSINSKAYA
HOUSE.
Vestibule.

KSHESSINSKAYA
HOUSE.
Entry stairs.

in St. Petersburg is the dacha of Count Polovtsov on Kamenny Island, designed by the gifted young architect Ivan Fomin and completed in 1916. He devised an *usadba* of great refinement in the spirit of Russian eighteenth-century Palladianism, featuring a delicate Ionic colonnade on the main façade, a domed vestibule, a large salon in white stone, an oval staircase, a dining room with Corinthian pilasters, and a Gobelin hall decorated with mural paintings. Count Polovtsov's city residence on Bolshaya Morskaya Street is less refined but features a gilded Louis xv salon and a French Renaissance dining room. The interiors of both these structures survive. An architectural club now occupies the townhouse, and the dacha is home to a retreat.

Other palaces in St. Petersburg underwent similar transformations, being allotted new occupants of various kinds or becoming museums. The history of the imperial capital came to an end, and the city was widely perceived as a grandiose monument to a Russia that was gone forever.

KAMENNY OSTROV. *The dacha of Georgi Borman, early twentieth century.*

KAMENNY OSTROV.
*Meltzer House. Built
in 1903 by the architect
for himself, the design
is intended to illustrate
a Russian legend as
an homage to indige-
nous traditions.*

8

TSARSKOE SELO

Examples of every sort of architecture are distributed through the park of Tsarskoe Selo, and this astonishing structural variety, which constantly creates new views, lends great charm to one's walks.

—Jacques Ancelot
Six mois en Russie, Paris, 1838

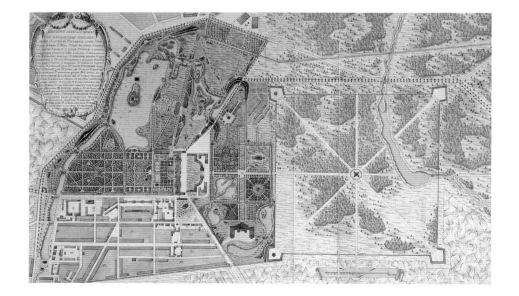

TSARSKOE SELO.
LEFT *Watercolor map from* Imperial Parks and Palaces Around St. Petersburg.
OPPOSITE *Aerial view. The property belonged to Catherine I at the beginning of the eighteenth century. Elizabeth Petrovna commissioned first Savva Chevakinsky and then, between 1751 and 1757, Bartolomeo Rastrelli to transform it into a palace. In 1762 Catherine II began to refurbish its interiors, and she continued to order new construction until her death in 1796.*

THE MYSTIQUE OF TSARSKOE SELO.

Tsarskoe Selo is the Russian Versailles. The pronouncement made by Viscount Olivier de Rohan —"Versailles is the supreme symbol of absolute power"— is more applicable to Tsarskoe Selo than to any other Russian imperial residence. This palace and its adjoining park were adored by all the Russian emperors with one exception: Paul I, whose hatred of his mother extended to Tsarskoe Selo as well.

For Russians, this ensemble is much more than a "perfect symbol of absolute power." They regard it as the birthplace of a part of the Russian soul. Tsarskoe Selo encompasses the whole of Europeanized Russian culture of the eighteenth and nineteenth centuries. It was not without reason that Alexander Pushkin wrote the following lines, at a time when he thought Russian culture was beginning to merge with European culture:

> *Wherever Destiny tosses us,*
> *Wherever Fortune leads us,*
> *We remain the same:*
> *For us the whole world is foreign,*
> *Our homeland is Tsarskoe Selo.*[1]

This was and remains true for the Russian intelligentsia.

Tsarskoe Selo is the most complete distillation of all that preceded and then accompanied the birth of Russian classical culture of the nineteenth century. It was here that sentiments given immutable form by several of Russia's greatest writers first saw light of day: Pushkin was educated at its lyceum, Lermontov served in the hussars of its imperial guard, and Turgenev was a frequent visitor to its park.

What other palace ensemble could claim to have fostered its own school of poetry? Russian poets of both the eighteenth century (Lomonosov, Derzhavin, Bogdanovich) and the nineteenth (Zhukovsky, Tyutchev) devised unforgettable images of its buildings and gardens. Whether exiled to the depths of Siberia or strolling along the bustling banks of the Neva, those who studied with Pushkin at the Tsarskoe Selo lyceum never forgot the home of their youth and initial aspirations. Anna Akhmatova, the most celebrated Russian poetess of the twentieth century, and her husband, Nikolai Gumilev, shot at a young age for having taken part in a counter-revolutionary plot, penned some striking lines about

Entry to the main courtyard, 1751–57.

GREAT PALACE.
Courtyard façade.

Tsarskoe Selo that prophesied the end of this culture. "By beckoning the minds of people toward such unexpected and melodious chimeras, Innokenty Annensky was the last of the swans of Tsarskoe Selo,"[2] wrote Gumilev about his teacher.

Tsarskoe Selo is a constellation of artistic worlds in its own right, a system of ensembles, each generating its own special world. In the middle of the eighteenth century "the baroque world of Tsarskoe Selo" was at the height of its splendor. Next to the baroque palace itself is one of the greatest exotic ensembles in all Europe, an Enlightenment Chinese "world of dreams," where exotic "Oriental fantasies" took place during the reign of Catherine the Great. The same years saw the appearance of "the world of political reveries," where historical and political events were reflected in park structures, and "the world of enlightened well-being," an idealized village. And at the center of the site—the nucleus of an ensemble embodying the antique ideal—is "the world of Greece and Rome revived" in the form of one of the most beautiful buildings of the European classical revival movement: the baths designed by Charles Cameron, the Scottish architect active in Russia for many years.

These "worlds" occupy sites within an overarching topographical configuration. In the center is the baroque palace and park of the Elizabeth Petrovna period; to the east is the nineteenth-century city; and to the west is the landscape park of Catherine the Great. This park extends, fanlike, from the classical west façade of the palace. To the far south, beyond the lake, are the remains of the ideal village of Sofia ("the world of enlightened well-being"), now in a sad state of disrepair. The park with political and sentimental allusions is arrayed around the lake. Farther north is the Chinese ensemble, situated at the extremity of the romantic nineteenth-century park, or Alexandrovsky Park, in which is a palace by the same name. At the eastern end of this park, where the contemporary city begins, are some "Russian-style" structures dating from the early twentieth century.

T HE TRIUMPH OF THE BAROQUE. The history of Tsarskoe Selo began on August 24, 1702, when Swedish troops abandoned the residence then extant on the site to Russian regiments advancing under General Apraksin. This episode occurred during

GREAT PALACE.
LEFT *Courtyard façade, central frontispiece.*
OPPOSITE *Main staircase, built by Monighetti in 1860.*
FOLLOWING PAGES *Grand Ballroom, with eleven windows on either side, realized by Rastrelli between 1751 and 1757.*

the famous Northern War, which pitted two early-eighteenth-century heroes against one another: Charles XII, king of Sweden, and Peter the Great, the first Russian emperor. Shortly after the Russian victory and the annexation of the northern shore of the Gulf of Finland, Peter I gave the former Swedish country house of Saar to his favorite, Alexander Danilovich Menshikov. But he changed his mind shortly thereafter—something he often did—and gave it instead to his wife, Catherine I, in 1708. From that point forward Tsarskoe Selo became the favorite residence of the emperors. For four decades, beginning in 1716, a series of court architects—Braunstein, Ferster, Tressini, Zemtsov, Kvasov, and Chevakinsky— rebuilt the palace one after the other, enlarging it and expanding the formal garden. By mid-century the modest residence of Catherine I had been transformed into a gigantic structure 984 feet (300 meters) long and consisting of three contiguous main buildings, an orangery, and a church linked by galleries. In 1751 the façades and interior decors were brought to completion in accordance with designs by Savva Chevakinsky.

Beginning on May 12, 1751, however, a complete reconstruction was undertaken on the orders of Elizabeth Petrovna, a project that was completed in 1757. Catherine II, who liked to emphasize her august predecessor's inconsistency, said that "it was like the work of Penelope: the next day the previous day's work was destroyed." She estimated that the palace had been destroyed and rebuilt from top to bottom six times before attaining the state "in which it is at present."[3] Elizabeth Petrovna did indeed have a penchant for excess. After her death, more than five thousand gowns were found in her wardrobe.

This pronounced taste for excess was characteristic of the baroque era. Awareness of this tendency is crucial to an understanding of Russian architecture of the period. The construction history of the Great Palace at Tsarskoe Selo under Elizabeth Petrovna exemplifies a boundless attraction to exaggerated grandeur, sumptuousness, and luxury. It also demonstrates an undeniable aesthetic sense.

As though for these marvelous edifices
It was necessary to multiply the number of stars,
Tsarskoe Selo deserves
To be a constellation on its own.[4]

These lines by the Russian poet Mikhail Vasilievich Lomonosov evoke the palace built by Rastrelli—a sumptuous, brilliant, and lucid ensemble, like the proof of some remarkably harmonious geometrical theorem.

The enormous park, disposed around an axis perpendicular to the palace, was composed of square and rectangular bosquets divided by paths that fan out in a star-shaped configuration. Their design was rigorous but various.

GREAT PALACE.
LEFT *View of enfilade
and detail of the decor
of the Grand Ballroom.*
OPPOSITE *Salon.*

The Hermitage and Grotto pavilions were the principal ornaments of the baroque park, and they survive unaltered. Their interiors are as interesting as their exteriors. The Hermitage was intended for intimate gatherings, and its furnishings included a "flying" chair and tables—"elevators" for guests and food. The former was an elegant armchair that rose lightly to the ceiling. The tables—a large one in the center and several small ones around the periphery—were designed to make the food and drink appear in the banquet room as if by magic. Elizabeth Petrovna made little use of the building, but its pleasures were much appreciated by her niece Catherine II.

All this is nothing in comparison with the interiors of the palace. Rastrelli conceived a single enfilade nearly a thousand feet (three hundred meters) long, all decorated in the same lavish style. The space was meant to flow from room to room "in a single breath."

When arriving from St. Petersburg for a gala reception, one mounted the main staircase situated at one end of the palace in a pavilion culminating in a star. Two sets of stairs led to a large landing. Marble flooring, carved and gilded banisters, and countless vases and statues immediately instilled a sense of luxury. The entire stairwell was inundated with light, for each of its forty windows was outfitted with thirty-three small mirrors.

At the top of the stairs began the second phase of the solemn advance. In the words of Alexander Benois, the celebrated early-twentieth-century historian of Russian art: "The first room opened onto an endless enfilade of richly decorated and gilded rooms. At the end of this mysterious labyrinth, beyond the innumerable doors and walls, resided a mythical creature, 'Her Extremely Pious Majesty the Empress herself.' On especially solemn occasions she emerged from this depth of depths as though from some looking-glass kingdom. Gradually she was transformed from a small, barely visible point sparkling with precious stones into a majestic, clearly outlined figure rustling with brocades and silks."[5]

After crossing the threshold of the main floor, one traversed five large antechambers linked by three doors (destroyed during World War II). Their walls were punctuated by gilded pilasters, their ceilings were painted, and by night they were illuminated by dozens of girandoles holding hundreds of candles. During the day their gilded forms sparkled with a muted grandeur. All this splendor was by way of preparation for entry into the principal room: the Grand Ballroom, viewed by all visitors

Beyond the Ballroom was the Silver Dining Room, which once led to one of the most astonishing rooms in the palace: the Chinese Salon, situated at the center of the building. It is no longer extant (in the late eighteenth century it was replaced by the main staircase that is still in use), but in the time of Elizabeth Petrovna the walls were covered with authentic Chinese lacquer panels and carvings executed by Russian masters in the Chinese style.

A bit farther along are some rooms that have recently been restored. The walls of most of them were covered in white damask within gold frames. In the Raspberry and Green dining rooms the panels were color coordinated with the decors. Also noteworthy are the Paintings Room, with its continuous mosaic of canvases, and the magnificently appointed chapel. The Amber Room was perhaps the most opulent and most celebrated of all. The circumstances of its disappearance during World War II have never been elucidated, but it has a remarkable history.

In 1716 the king of Prussia, Friedrich Wilhelm I, gave Peter I a set of amber panels and reliefs sufficient to decorate a whole room. In return, Peter I sent him fifty-five of his finest soldiers and his *kammerjunker* Tolstoy for induction into the king's personal guard. Peter used the ensemble to decorate a room in his Winter Palace. Subsequently, Elizabeth Petrovna asked Rastrelli to oversee installation of the panels at Tsarskoe Selo, and the result was the famous Amber Room. There they were

to Tsarskoe Selo, now as then. Eleven immense windows on each side illuminated the room during the day, but for evening receptions and balls it was lit by 56 girandoles containing a total of 696 candles. These figures convey some idea of the decorative excess of the room in question, which impresses the visitor by its gigantic size, its countless decorative details, and the continuous reflection of the gilded sculpture in its sparkling mirrors.

GREAT PALACE.
LEFT *Reconstructed fragment of Amber Room. The original amber panels used in this decor were given by Friedrich Wilhelm of Prussia to Peter the Great in 1716. They were first installed in Peter's Winter Palace, but his daughter, Empress Elizabeth Petrovna, had them transported to Tsarskoe Selo and incorporated into a room designed by Rastrelli. It is currently being reconstituted.*
BELOW *Paintings Room, as arranged by Rastrelli.*

GREAT PALACE.
RIGHT *Green Dining
Room. Its decor was
designed by Charles
Cameron in 1780.*
FOLLOWING PAGES
*Garden façade,
designed by Rastrelli.*

THE PARK.
*On the left, the façade
of the Great Palace.
On the right, at the far
end of the lake, the
Upper Baths, built by
Ilya Neelov between
1777 and 1779.*

combined with new amber carvings and mirrored pilasters to create a decor showcasing their color, their matte surfaces, and their superb workmanship. Thus was born the most extraordinary room in the entire palace, one of undeniable splendor and refinement.

In the 1750s Tsarskoe Selo was a strikingly unified baroque ensemble, displaying an exuberance so extreme as to border on the barbaric.

CATHERINE THE GREAT'S CHINESE CAPRICE. Catherine II's accession in 1762, a turning point in Russia's destiny, was feted at Tsarskoe Selo amid Elizabeth Petrovna's baroque decors. But the new empress loved all that was new and unexpected. One example was the Chinese Caprice.

In the 1760s the park at Tsarskoe Selo became home to the largest ensemble of exotic structures in eighteenth-century Europe. Almost half of these buildings survive. Originally there were fifteen of them, including a Chinese theater, a few Chinese bridges, an entire Chinese village, and the Small and Great Caprices. All of these structures were begun in the 1760s and 1770s.

The term *caprice*, used to designate two of the buildings, conveys something central to the conception of the entire ensemble. Legend has it that "the name 'caprice' for these lofty pavilions came from Catherine herself, who, examining the gardening estimates for Tsarskoe Selo, first hesitated and then authorized the expenditures, saying: 'So be it, it's my caprice.'"[6]

The Chinese village was built between two "artificial mountains," the Small and the Great Caprices. The topography seems more complex than it is in reality. Arriving from St. Petersburg, one passes in front of the arch of the Great Caprice. This artificial rock mountain is pierced by a gate "overgrown" with trees and undergrowth made to appear wild. Perched above is a Chinese pavilion with a characteristic peaked roof supported by marble columns. After passing beneath it via a short, dark tunnel one saw on the left, close to the road, the brightly colored structures of the village, bristling with frightful dragons and fish. Straight ahead was the Small Caprice; on the right was the park, with its picturesque lakes and islands, and the Squeaking Pavilion built by Velten. The village consisted of several buildings along a short street and an octagonal square with a pagoda in the center. The history of its construction is complex. The first design is attributed to Rinaldi, but subsequently the Neelovs, who were familiar with the Chinese pavilions in English parks, became involved. Through the Russian ambassador in London, a model was ordered of the pagoda designed for Kew Gardens by William Chambers, the only Western architect of the eighteenth century to have visited China. In 1780 all work in the Chinese style was assigned to Cameron.

THE PARK.
Lake façade of the
Upper Baths.

Cameron integrated all the component elements of the Chinese ensemble by building four exotic bridges decorated with Chinese figures, depictions of exotic plants, and pavilions. The bridges were placed so as to facilitate a "Chinese" promenade, starting from the palace, along which fantastic "Oriental" structures would always be visible.

Arriving at Tsarskoe Selo or walking through its park, one was encouraged to undergo a kind of artistic metamorphosis. To reach the palace, whether on foot or by carriage, one first had to negotiate this unexpected landscape of marvelous exotic buildings and "capricious" follies, for the main road from St. Petersburg traversed this imaginary China. Elsewhere on the grounds, however, the object of celebration was very different: an idealized vision of antiquity.

THE RETURN TO ANTIQUITY. From the beginning of the 1770s Catherine II resolved to build "a Greco-Roman rhapsody" in the garden of Tsarskoe Selo. An announcement forwarded to Paris on Catherine's behalf described its program: "We are seeking one or several . . . artists to find in Greek or Roman antiquity a completely furnished house. . . . It must summarize the era of Caesar, Augustus, Cicero, and Maecenas, and be a house in which all of them could be found in person."[7] Many famous architects were seduced by the prospect of erecting something splendid in the gardens of the "Semiramis of the North." Charles de Wailly proposed an edifice consecrated "to the sciences and the arts" and their protector, Minerva. Charles Clérisseau, who was well versed in antiquity, struck a characteristically pedantic note in his submission. Taking the wording of the announcement literally, he opted for baths, this being the only building type in which all these illustrious Romans might have encountered one another. He modeled his design after the baths of Diocletian and envisioned it on a scale exceeding that of Rastrelli's Great Palace. It was rejected for this reason, of course, but Clérisseau's notion that neo-antique baths would be the best way to implement the program was retained.

Doubtless Clérisseau would have been willing to produce a more modest design along similar lines, but

THE PARK.
View down the main axis. The Hermitage Pavilion can be glimpsed in the distance.

GREAT PALACE.
*Garden façade viewed
from the far side of
the terrace.*

the empress did not want to pay the exorbitant fees he demanded for his services. Instead she engaged Cameron, "known for his book on ancient baths" (1772), to realize Clérisseau's idea.

Cameron was only thirty-six when he began to draw up his plans for the baths at Tsarskoe Selo, and he had yet to build anything. No matter, for the ensemble that he devised for this commission—consisting of baths, a garden, and a gallery-promenade—was to make his reputation.

He worked on the baths between 1779 and 1792. First he built a small two-story pavilion with baths on the ground floor and small rooms on the floor above. His design called for the two levels to be treated quite differently. The ground floor was heavy, faced with roughly worked, porous stone, seemingly battered by wind and rain. This was to be a "pedestal of time," and the design was meant to create the illusion of an authentically "ancient" building. The upper floor, however, was light and luminous.

No matter how perfect the exterior architecture of the baths, contemporaries found it less striking than the interior decor, which was ornamented with semipre-

cious stones, including red, green, and green-veined-with-red jasper, dark red agate, rock crystal, and various marbles, as well as with bronze, porcelain, and gilt. The building became legendary in the empress's own lifetime and soon came to be known as the Agate Pavilion. The poet Derzhavin called it a "*terem* [tower] equal to Olympus," where the semiprecious stones sparkled like "clouds of stars."

These interiors are remarkable not only for their extravagance but for the quality of their design, and they are unique in Russia in that they combine ancient decorative forms with a function paralleling ancient usage, namely the Roman rite of ablution.

In 1784 Cameron designed a two-story gallery-promenade for a site next to the baths. On instructions from the empress, he used an unusually delicate version of the Ionic order for its upper floor. "This colonnade," Catherine wrote to Baron Grimm, "is all the more agreeable because in cold weather there is always one side on which the cold is less penetrating than on the other. The middle of my colonnade is glazed; below and to the side there is a flower garden; the lower part of the

colonnade is occupied by ladies close to me who there seem like nymphs amid the flowers; inside the colonnade are busts of the great men of antiquity: Homer, Demosthenes, Plato."[8]

These busts were among the curiosities of the Cameron Gallery, which was haunted by the ghosts of generals, emperors, writers, philosophers, and even a few political men of the ancient world. "If you are curious to know the identity of these honorable persons, here is a list I made while promenading," added the empress. Most of those honored were Roman emperors, from Julius Caesar to Vespasian, from Antoninus Pius to Septimus Severus, but there were also likenesses of Socrates and Plato, Heraclitus and Ovid, Apollo, Minerva, Bacchus, and Heracles.

At the beginning of the 1790s the narrow passage linking the Agate Pavilion to the Cameron Gallery was transformed into a roof garden planted with parterres. Contemporaries could not resist comparing it to the hanging gardens of Semiramis. A gently sloping ramp linked the park to the roof garden. Walking up it, one passed bronze statues of the muses, figures of Venus, Mercury, and Flora, and enormous neo-antique vases. The architecture also made a strong impression. The low, rusticated arcades emerging from the earth, flanked by squat columns, and the fantastic masks on the keystones created a powerful romantic image. It seemed that antiquity had been reborn, that it had thrown off the

intervening centuries to emerge once more, slowly but surely, from the ground at Tsarskoe Selo.

ROOMS FROM THE ERA OF CATHERINE THE GREAT. The great Italian architect Giacomo Quarenghi displayed considerable magnanimity when Cameron completed his rooms in the Great Palace, for he told the empress that these productions by his most dangerous rival "were as beautiful as they were original."[9] And Catherine herself commented in a letter to Paris: "Anyone who has not seen them can have no idea of them."[10]

Most of the rooms in the Great Palace were destroyed during World War II and have not yet been reconstituted, notably Catherine's own apartments in the new part of the palace, the Zubov wing. But the rooms of Grand Duke Paul Petrovich and his wife, Maria Fedorovna, have been restored and are accessible to the public.

The surviving rooms, conceived by Cameron in the early 1780s, include the Green Dining Room, the office, the Dark Blue Salon, the Light Blue Salon, the bedroom, and the studios for painting and ivory carving. Art historians have assessed the degree to which their decors are indebted to Cameron's contemporaries the Adam brothers. In their published work, Robert and James Adam laid out their ideal program for interior decoration,

RIGHT *The Hermitage Pavilion, begun in 1743 by Mikhail Zemstov and completed by Savva Chevakinsky in 1746. The façades were modified in 1748 by Rastrelli, who added the paired columns and pediments.*

BELOW *Ceiling of the Large Salon in the Hermitage Pavilion. Painted by Giuseppe Valeriani in 1752–53, it represents a "Feast on Olympus."*

AGATE PAVILION,
OR COLD BATHS.
LEFT *Built by Charles
Cameron between 1780
and 1785. View from
the sloping ramp.*
OPPOSITE *Ceiling of
one of the two ante-
chambers.*

224

AGATE PAVILION.
*View of the Large Room and
a detail of the ceiling in one of
the two antechambers.*

which combined fidelity to antique models with "picturesque" details. Cameron was much influenced by their designs, and he set about adapting their idiom for Catherine, utilizing the unlimited means she left at his disposal.

The Green Dining Room is the most remarkable of these decors. From the moment one enters, one's eyes are drawn to the striking white relief figures, almost lifesize, fixed to the pale green walls. Then one notices other elements, notably smaller figures contained within pink-ground medallions. The large figures are static and serene, whereas the small ones are full of animation. The spectator is invited to participate in the various mythological episodes unfolding in these diminutive compositions, thereby becoming involved in metamorphoses like those prevalent in Roman grotesque decorations.

The architect used a different "manner" in each of the rooms comprising the apartments of Paul Petrovich and Maria Fedorovna. In the Chinese Salon and the Light Blue Salon, the walls were covered with fabric, sky blue in the latter case and painted with a Chinese motif in the former. In the bedroom the architect conceived a variation on the "antique revival" theme, creating a

decor that brought to life illusionistic ones in Pompeian murals, thereby giving new currency to an idiom that had seemed fantastic to the Romans.

Between 1780 and 1788 Cameron decorated other apartments for Catherine that have not been preserved: the Arabesque Room, the Lyons Room, and the Chinese Room. To the right of the latter was the Domed Dining Room; to the left, the private rooms of Catherine the Great; the Silver Study, the bedroom, the "Tabakerka," or Snuff Box, Study, and the Mirror Room, which opened onto the roof garden and the Cameron Gallery.

The impressions of the mistress of the house are worth citing. Here is Catherine's description of her Silver Study: "I write to you from a study of solid silver imprinted with red leaf motifs; four columns with the same motif support a mirror serving as a canopy for the divan, which is covered with a red-and-green fabric with some silver, produced in Moscow; the walls are covered with mirrors framed by silver pilasters with the same red leaves. The balcony overlooks the garden, the door is made of two mirrors so that it always seems open even when it's closed . . . the study is very luxurious, brilliant,

CAMERON GALLERY. *This two-story gallery-promenade, built by Charles Cameron beside his baths beginning in 1784, shelters busts of celebrated men of antiquity.*

RIGHT
THE PARK.
*Copies of antique
statues on the
balustrade of the
granite terrace,
designed by Luigi
Rusca in 1809. In the
distance, the Cameron
Gallery.*

BELOW
*The sloping ramp
beside the Cameron
Gallery, painting by
Vasily Petrov, 1794.*

gay, it is not overloaded with heavy ornamentation and is quite agreeable."[11]

Beyond this study was the bright white bedroom with dark violet columns and solid bronze details in a pale gold color. It accessed the famous tiny study known as the Tabakerka, which Catherine described as follows: "I have another study where, as on a snuff box, white and light blue are combined with bronze and white and light blue glass, and arabesques have free play."[12]

At the beginning of the 1780s there was also, behind this room, the Palm Room, one of the strangest of Cameron's interiors. It was appointed with twenty-eight palm trees made of painted tin, and the walls were covered with mirrors reflecting this "palm grove" into infinity. At the end of the decade it was transformed into a mirrored study, marking the end of work on the empress's personal apartments.

The artistic environments conceived by Cameron were much richer and more idiosyncratic than was usual in neoclassical decors of the period. He incorporated many materials not used in ancient buildings: porcelain, Chinese lacquer, Russian semiprecious stones, colored glass, inlaid floors, and silk wall coverings. He covered walls and doors with mirrors to make the space seem larger. He did not hesitate to place a "Chinese" room in the center of a suite of neoclassical decors, and he transformed another interior into a veritable palm grove. Most remarkably, he managed successfully to adapt ancient Roman decorative schemes for use in rooms whose purpose, scale, and general character were completely different from those of their models.

THE MEANING OF THE PARK. "The next day, at an early hour, Maria Ivanovna woke, dressed, and slipped out into the gardens. The

morning was wondrous, the sun lit the tops of the linden trees, already yellowed by the cool breath of autumn. The large lake shone motionlessly. The swans awoke and proudly sailed out from under the bushes shading the bank. . . . Maria Ivanovna walked around the wonderful meadow. . . . Suddenly a little white dog of English breed ran toward her, barking. Maria Ivanovna took fright and stopped. At that moment she heard a woman's pleasant voice: 'Don't be afraid, he won't bite.' And Maria Ivanovna saw a lady sitting on a bench opposite the monument. . . . She wore a white morning dress, a nightcap, and a wadded coat. She seemed to be about forty years old. Her face, plump and ruddy, wore an expression of majesty and serenity, her blue eyes and slight smile had an ineffable charm."[13] So Pushkin described Catherine the Great strolling through the park at Tsarskoe Selo in his famous story, "The Captain's Daughter."

The technical difficulties involved in creating the garden call for some discussion. The site, a dreary plain covered with a forest of trees stunted by a scarcity of water, was not conducive to such a project. The ungrateful topography, however, did not stop the architects and garden designers. Powerful hydraulic works were constructed. Canals—in places flowing into vaulted underground galleries that were structural feats at the time—were built to transport water from springs twenty miles (fifteen kilometers) away. Several lakes were excavated, all linked by waterfalls with the Large Lake, whose shores were notched by promontories and bays. Artificial hills were constructed. Finally, wooded groves were planted. These works were overseen by the architects Rinaldi, Cameron, and the Neelovs (father and son), by the engineers von Bauer and Toll, and the English landscape designer John Bush. The New Garden at Tsarskoe Selo was the first large English-style park in Russia. It served as the model for similar "natural" designs undertaken at countless aristocratic estates. This landscape conception did not come directly from England, however. The empress knew of it only by way of French examples like the Parc Monceau in Paris and the Désert de Retz. It should also be noted that she scattered her park with allegorical tableaux alluding symbolically to both her political and her emotional life.

The designs for these *fabriques*, or garden follies,

THE PARK.
Aerial view. In the foreground the Turkish Bath and the port, in the background the Marble Bridge.

tended to mirror her changing moods and tastes. In the 1770s she was partial to evocations of the age of chivalry, as evidenced by the neo-Gothic Admiralty and Hermitage kitchens. The Palladian Bridge over a stream emptying into the Large Lake is of classical inspiration, however, and a pyramid reminiscent of the ancient Tomb of Cestius in Rome was also built. It served to mark the cemetery of the empress's dogs, and it bears an epitaph: "Here lies Zemira, and the melancholy graces should throw flowers on her grave. Like Tom, her grandfather, like Lady, her mother, she was constant in her preferences and had but one fault—she was a little cross. . . . May the gods, witness to her tenderness, reward her fidelity with immortality."[14] All these follies and inscribed monuments add to the garden's sentimental overtones.

One part of the park was conceived as a reflection of Catherine's political dreams. This was the time of the war with the Turks, in which the Russian army gained one striking victory after another. The empress wrote: "If this war continues, my garden at Tsarskoe Selo will resemble a board game, for after each glorious engage-

ment a monument is erected there."[15] But it is not easy to decipher the allegories of eighteenth-century parks and gardens without their "key." Luckily, surviving notes taken by Catherine's personal secretary, Khrapovitsky, clearly indicate her intentions. We know, for example, that she once ordered "the marble gates at Tsarskoe Selo to be illuminated, decorated with naval and military trophies, and have this verse written on a screen: 'You will penetrate through the crashing waves into the Temple of Sophia.'"[16]

This last line provides the key to an allegorical conceit that began to take shape in the 1770s. It means, in effect, "You will reach Constantinople by sea," for the "Temple of Sophia" is the famous basilica Hagia Sophia, since transformed into a mosque. Note that in the course of the Russo-Turkish hostilities a maritime invasion of the capital of the Ottoman Empire was proposed time and again. The idea appealed to Catherine, or at least she wanted to create the impression that it did. Hence this decoration at the entrance to the park, which alluded to a politico-military possibility.

Just beyond these Triumphal Gates was the Ruined

THE PARK.

LEFT *The Marble Bridge, also known as the Palladian Bridge, built by V. Neelov between 1772 and 1774 to link the Large Lake with the water labyrinth.*

OPPOSITE *The Marble Bridge, also known as the Palladian Bridge. Neelov based his design on a project by the great sixteenth-century Italian architect; the marble used to build it came from the Ekaterinburg quarry.*

Tower, built by Velten, which still exists today. It was made to resemble gigantic, half-buried ruins. The capital of a Doric column and an arch emerge from the earth in front of the spectator, who is struck by these cyclopean forms. Above, on a small clearing shaped like a colossal capital, is a pavilion with lancet windows in the conventional Turkish mode. This ensemble was conceived as an allegory of the occupation of Greece—formerly powerful and renowned for its ancient culture —by the Ottomans. A bit farther along the stroller came upon a Turkish pavilion beside a waterway. This structure, no longer extant, was a faithful replica of a building that stood on the banks of the Bosporus, and the adjacent canal was embellished with a Turkish waterfall framed by small towers of a vaguely Eastern character.

These constructions were meant to create a "Turkish" mood. Beyond them was the portion of the park harboring references to political dreams. A long Ionic colonnade on a low stylobate was the Temple of Memory, an apotheosis of the victory over the Turks (unfortunately, the structure was destroyed in 1797 on the orders of Paul I). Below, by the lake, stood a symbol of Russian naval prowess, a rostral column erected by Rinaldi in commemoration of the Battle of Chesme. In the distance beyond the lake one could distinguish the dome of a cathedral built by Cameron, dubbed St. Sophia. The implication was clear: the lake was meant to represent

the Black Sea, which provided access to the capital of the Turkish empire.

Also beyond the lake was "the world of enlightened well-being," the model village of Sofia. Founded in 1780 by Catherine II beside Tsarskoe Selo, it is now all but forgotten, for it survived only twenty-eight years. It had already disappeared by 1808, most of its houses having been taken apart for the bricks. But at the end of the eighteenth century it was the district seat and played a rather important role. Sofia was supposed to become one of the centers of "Enlightenment" in Petersburg Province and all of Russia. Schools and model factories were built, merchants and craftsmen were settled there. The intention was to devise a vision of life as it should be for the edification of the court, a model village rather than a real one. From the Cameron Gallery the attention of foreign visitors—the Prince de Ligne, for example—was directed toward "the view of a small town" arrayed in a semicircle around the park of Tsarskoe Selo.[17] Its streets were outfitted with lanterns—quite a novelty in the Russia of the 1780s—but they were lit only when Catherine II was in Tsarskoe Selo, a telling illustration of the theatrical nature of the whole complex.

It mattered that the view from the Cameron Gallery encompassed far more than the park and the town. Catherine wrote Voltaire that "sitting in the colonnade, I can see about a hundred versts [sixty miles] around me."[18]

THE PARK.
LEFT *View of the Turkish Bath from the Marble Bridge.*
OPPOSITE *The Turkish Bath, built to a design by Monighetti between 1850 and 1852 to commemorate Russia's victories over the Turks.*

Doubtless she was exaggerating, but the remark is still revealing about her attitude toward space. A panoramic impression is also evident in an idyllic eighteenth-century description of Tsarskoe Selo: "From there one can see the surrounding villages in the distance, and in them well-cultivated orchards and kitchen gardens, wheat being sown, and the surrounding woods."[19] Here, too, hyperbole is in evidence, but it reflects the degree to which Tsarskoe Selo was meant to mirror Russia in miniature.

CLASSICISM AND ROMANTICISM.

In 1792 Quarenghi began to build an only slightly less grandiose structure not far from the Great Palace. This was the new palace Catherine intended for her grandson Grand Duke Alexander Pavlovich. When one sees this enormous building, situated beside the empress's own gigantic residence, one cannot help but wonder about the reasons for such a costly undertaking.

It is well known that the relations between Catherine II and her direct heir, the future Paul I, were terrible. Many contemporaries maintained that the empress wanted Alexander to succeed her instead. No concrete evidence of an actual plot survives, but the decision to build a colossal palace for her grandson directly beside her own speaks volumes about the political tensions in the last years of Catherine's reign.

At the beginning of the nineteenth century this neo-antique colossus was given new surroundings. Its heroic classicism was set off against gardens in a "chivalric Gothic" mode. A picturesque park incorporating a menagerie of the baroque era was laid out around it by Ilya Neelov, Adam Menelas, and I. Ivanov, and in the 1810s and 1820s Menelas filled it with countless neo-Gothic structures. They included a five-story white tower surrounded by fortifications and a moat, and entered through a "Gothic" gate protected by two round towers. There was also a chapel designed to evoke a ruined Greek temple. Nearby, at the junction of two shaded walks, was an arsenal with hexahedral towers, a quadrangular inner courtyard, and crenelated fortifications. The lama pavilion was reminiscent of medieval fortresses. And there were even more structures, among them pensioners' stables and a farm, answering to the typical romantic taste for things medieval. The imagery of Walter Scott was perfectly at home in this park, all the more so as these structures were built by a Scot, Menelas.

A CITY OF PARKS AND SALONS.

Tsarskoe Selo experienced its "golden autumn" in the middle of the nineteenth century. The hour of lavish construction had passed, but the place

THE PARK.
*Views of the Music Pavilion,
left, and, below, a fountain
by P. Sokolov inspired by
La Fontaine's fable of a
milkmaid who breaks her pot.*

continued to inspire poetry. It succeeded in expressing whatever the language of stones had not been able to. The poet Fedor Tyutchev captured well its nostalgic appeal:

> *The sun glistens gold*
> *The currents in the lake sparkle;*
> *It's as though grandeur*
> *Were breathing in oblivion.*[20]

As time passed and the twentieth century grew near, the poetry of Tsarskoe Selo acquired a sadness that only intensified its mystique.

And while the culture of Tsarskoe Selo became more immersed in the fin de siècle atmosphere, court life continued to follow its immutable rhythms with fetes and parades, intrigues and changes of the guard. The palaces were filled with new furniture, but happily the architecture was left largely untouched. However, many new buildings intended to serve the court made their appearance. The most interesting of these were built for the tsar's personal guards.

Between 1895 and 1912 an entire community, called Fedorovsky, was erected for part of the imperial guard. First barracks were constructed, then the "city" itself rose in the style of seventeenth-century Russian architecture. It had its own infirmaries, chancellery, and officers' mess.

ALEXANDROVSKY PARK.
LEFT *Chinese Pavilion, dubbed the Squeaking Pavilion because of the noise made by the standard flying from its roof. Begun in 1778 by Ilya Neelov after a design drafted as part of the Chinese ensemble by Georg Velten, it was completed only in 1786.*
BELOW *Detail of the Dragon Bridge.*
OPPOSITE *Detail of the Large Chinese Bridge, redesigned in 1780 by Charles Cameron.*

Surrounded by walls with round towers, it resembled an ancient Russian fortress. In its center, the architect V. Pokrovsky built a temple combining elements of the sixteenth-century Cathedral of the Annunciation in the Kremlin in Moscow and features typical of the ancient churches of the Pskov region in northwestern Russia. The designs of these structures appealed both to the neo-Romantic taste for the national past and to the official historicizing mode that became prevalent before World War I in conjunction with the tricentennial of the rule of the house of the Romanovs in 1913. This jubilee was celebrated with much fanfare at Tsarskoe Selo, but a funeral march could already be heard amid the festivities.

THE EGYPTIAN
GATES.
*Built between 1827
and 1830 by Adam
Menelas, the gates
mark the entrance to
the property of Tsarskoe
Selo and are covered
with cast-iron reliefs
depicting scenes from
Egyptian mythology
realized by the sculptor
V. Demut-Malinovsky.*

9

ORANIENBAUM

Grand Duchess Helen has made a charming habitation at Oranienbaum, despite the sadness of the landscape and the obsessive memory of the dramas that were played out in this place.

—Marquis de Custine
La Russie en 1839, Paris, 1843

GREAT PALACE.
LEFT *View from the Gulf of Finland, print by Chelnakov and Knunov after a drawing by Makhaev.*
OPPOSITE *Begun in 1710 for Alexander Menshikov by Giovanni Fontana and completed in 1727, it was given to the future Peter III by Elizabeth Petrovna in 1743 and subsequently remodeled by Bartolomeo Rastrelli. Just out of view is the canal linking the gates to the Gulf of Finland.*

THE PALACE OF
PETER III.
*Known as Peterstadt,
it was built by Antonio
Rinaldi between 1748
and 1752 and was
situated within a small
fortress in the park at
Oranienbaum that
was intended for use
by the future emperor
for the training of his
personal troops.*

THE PALACE OF VICISSITUDES. Of all the palaces in the environs of St. Petersburg, Oranienbaum most closely reflects the vicissitudes of its successive owners in its architecture. It was founded by Alexander Menshikov, who as we have seen was extremely close to Peter the Great. Doubtless the emperor's attachment to Menshikov was largely a function of his having "made" him, raising him from the humblest parentage to great power, wealth, and distinction. The emperor loved Menshikov as one loves one's own creation. They were the same age, but Peter called him *mein Herzenkind*, German for "child of my heart."

Menshikov had been plucked from the streets of Moscow, where his father was probably a groom. Contemporaries recount that as a youth he sold small pies of dubious quality made by his mother or his aunt. He became one of Peter's valets during the period when Sophie, Peter's elder sister, governed Russia and was attempting to oust her brother from the throne for good. Peter knew very well that she might imprison him in a monastery or even have him killed, as his mother's family had been. He was afraid; he needed supporters who could be trusted, and Menshikov was among the first. As Peter's power increased, so did that of his favorite.

Early on, Menshikov distinguished himself in the tsar's entourage by his readiness to share his tastes and way of life. This was anything but a given, for Peter's youthful conduct was quite scandalous by the standards then prevailing in Moscow. He struck up friendships with foreigners, smoked tobacco, and loved grandiose drinking bouts; he did not wear a beard; he indulged in unbridled revelry and regarded ceremony with contempt, all of which was nothing less than astonishing in late-seventeenth-century court circles. Noteworthy among these "innocent amusements" was the custom of firing stewed turnips and macerated apples on boyars curious about what the young tsar was doing. Menshikov, of course, was his main accomplice in all of these pranks.

But he also distinguished himself in more serious ways. When he accompanied Peter the Great to Holland, where they worked as carpenter's apprentices in a shipyard, Menshikov received a letter of praise from the master carpenter. He also displayed bravery under Turkish fire during the siege of a fortress in southern Russia, and the same spirit and bravura marked his comportment during the war with Sweden. When the new capital was founded, he became its first governor.

Advancements, titles, and riches showered down on him as from a cornucopia. He was named in turn general field marshal, vice admiral, grand master of the court, secret adviser in service, and senator; he received the titles Prince Izhorsky and count of the Holy Roman Empire; and he was decorated with countless orders. He was given outright about a hundred thousand peasants as

THE PALACE OF
PETER III.
RIGHT *Study.*
BELOW *The Painting
Gallery.*

well as various estates, palaces, and properties throughout Russia, Ukraine, and the Baltic countries. All this seemed insufficient to him, despite the fact that he lived much more luxuriously than the emperor himself—as evidenced by the palace of Oranienbaum. He was caught stealing money from the treasury on several occasions, and he organized fraudulent schemes in provisioning the army. When discovered, the emperor had him tried but always commuted the sentences, saying to the judges: "When you condemn Menshikov you condemn me," after which he went to his friend's house and beat him mercilessly with his own hands.

The death of Peter the Great in 1725 only strengthened Menshikov's power. He had the emperor's widow named his successor, and he himself received the title of general in chief and colonel of all the regiments of the guard.

Catherine I did not survive her husband for long, and the throne passed to an eleven-year-old boy—Peter II, grandson of Peter the Great and son of Peter's eldest son, Alexis, who had been executed. Menshikov moved the young tsar into his palace and arranged a marriage with his own daughter Maria, then sixteen, for whom he ordered prayers said throughout the empire as for His Majesty.

Menshikov fell gravely ill when his fortune was at its peak, and while he was at death's door the courtiers turned the young tsar against him. The general in chief recovered from his illness and joyfully traveled to Oranienbaum to celebrate the consecration of a new chapel there. All was ready, and the emperor's arrival was eagerly anticipated. But he did not come, and neither did the dignitaries of the court. This episode marked the beginning of Menshikov's fall, and Oranienbaum became the witness of his disgrace.

He was quickly stripped of all his titles, and on September 9, 1728, he was exiled to one of his estates. He never reached it, however; on the way his money and property were seized, and he and his whole family were taken to Siberia, where they were obliged to live in appalling conditions. After living for a year in the village of Berezov, on the banks of the Ob close to the Arctic Circle, he died and was buried in the permafrost. Oranienbaum, then the most luxurious of all the palaces in the environs of St. Petersburg, was confiscated by the emperor and became a royal residence.

Fourteen years passed. Three Russian sovereigns suc-ceeded one another: Peter II, Anna Ivanovna, and Elizabeth Petrovna. The latter never married and so left no legitimate children. Her heir was the son of her deceased sister, her nephew, Peter, the Duke of Holstein, known in Russia prior to his accession as Grand Duke Peter Fedorovich and afterward as Peter III. In 1743 his august aunt made a gift to him of Oranienbaum. Like its previous owner, he was to lead a short life marked by sudden changes of fortune.

The adolescent heir to the throne of a small principality in northern Germany, Peter now found himself master of all Russia. He was, however, singularly ill suited for such a role. Of fragile health, the grand duke, even as a grown, married man, displayed little interest in education, preferring to indulge his passion for toy soldiers. Model fortresses were built in his bedroom, over which he maneuvered battalions of wax figures in uniform. Disciplinary lapses in this "army" were severely punished. The future Catherine the Great, brought to Russia to marry this man, caught him shortly after the wedding in the course of condemning an offender. He was personally conducting an interrogation about an attack against

THE CHINESE PALACE.
Built between 1762 and 1768 by Antonio Rinaldi for Catherine II to the rear of the park.

One of the allegorical sculptures beside the pond in front of the Chinese Palace.

sentinels in the model fortress and pronounced a death sentence on a rat who had eaten the wax head of one of his soldiers. The rat was caught and hung to the accompaniment of a loud drumroll. This episode transpired in the Winter Palace in St. Petersburg, but during the summer the grand duke could indulge in "real" war games. Oranienbaum had been given to him for this purpose, and everything needed for these operations was installed there, including small forts, an artillery battery, and a detachment of soldiers.

These martial amusements continued on an even larger scale after Peter III was crowned emperor. A model regiment was established at Oranienbaum whose uniforms and formations imitated those of the Prussian army, for Frederick the Great was the absolute idol of Peter III throughout his life. He could have made a worse choice. The ruler of Prussia, after all, was capable of charming the likes of Voltaire, Maupertuis, and Algarotti. Peter III, however, was seduced by superficialities associated with Frederick's regime. The rigor of Prussian military discipline attracted him greatly, especially its elaborate protocols, drill formations, and fanatical attention to details of dress and appearance: everything relating to "the science of the parade." The rest of Frederick's many qualities were a matter of indifference to him. This passion for exteriors, this tendency to mistake appearance for reality, was characteristic of many Russian rulers. It made it easier for them to sustain the illusion that they had attained genuine order and social well-being.

Peter III was a limp-willed, ill-educated boy who cultivated appearances to the point of indecency. It must be admitted, however, that all the Romanovs, to one degree or another, were preoccupied with constructing a land of illusions where "maneuvers and mazurkas" took the place of substantive reforms. This fact lies near the heart of the lamentable tragedy that has been Russia's destiny. Nicholas II and his family paid dearly for the folly of the imperial family, but the retribution began much earlier, starting with Peter III.

While the emperor drilled his six hundred soldiers at Oranienbaum in the Prussian manner and multiplied politically aberrant acts such as the annulment of Russian conquests made during the Seven Years War (he objected to Russian sovereignty over eastern Prussia and the establishment of a Russian government in Königsberg), a plot was organized against him. It was masterminded by none other than his wife. Catherine had never loved her husband. When brought to Russia as a young girl she had had no choice but to marry him. She had been trapped, much like the duke and duchess of Brunswick two decades before, who arrived with their infant son, the designated heir of Empress Anna Ivanovna, only to spend most of their subsequent lives in prison.

The only possible solution for Catherine, the only way for her to lead a "normal" life, was for her to engineer

THE CHINESE PALACE.
LEFT AND BELOW *General view and detail of the pond façade.*
FOLLOWING PAGES *Salon of the Muses, with a decor by the Italian Stefano Torelli.*

THE CHINESE
PALACE.
RIGHT *Portrait Room.*
OPPOSITE *Ceiling of the
Salon of the Muses,
incorporating a*
Triumph of Venus
by Torelli.

her own accession. In the end fortune rewarded Catherine's incredible patience and cleverness, but the risk for the conspirators was great. On June 26, 1762, their plan was all but exposed. At the time Peter III was at Oranienbaum and Catherine was at Peterhof. Its greater proximity to St. Petersburg gave her a momentary advantage, and her party turned it to account. Count Orlov had time to rush her to the city and organize the troops sympathetic to the plot. After having received guarantees of their allegiance, Catherine led them to Oranienbaum. Peter III tried to resist, but his forces were soon obliged to surrender. He was taken to the often vacant Ropsha Palace and placed under the guard of Alexei Orlov, the brother of Catherine's lover Grigori Orlov, who had played a crucial role in the plot. A few days later the dethroned emperor died a quick and violent death.

For reasons that remain obscure, in the early years of her reign Catherine elected to make her murdered husband's palace her principal summer residence. Clearly she had no fear of ghosts, and she proceeded to allow her fantasy free play at Oranienbaum. Antonio Rinaldi, the architect who had worked there for Peter III, built the extravagant Chinese Palace for its new occupant.

THE MENSHIKOV PALACE. The palace built for Peter the Great's powerful protégé is known as the Great Palace of Oranienbaum. It is the most important suburban ensemble of the first quarter of the eighteenth century to have survived more or less intact, and thus merits discussion here. The Italian architect Giovanni Fontana oversaw its construction beginning in 1710. Menshikov's decision to build such a luxurious residence on recently conquered territory was audacious, but it was precisely actions of this kind that won the emperor's affection. By undertaking to build a country house as well as another residence in St. Petersburg at this time, when the outcome of Peter's conquests in the Baltic was still in the balance, Menshikov demonstrated his faith in Peter's continuing good fortune as well as in the irrevocability of his victories.

We have a precise contemporary description of the palace penned by a *kammerjunker* at the Russian court, F. Bergholtz, who in addition to his diplomatic service there provided the Swedish government with precise reports concerning Russian affairs. His facts tend to be trustworthy. "The house is built on a hill from which there is a splendid view. It consists of a two-story block and two semicircular galleries leading to two round wings that are comparatively too large. A chapel will be built in one of them and the other will be occupied by a large room. Below, in front of the residence, there is an enormous garden. . . . One descends from the eminence on which the palace is sited via two stone terraces, built one above the other, to a large wooden porch, and from there to the garden, which is not yet completed. Above, from the palace's central room, one can see Kronschlot, which is almost . . . opposite, less than five versts away. The rooms in the palace are small but beautiful and decorated with marvelous paintings and furniture." The author does not seem to have omitted anything important from his report. The palace was indeed built near the shore of the Gulf of Finland, just opposite the island on which Peter the Great situated the Kronschlot Fortress (subsequently renamed Kronstadt) to protect St. Petersburg.

A canal ran from the shore to the palace, making it possible to sail almost to the gates of the garden. This, known as the Lower Garden, was formal in conception. The work of Dutch designers, it featured low, clipped groves in complex geometric patterns and ornamental parterres. Behind the palace, on more elevated ground, was the so-called Upper Garden.

Traversing the Lower Garden via its main walk, one arrived at a formidably steep and high stairway—since replaced by a more complex tiered stairway—leading to the vestibule of the principal block of the palace. This was divided into three interior volumes by heavy columns and

THE CHINESE
PALACE.
Large Oval Room.

254

THE CHINESE
PALACE.
*Partial view of the
main enfilade from
the Large Oval
Room. The marble
portrait medallion
of Catherine II is
by Marie-Anne
Collot, a student of
Etienne Falconet.*

THE CHINESE PALACE.
LEFT *Details of the Small Chinese Room and the Large Chinese Room.*
OPPOSITE *The walls of the Large Chinese Room are entirely covered with "Chinese" marquetry.*

covered by a groined vault. The main staircase was at the back of the building. Its steps were made of oak, and its banisters and balconies were of walnut carved in an attractive pattern. In the center of the main floor was a large room decorated with pilasters. It was flanked by a salon and a dining room, and the windows of all three interiors faced the sea. The remainder of the floor space was occupied by two dozen symmetrically disposed rooms of small dimensions, some of which could even be described as minuscule. The original interiors do not survive, but they are known to have been exceptionally lavish. The room occupying one of the side wings was decorated with lacquer and porcelain from the Far East, and for this reason was known as the Japanese Pavilion. Situated in the corresponding space in the other wing was the chapel, which boasted a remarkable carved and gilded iconostasis consisting of four tiers of icons, a collaborative effort by two of the most remarkable artists of Peter's reign: Ivan Zarudny, also responsible for the sculpture in the Peter-Paul Cathedral in St. Petersburg, and the painter Ivan Vishnyakov. The day of the chapel's consecration marked the beginning of Menshikov's fall from grace, as we have seen. It also marked the end of the first period of Oranienbaum, for Menshikov never returned to the palace.

The architects of Oranienbaum included not only

Fontana but also the German Gottfried Schädel and, probably, the celebrated Prussian architect and sculptor Andreas Schlüter, who arrived in St. Petersburg in 1713. It is difficult to determine with any degree of precision the role that each one played. The building was subsequently remodeled by Mikhail Zemtsov and Pyotr Eropkin. Rastrelli refurbished the interiors in the middle of the eighteenth century. Oblong, one-story extensions were built behind the palace at that time. Rinaldi worked there between 1762 and 1789. He is the author of the tiered stairway now in front of the main façade, and he demolished the west wing, which contained the chapel, replacing it with a structure perfectly symmetrical to the Japanese Pavilion.

These were apparently the most significant alterations, but further changes were made from time to time, and many of the rooms were redecorated by the three most prominent architects of the nineteenth century: Vasily Stasov, Andrei Stakenschneider, and Harald Bossay. But the principal features of the building were preserved. It remains, above all, one of the most successful productions of the Russian baroque of the era of Peter the Great. It also exemplifies the transitional style between Russian late medieval architecture and the contemporary European idiom, one shaped by imported masters trained

in both the Italian and German traditions. These influences can be discerned in the Great Palace of Oranienbaum as it stands today, an immense but wonderfully harmonious composition whose massing is reminiscent of Italian models but whose spare façade treatments are more characteristic of the northern baroque.

PETERSTADT, OR THE DREAM OF PETER III. The subsequent history of Oranienbaum unfolded to the south of the Great Palace, in the Upper Garden. Immediately after the property was given by Elizabeth Petrovna to her nephew and heir, Peter Fedorovich, "divertissements" of a most peculiar character began to be built there, and it was not long before another historic ensemble was envisioned. We have already discussed the grand duke's love of war games. To humor him, a fortress was built with earth ramparts and surrounded by moats and a defensive line of wooden spikes. This was in 1746, and the heir made use of it for the next ten years. But the more he indulged his taste for military games, the less satisfied he became with this facility. In 1756 Rinaldi arrived in St. Petersburg, and he proved an adept courtier. He knew how to please Peter Fedorovich, and before long he was named

architect to the heir to the throne. His first project was to build a fortress of very different character, one as real as could be. The Italian took the project seriously, devising a veritable miniature country, refined and charming, very much in line with contemporary European architectural taste.

The complex was situated in a rococo garden beside a lake known as the "little sea of diversions." Geometric parterres and clipped groves were bordered by picturesque paths—perhaps a bit *too* picturesque. In the center, five genuine earthwork bastions were raised, complete with moats and drawbridges. Behind them, arrayed in a pentagonal configuration, were all the essential service facilities: barracks, officers' lodgings, an arsenal, and a powder magazine. It was a German master, Martin Hoffmann (from Holstein, which belonged to Peter Fedorovich), who oversaw the construction of this fort. The soldiers and officers were also from Holstein, and the chapel in the complex was Lutheran.

Rinaldi, in addition to devising the overall plan of the complex, between 1758 and 1762 also constructed the fortress's principal buildings, including a palace and ceremonial gates. The palace of Peter III is a very small, two-story structure shaped like a cube, yet it is one of the most fully realized rococo buildings in Russia. Its intimate

scale facilitated great refinement in its detailing. The continuous rustication of the low ground floor gives it a pronounced horizontal emphasis. The main floor is decorated with twinned pilasters without capitals and window treatments that are sumptuous yet light. The roofline is ornamented with a balustrade. Above the entrance is a rather large balcony with a cast-iron railing in an arabesque design, flanked by deep niches sheltering marble busts.

The interior is even more interesting. From the vestibule, ascending a spiral stairway to the right, one arrived at the principal rooms: an antechamber, a pantry, a room for the display of paintings (doubling as a dining room), a bedroom, and a boudoir. The decors of the small rooms were quite extraordinary. In addition to painted overdoors, stucco ceilings, and entire walls covered by contiguous paintings, they featured many decorative compositions in a "Chinese" mode, from the doors and dado of black lacquer heightened with gold in the paintings room to the fabric on the walls of the bedroom, which were painted with Chinese landscapes, pavilions, and diminutive figures, and the incorporation into this same room of gilded incrustations and mural painting. The result perfectly justified the nickname given Peter III's residence, the "palace in a snuffbox."

It is rather strange that people as different as Peter III and Catherine the Great, whose relations were so hostile, should have had such similar youthful tastes in the matter of architecture. Catherine's preferences evolved after the death of Peter III, and continued to do so throughout her long reign. She cultivated her own tastes and was continually on the lookout for diversity and novelty. But in the 1760s, when the young empress had her own palace constructed at Oranienbaum—the third to rise on the property—she developed both the style and the ideas of the palace of Peter III.

C ATHERINE THE GREAT'S PERSONAL DACHA. Even prior to her seizure of power, Catherine wanted a palace of her own, one in which she could feel mistress of the house and find momentary freedom from her husband and her august empress-aunt, one that would be hers alone. This dream became realizable only about 1760, when she purchased a piece of property abutting the imperial domain of Oranienbaum from the Golitsyn princes. Plans for both a park and a palace were drawn up by Rinaldi and realized between 1762 and 1774. The result was one of the most important rococo ensembles in all of Russia.

The overall conception was quite beautiful. The master drew upon all the latest developments in garden

SLIDING HILL PAVILION.
View of the ceiling of the Rotunda, decorated by S. Barozzi.

design, above all as developed in France and Germany. Both Catherine and her architect were persuaded that recent gardens in those two nations were an accurate reflection of the English picturesque, with its ideal of the close imitation of nature, but such was not the case. The park brought together elements characteristic of German gardens of the late baroque and rococo eras on the one hand, and on the other, the "Anglo-Chinese" garden, with its obsessive preoccupation with the "natural," a conception that in fact had been elaborated in France. Rather than being integrated, the two approaches were kept distinct from one another, with one prevailing on the eastern side and the other on the western side. An enormous "sliding hill" 1,745 feet (532 meters) long divided the park in two.

To the right of the sliding hill, on the park's eastern side, was a very pretty ornamental garden design based on the interplay of straight and curved lines, featuring cross, triangle, and lozenge configurations arranged in a

SLIDING HILL
PAVILION.
*Detail of the faux
marble decor of
the Rotunda.*

sumptuous geometric pattern. Its component elements were more crisply delineated and compartmentalized than in French formal gardens, making for a result that more closely resembled German rococo designs.

To the left, in the western portion of the park, the crisscrossing patterns of the paths were no less picturesque and capricious. But here each line meandered around groves of trees and along paths or the shores of ponds. In the eastern portion of the park, at the end most distant from the sea, Rinaldi built Catherine's Chinese Palace with its wings and kitchen situated around a small, rather formal pond. It survives, and is now the principal curiosity at Oranienbaum.

The park devised for the youthful Catherine does not survive, for in the early nineteenth century it was transformed into a landscape park perfectly integrated with the natural setting but far less "diverting." It was the work of one of several English landscape designers who worked in Russia, Joseph Bush, the son of John Bush, who was responsible for the parks at Tsarskoe Selo and Gatchina. This artist displayed great skill in his design for the Alexander I Park on Elagin Island in St. Petersburg, but his design for Oranienbaum was no match for Rinaldi's original fantasy.

THE CHINESE PALACE. "The authentic marvel of eighteenth-century marvels": this is how Igor Grabar, the celebrated historian of Russian art, described the palace almost a century ago. It bears a resemblance to the residence of Frederick the Great at Potsdam but is more elegant, especially its interiors. Rinaldi surpassed himself here. Nowhere else in Russia can one find well-preserved interiors of such supreme architectural inspiration. Clearly Rinaldi put all his heart into this project for his young but all-powerful patron. World War II spared the Chinese Palace, which makes it unique in the environs of St. Petersburg. Battle was waged literally all around it for three years, but it emerged intact, preserving for posterity one of the eighteenth century's most charming creations.

In plan the design resembles a bird in flight. An enfilade of seven rooms extends the length of the northern façade. In the center is a large oval room, on either side of which are three more rooms. There are also two other, shorter enfilades perpendicular to the main axis of rooms. These constitute the southern wings of the palace, between which is the principal entrance facing the pond. The glazed gallery on this façade is a mid-nineteenth-century addition.

THE SLIDING HILL PAVILION. This structure wonderfully captures the tone of the young
Catherine's court. A high, elegant pavilion in blue
and white, it is all that survives of an ensemble designed to
accommodate the popular Russian amusement that gave
the building its name. Its first floor is surrounded by an
open white colonnade. The façade of its second floor is
decorated with white pilasters, and the whole is crowned
by an eccentric little cupola. Next to the large central
room decorated in faux marble was a large spiral staircase. This originally led to the "starting platform" and a
gallery ideally situated for viewing the roller-coaster-like
diversion for which the pavilion had been built. It involved descending an undulating wooden ramp half a
kilometer in length, in winter by sled and in summer by
special four-wheeled carts developed by the celebrated
Russian technician A. Nartov. A colonnade surmounted
by a spectators' gallery extended the ramp's entire length.
In the summer the little vehicles flew down the smooth
surface so quickly that "it took one's breath away." Some
courtiers were afraid to take part, much to the delight of
the younger members of the court.

10

GATCHINA

We are at Gatchina, where the tsar is currently in residence. From this point to St. Petersburg sentinels have been posted every hundred feet, and small tents of white canvas, to which the soldiers retire when relieved from their watch, create the impression of a camp.

—Armand Silvestre
La Russie: Impressions, Portraits, Paysages, Paris, 1892

LEFT
PLAN OF THE PARK.
Attributed to G. S. Sergeev, 1798. Around the parallel White Lake and Silver Lake, separated by the Long Island, are (from right to left) the town with its regular street grid, the botanical gardens with their two geometric pools, the Black Lake, Constable Square, the Dutch gardens and the private garden, the greenhouses, the amphitheater, and the Sylvia Park.

OPPOSITE
GATCHINA.
Aerial view of the palace, built between 1766 and 1781 to designs by Antonio Rinaldi for Grigori Orlov, Catherine the Great's favorite. Its present appearance reflects alterations made by Vincenzo Brenna beginning in 1796 and by R. Kuzmin in the mid-nineteenth century.

THE MASTERS OF GATCHINA. Even now, the word *Gatchina* makes those familiar with Russian history tremble. In the nineteenth century the expression *Gatchina order* was synonymous with the most extreme severity, with formal discipline taken to the point of absurdity and even madness. In Russian memory it is inextricably linked with the short reign of Emperor Paul I—his eccentric pranks, unjustified cruelty, and strange behavior, which ultimately prompted the revolt of both aristocrats and the army that led to his assassination.

Gatchina had existed long before Paul I, and its earlier history is full of premonitions. It changed hands constantly. In 1708 Peter the Great gave the property to Grand Duchess Natalya Alekseevna, the only one of his many sisters whom he loved. But Natalya died in 1716, and the tsar then gave the residence to his doctor, Robert Areskin, who also died soon thereafter. Gatchina was then bestowed as a country house upon another court doctor, Johann Blümentrost. After the death of Peter I, it was here that his niece Anna Ivanovna bid Russia a solemn farewell. The daughter of Peter's brother Ivan, she left her native land to marry the Duke of Kurland. After returning to Russia to rule as Anna I, she reclaimed Gatchina from Blümentrost and presented it outright to Prince Alexander Kurakin, Peter's ambassador to Paris from 1719 to 1724. It remained in his family from 1734 to 1765, when Catherine the Great acquired it for Grigori Orlov, a key player in the coup that brought her to the throne as well as her lover and adviser for ten years. Even so, we should not overestimate his influence on the empress. Catherine was well aware of the dangers involved in mixing personal and political interests. The history of Gatchina demonstrates that it was the empress who made the decisions and that her will determined everything, including the appearance of the residence. Grigori and Catherine had a son, who was given the title Count Bobrinsky and endowed with considerable property, but his existence was kept secret until Catherine's death. After acceding to the throne, Paul I recognized him as his brother.

Orlov remained close to Catherine until 1772, when, having ceased to love him, she exiled him from the court. He died on April 13, 1784, reportedly of sadness. Soon thereafter Catherine repurchased Gatchina, this time for her son Paul, and at about the time he wrote Field Marshal Rumyantsev, who was very close to the empress, "Here I am, thirty years old, and I have nothing to do,"[1] a remark occasioned by his mother's determination not to involve him in affairs of state. It is difficult to imagine the feelings that this gift must have prompted in Paul Petrovich. He cultivated a morbid love for his father, whose memory he venerated, and now he was offered the former domain of Prince Orlov, whom he suspected of having been a party to his father's death. Nonetheless Paul lived at Gatchina for some time, even making it his principal residence.

From his early youth Paul idolized Frederick the Great of Prussia, largely because his father had done so. At Gatchina he took steps to give this admiration material form. German visitors to the estate were amused by his mania for all things associated with the Prussian military. When they arrived in Russia its rigors were reawakened in their memory. The princess of Saxe-Coburg noted: "The grand duke . . . distinguished himself by his incomprehensibly bizarre behavior, for example his idiotic idea to organize everything in his entourage along old Prussian lines. On his estates one currently sees barriers painted black, red, and white, as in Prussia."[2]

This atmosphere crushed everything at Gatchina. The empress understood the situation and wanted her grandson Alexander to succeed her instead of his father, but such an outcome could be envisioned only if the grand duke were eliminated. As a result, Paul lived each day in fear of suffering a fate like his father's. When Count Nikolai Zubov—the brother of Catherine's last favorite, Platon Zubov—arrived at Gatchina unexpectedly on November 5, 1796, Paul was terrified and said to his wife, "We are dead." However, the count had come not to arrest the heir to the throne but to inform him that the empress was on her deathbed. Paul rushed to St. Petersburg, and soon the "Gatchina order" was imposed on all of Russia. There was one more brilliant page in the history of the estate during Paul's reign, for it became the capital of the priory of the Russian Order of Malta when Paul received the title of grand master.

It remains a singular oddity that most of Gatchina's owners came to a bad end. Orlov ended his days in disgrace. Paul I was assassinated. The property's final owner was Grand Duke Mikhail Alexandrovich, the brother of Nicholas II. On abdicating, the emperor transferred the throne to this brother, who declined it. He was shot on the same night as Nicholas II. Countess Natalya Brasova, whom the grand duke had married for love, managed to escape to France with their son, but he was to die near Paris in peculiar circumstances in the 1920s, when he was about to attain his majority. He was the last heir to whom Gatchina belonged by right.

The "curse" affected only the owners, not the palace, whose history can still be traced through its many remarkable interiors, artifacts, and garden buildings.

Count Orlov, wishing to compete with Louis de Girardin, the owner of Ermenonville in France, invited Jean-Jacques Rousseau to settle at Gatchina. His offer was cast in the following terms: "I venture to inform you that sixty versts from Petersburg I own a property where

the air is clear, the water is astonishing, and the hills surrounding the lake form small nooks propitious for walks and conducive to reverie. . . . If such nooks are to your taste, Dear Sir, you have only to settle there."[3] These lines convey some idea of what Gatchina was like at the time, or at least the way its owner wanted to see it. When Catherine acquired the property in 1765 for Count Orlov, she probably envisioned transforming it into an ideal country residence for her lover. Opting for what then seemed to her the most elegant examples of European design, she commissioned the Italian architect Antonio Rinaldi to design the palace. His plans were ready by the end of 1766. Rinaldi's designs for the park were in a rococo spirit, but Catherine was more interested in English landscape gardens, especially since her favorite's brother Vladimir Orlov, having recently returned from England, had told her about them. In the end she decided to have a real English garden designer oversee the creation of the park at Gatchina. In 1768 the Irishmen John and Charles Sparrow arrived from England, and a year later they were followed by the Englishman James Heket. Through their efforts Gatchina became, along with Tsarskoe Selo and until the garden subsequently created at Pavlovsk, one of the first large landscape parks in Russia. But the most

important development in the period of Orlov's occupancy was the construction of the Great Palace, which continued under Paul's reign.

T HE PALACE AT GATCHINA. A plaque bearing the inscription "Founded on May 30, 1766, completed in the year 1781" is now visible on the park façade of the palace. These fifteen years were important ones in the evolution of Russian architecture. A new manner of building was being sought, and Gatchina represents a stage in its development.

The palace is far more austere than was typical of the work of Rinaldi's teacher, Luigi Vanvitelli, and his Neapolitan school. Two scholars who have studied Gatchina, D. Kyucchariants and A. Raskin, provide us with the key to this relative severity. "It was, first and foremost, a palace-castle; moreover, it was the only castle in the environs of Leningrad. The idea of erecting a palace-castle in the depths of an isolated forest, far from the bustle of the capital and also from the festive life of the imperial residence at Tsarskoe Selo, proposed by Rinaldi as a point of departure for the project, impressed G. G. Orlov greatly." It is true that the somber images of the palace are quite

different from the extravagant chinoiserie devised for Oranienbaum and Tsarskoe Selo in these same years. It has been suggested that this shift in tone was connected with the English influence, that it reflects an intention to imitate the royal residences on the outskirts of London. It has even been proposed that Rinaldi's model was Hampton Court. This idea is questionable, however, for Gatchina seems closer to English country residences by Vanbrugh and Hawksmoor, for example Blenheim Palace and Castle Howard. A trip by Rinaldi to England has been hypothesized, but there is no hard evidence to support it. The architect could have familiarized himself with English baroque models without leaving Russia, for the publication *Vitruvius Britannicus* was known to Catherine and her entourage. This contained plans of the most beautiful of England's baroque country houses. In any event, the plan of Gatchina demonstrates that its author knew the work of Vanbrugh and Hawksmoor.

Like Blenheim and Castle Howard, the palace consists of a central block and small semicircular galleries providing access to two large service buildings that are square in plan. Their corners are punctuated with towers. There are three courtyards: a large, open one in front of the main block and two others enclosed within the square service wings. The palace is situated on a rise that descends on the north toward the lake.

Rinaldi set off the volumes of the three principal masses with exceptional skill. All of the original architectural detailing is flat and so closely adjoined to the façades that it seems the architect carved it out of the stone mass of the building. The palace is a rare phenomenon in the history of Russian eighteenth-century architecture, for its facings are entirely of stone, whereas most buildings erected in the St. Petersburg region at the time were built of stucco-covered brick. The combination of stone and assertive massing is among Gatchina's most remarkable features.

The southern façade of the palace, which faces the central court, is 886 feet (270 meters) long. The three-story central block is treated in the Roman mode, with Tuscan pilasters on the first floor, Ionic pilasters on the main floor, and pilasters without capitals on the third. The central portion of the building is concave, which defines it as the heart of the entire composition: its horizontals, prolonged over the façades of the galleries and service buildings, bind the whole into a unity. In Rinaldi's day the second floor of the curving wings consisted of open galleries supported by Ionic colonnades. It was Vicenzo Brenna—the same architect who added a story to Charles Cameron's gallery at Pavlovsk—who had them walled and glazed. Rinaldi's design called for service quadrants of a single floor. In 1796, on the accession of Paul I,

Brenna added two additional floors. He was remarkably successful in destroying the harmony of his predecessor's work. In the mid-nineteenth century the architect R. Kuzmin remodeled the service buildings again, fundamentally altering the appearance of the palace.

The northern park façade, however, survives intact in the form given it by Rinaldi. It is dominated by the three-story central block with its high projecting corner towers, known as the Clock Tower and the Signal Tower. This volume is framed by the backward-curving façades of the galleries leading to the service buildings. The clarity, austerity, and force of the conception mark it as an anticipation of Russian neoclassicism. Rinaldi here was consciously moving toward a restrained classical idiom, so different from his highly decorative work at Oranienbaum.

The central block contained the public rooms, originally accessing the open side galleries. The two service quadrants were occupied by kitchen facilities and stables. At the end of the 1790s, just after the accession of Paul I, the public rooms were expanded. The stables were converted into an arsenal containing not only an arms collection but the quarters of the grand dukes, the emperor's children. The rooms in this building, including the theater, were refurbished again in 1850 by

GREAT PALACE.
LEFT *Relief overdoor in the White Hall, representing the sign of Cancer.*
OPPOSITE *The White Hall. Despite late-nineteenth-century alterations, much of Antonio Rinaldi's original decor survives.*

Kuzmin in accordance with the historicizing taste of the mid-nineteenth century. He also renovated the interior of the kitchen building, in which the palace chapel was located.

The vestibule is a high, whitewashed room with a vaulted ceiling and decorated with pilasters. Paul's private apartments were situated next to it on the first floor. The main stairway, made of porphyry, led to an antechamber with a sumptuous floor inlaid with precious woods and a painted ceiling. The ceiling was destroyed during World War II but is now being restored after a sketch by eighteenth-century Italian artist Stefano Torelli. An adjacent passage provides access to the Marble Dining Room, whose decor features marble Corinthian columns. The end of the room originally used as a pantry is outfitted with a marble balustrade, and the walls are decorated with reliefs of intertwining laurel branches and emblems of pastoral diversions: musical instruments, gardening tools, and baskets of flowers. There is also a discontinuous frieze of reliefs depicting episodes from the life of Bacchus, who is the focus of the room's iconography. Two oval paintings were set into the elaborate ceiling, *Bacchus and Ariadne* and *Apollo and the Muses*. Designed by Brenna at the very end of the eighteenth century, this room must be numbered among the finest monumental interiors of its period.

The adjacent Throne Room of Paul I, also refurbished by Brenna, was originally Count Orlov's study.

The original inlaid floor, featuring a design of exquisite refinement, was retained. After its conversion the room was dominated by the throne, surmounted by a red-and-gold canopy, and was decorated with large tapestries set into heavy gold frames. The rest of the wall surfaces, doors, overdoors, cornice, and ceiling were newly appointed with rich neoclassical designs. Next in the sequence is the Crimson Room, which takes its name from a set of tapestries woven in France to designs by Charles Coypel (1694–1752). The French court presented them to Paul Petrovich and Maria Fedorovna during their sojourn in Paris. Beyond was the ceremonial bedroom, with its gilded sculptural detailing. The walls, punctuated by pilasters with gold capitals and decorated with arabesques, were covered with sky blue silk embroidered with silver thread, and the same fabric was used to upholster the chairs. Above the bed, set apart by a gilded balustrade, was a canopy designed by A. Jacob. On the ceiling was *The Marriage of Psyche*, a painting commissioned from François Doyen. Both the Crimson Room and the ceremonial bedroom were the owners' homage to French taste of the old regime. They were followed by the five rooms of Maria Fedorovna: an oval boudoir, a study (situated in one of the towers), a dressing room, a hallway, and a green corner room, through which one passed when entering the main block from the lateral gallery leading to the arsenal.

One could also proceed around the periphery of the

LEFT
GREAT PALACE.
Paintings Gallery.

OPPOSITE
*Aerial view of the water
park with the palace in
the distance.*

palace to enter the throne room of Maria Fedorovna, formerly the Chinese Room designed by Rinaldi for Orlov, and then the White Hall, the largest in the palace. Of all the public rooms, this is the best preserved interior from the era of Count Orlov. The parquet floor was restored at the end of the nineteenth century after an old drawing. The wall treatments feature rhythmically spaced paired Corinthian pilasters—Rinaldi's favorite—and a simple cornice. A broad ceiling cove is decorated with an elegant pattern of garlands and rolling acanthus. Between the pilasters the walls are decorated with stucco garlands and wreaths, below which are inset reliefs of ancient subjects. Embedded in one of the narrow walls, above the mantel, is an ancient Roman relief depicting *Emperor Vespasian Offering a Sacrifice,* further evidence of the interest of both Rinaldi and his patrons in classical imagery.

However unfortunate Brenna's enclosure of the lateral colonnades, the interiors he devised for them are of some interest. His decorative work at Gatchina is typical of his style, which was nourished by the classical Italian tradition. Its opulence and coloristic brilliance corresponded to Paul I's notion of an "imperial" style, as did Brenna's penchant for baroque-inflected reminiscences of classical forms. His manner was anything but old-fashioned, however; it was very much in the spirit of the historicist sensibility that was to prevail in the following century.

When he rebuilt the service quadrants, Kuzmin gave them a distinctly mid-nineteenth-century character. He devised a long Gothic gallery with a fan-vaulted ceiling in the spirit of late English Gothic; a Chinese gallery for the display of countless objects from the Far East, arranged as in a museum; an Arsenal Hall for the arms collection; and a theater conceived along late classical lines. He also devised apartments for three emperors: Nicholas I, Alexander II, and Alexander III.

The interiors of the palace were destroyed by fire during World War II. Those in the main block are now being reconstituted. Many precious objects in the palace were saved, having been removed prior to the German occupation for safekeeping, but many more were lost forever.

THE PARK AT GATCHINA. Both the size and the picturesque quality of the park at Gatchina make it extremely seductive. It is almost as large as the park at Pavlovsk, covering some seven hundred hectares. In the 1760s two winding rivers and a string of narrow lakes fed by clean, cold spring water—the White Lake, the Silver Lake, and the Black Lake—cut through its dense forests. In addition, the White Lake boasted a number of islands. All the notable topographical features at Gatchina—hills, valleys, and the high banks of the lakes—were natural, making the site highly unusual for the region surrounding St. Petersburg, which consists primarily of flat plains.

The palace is situated at the southern end of the property. The White Lake extends in front of it, slightly to the left. The landscape park adjacent to the palace, known as the Palace Park, encompassing half the domain's property, borders this lake. The wooded area between the lake and the palace is called Sylvia in honor of the god Silvanus, the protector of forests. Beyond is a large hunting preserve known as the Menagerie. To the right of the palace, on the shores of the Black Lake, is the Priory Park, which surrounds a small palace intended to house the prior of the Order of Malta, headed at the time by Paul I.

The Palace Park is the most elaborate. It is unusual in that a third of its surface is occupied by the White and Silver lakes, making it a veritable "water park." Immediately in front of the palace is a string of narrow islands, on which are the Large Terrace, which offers wonderful views, and the Eagle Pavilion, a semicircular Tuscan colonnade backed by a deep niche with an eagle perched atop it. Linked by bridges, the series of islands is usually referred to simply as the Long Island, and it leads to another large island that is perpendicular to it.

The islands afford wonderful and various views of the lake. In the distance, close to the opposite bank, are still more islands. One of them is known as Silver Fir, after

the trees planted there. Another, consecrated to Cupid, is the site of a Pavilion of Venus. In a cove nearby are three small islands composing the Water Labyrinth. The Pavilion of Venus was modeled after the one at Chantilly, which Paul Petrovich and Maria Fedorovna had seen during their Parisian sojourn. Following the near shore to the left of the palace, one arrives at a promontory on which stands an obelisk erected by Rinaldi about 1770 to commemorate the naval victory at Chesme. Not far from there, hidden in the brush, is a forest orangery built to a design by Brenna.

All these buildings reflect an underlying program conceived around three themes: heroism, embodied in the commemorative monument and quite canonical in Russian eighteenth-century gardens; sentimental affect, represented by the island consecrated to Cupid and Venus, more or less obligatory in European gardens of the period; and a theme far rarer in contemporary garden iconography—the sacred forest.

The Birch Walk on Silver Fir Island harbors one of the most curious of Gatchina's garden pavilions: the Little Birch House, constructed of logs. Huts of one kind or another figured in many European parks of the period; there were also examples at Pavlovsk and Peterhof. But only a few of these "primitive" structures, recommended in many Enlightenment texts on gardens, have survived. From the outside the one at Gatchina resembles a large stack of birch firewood, but the birch shutters open to reveal large windows and a striking interior featuring a high cupola painted on the ceiling with Zephyr flying amid garlands of flowers, mirror walls painted with more flowers, soft divans, and parquet floors covered with fine carpets. The conception, realized in the 1780s, has been attributed to the French garden designer A. Viollet, who worked for Maria Fedorovna. The structure was destroyed during the war but has since been rebuilt.

Nearby are the Forest Labyrinth, the Water Labyrinth, and, near the far end of the White Lake, a botanical garden, which bordered a canal that boasted a small harbor where the fleet of Gatchina once dropped anchor. In the eighteenth century a great many sailing vessels were to be found on the lake, including *The Pacifist*, an eight-cannon yacht, and *The Impregnable*, a frigate equipped with sixteen cannons. On festive occasions they fired salute salvos. In the 1790s an admiralty was built near the harbor; it was known as Holland, the habitual name for such facilities in Russian gardens, a usage that reflects Peter the Great's respect for this maritime power.

To reach Sylvia one had to pass through the gates in a stone wall built to designs by Brenna in 1792–93. The gates are made of crudely squared timber, rustic material considered appropriate for the Roman god Sylvanus, whose mask is fixed above them. Once again it is tempting to evoke the part of the park at Chantilly called

THE PARK.
The masking portal and the Little Birch House, 1794.

THE PARK.
*The Island of Cupid
and the Pavilion of
Venus, 1792.*

THE PARK.
LEFT *Eagle Pavilion
on the Long Island.*
OPPOSITE *Pink marble
obelisk commemorating
Aleksei Orlov's naval
victory over the Turks
at Chesme in 1770.
Situated to the west
of the White Lake,
it was designed by
Antonio Rinaldi.*

Sylvie, for French traditions seem to be reflected in the regular crow's-foot configuration used here. In 1797–98 Adrian Zakharov built a farm, reminiscent of Marie-Antoinette's at Versailles, and an aviary, linking the two by a ruined bridge with a waterfall, no longer extant.

At this point one is quite close to the Menagerie. Covered with forest, it is the largest and most distant portion of the park. Paths dividing it into large squares were cut through it in the eighteenth century, but it did not acquire celebrity until the second half of the nineteenth century, when it became the official territory for royal hunts.

The Priory Park, planted beginning in 1798 in the forest of the Black Lake, was conceived in a picturesque mode. Its design was probably a collaboration between Brenna and the English landscapist James Heket. The Priory Palace is its main point of interest. The Prince of Condé bore the title grand prior of the order, and after the French Revolution Paul I hoped that he would reside in emigration at Gatchina. In anticipation of his arrival he had suitable lodgings built for him. Thus, the Priory Palace was intended for the Prince of Condé, whose hospitality had made such an impression on Paul during his stay at Chantilly. It was constructed in accordance with the unlikely "beaten earth" technique invented in France, which involved the compression of earth in special molds. It was sometimes used in eighteenth-century houses. One of the most brilliant figures of the Russian enlightenment, Nikolai Lvov (architect, musician, poet, and inventor), had learned of the technique from a French treatise and decided to try it at Gatchina. The result was a romantic Gothic castle on an isthmus between two lakes. Its walls are decorated with the coat of arms of the Russian empire—the two-headed eagle—complete with a Maltese cross on its breast.

The property at Gatchina was not limited to the park. In the years prior to Paul's accession, an entire "country" rose around it with its own frontiers, fortifications, and military support facilities. The largest of these, the stone Ingeburg Fortress, guarded the approach to Gatchina from St. Petersburg. The servants resided in a veritable town of their own, replete with workshops and factories where cheese, canvas, cloth, and glassware were produced. Zakharov even built a "pedagogic village" there for orphans and children of the poor. But Paul imposed strict rules on the domain. All the inhabitants of Gatchina had to abide by them, in the smallest details of their work as well as in their everyday lives.

11

PAVLOVSK

I assure you that, far from having spoiled Pavlovsk for me, Italy has led me to feel still greater affection for it.

—Letter from Maria Fedorovna to Karl Kyukhelbeker, the overseer of Pavlovsk

PAVLOVSK.
LEFT *Plan of the Park, print by A. Bugreev, 1803. Above the large park with its central star configuration are, proceeding from right to left, the town with its regular street grid, Bip Fortress, Marienthal Lake, the palace (newly enlarged by Vicenzo Brenna), the Temple of Friendship, and the other garden pavilions along the vale of the Slavyanka River.*
OPPOSITE *Aerial view of the palace. Begun in 1782 by Charles Cameron, who was replaced in 1786 by Brenna, the personal architect of the future Paul I.*

PAVLOVSK AND ITS DOMAIN. John Low-don, the famous early-nineteenth-century English garden specialist, informed readers of his 1827 *Encyclopedia of Gardening* that "Pavlovsk is the most beautiful park in the English style not only in the environs of the Russian capital but, it would seem, in all the empire."[1] Lowdon could hardly have chosen a worse moment to assess Russia's gardens. He crossed the country's western border only shortly before Napoleon's armies, and his tour was conducted during the War of 1812. When he visited Moscow the city was in ruins, having been largely destroyed by fire. According to his wife's memoirs, the couple barely escaped being eaten by wolves on the road to St. Petersburg. Despite all these misadventures, the author seems to have retained his powers of judgment, for Pavlovsk is indeed the most beautiful landscape park in Russia.

He liked it so well, in fact, that he attributed it to Lancelot Brown, better known as Capability Brown, the designer of several of the most famous landscape parks in Britain. Lowdon maintained that the Russian court had summoned this celebrated English master through a student of his who was gardener to Prince Potemkin, the favorite of Catherine II. The story was pure invention, although it gives an accurate idea of the character of Pavlovsk. But the question remains: Who was responsible for the special charm of the place?

There is no simple answer, for Pavlovsk was the fruit of a collaboration among Russian, British, French, German, and Italian designers. Among the architects active there one must first cite the Scot Charles Cameron, who also worked for Catherine II at Tsarskoe Selo. He was succeeded by two Italians: Vincenzo Brenna, who hated Cameron and tried to modify everything he had done, and Pietro di Gottardo Gonzaga, who by contrast found the Scot's designs charming and tried to implement them. In the late eighteenth century Giacomo Quarenghi was employed there, and in the nineteenth century Carlo Rossi, Andrei Voronikhin, and Andrei Stakenschneider, authors of the most famous urban ensembles in St. Petersburg, also contributed to its development. This list comprises most of the finest architects practicing in Russia during this extended period. Even so, there is another personality whose tastes and interventions were more

THE PALACE.
West façade. Viewed from the foot of the hill, as here, this façade gives an idea of the Palladian villa originally conceived by Cameron.

THE PALACE.
Italian Hall.
RIGHT *The Dome.*
BELOW *The volume
was conceived by
Cameron but the
room's first decor was
designed by Brenna.
It was damaged in the
fire of 1803 but restored
shortly thereafter by
Andrei Voronikhin.*

instrumental than theirs in shaping the "Pavlovsk style": the princess of Wurtemberg, niece of Frederick the Great, king of Prussia, who in 1776 married the heir to the Russian throne, Catherine II's son Paul Petrovich. The grand duchess interested her husband very little. After his death, however, thanks to her sons' respect for her, Maria Fedorovna set the tone in the upper echelons of St. Petersburg society for a quarter century and even influenced political policy. It was she who undid Napoleon's plan to marry one of Alexander I's sisters, Grand Duchess Anna.

Maria Fedorovna was a captivating figure. Admittedly, she sometimes brought to mind the kind of princess generally associated with small German principalities of the late eighteenth century, which is to say she was proper to a fault. Devoted to moral respectability, conjugal fidelity, thriftiness, and resourcefulness, she was also extremely sentimental. Partial to lace curtains and white porcelain decorated with blue or gold, she cared about orphans and the poor, and she was given to springing surprises on those close to her. More pertinent to our purposes, however, she was persistent and far from indifferent to artistic matters. In a very real sense Pavlovsk was her creation.

But one cannot dismiss the influence of the tastes of her husband, Paul Petrovich. Although the estate belonged to Maria Fedorovna, it was named Pavlovsk

THE PALACE.
*Greek Hall. The sixteen
wooden columns
painted to resemble
green marble are purely
ornamental, supporting
only the decorative
corbel. They were
incorporated by Brenna
to create an impression
of antique solemnity.*

(literally, "of Paul") in honor of him. The personality of Catherine's son is most closely reflected in Gatchina, his favorite residence, but his idiosyncrasies also had an impact at Pavlovsk, including the introduction of facilities for military exercises. His preferences, along with those of his wife, set the boundaries within which the architects and gardeners were obliged to work.

The construction history of Pavlovsk falls into four brief but distinct periods. The first extends from selection of the property in 1777 until the beginning of construction in 1782. The second encompasses Cameron's work there between 1782 and 1787. This was followed by a phase dominated by Brenna's interventions, stretching from the late 1780s to the death of Paul I in 1801. The final period, which continued until Maria Fedorovna's death in 1828, was a crucial one in the domain's cultural history. Pavlovsk was converted into a museum in 1918. During World War II the palace was destroyed, but in the decades following the war it was scrupulously restored.

T HE FIRST YEARS AT PAVLOVSK. Maria Fedorovna fulfilled the hopes of Empress Catherine. A son was born to the royal couple on December 12, 1777: Alexander, the empress's first and favorite grandson. To express her joy, Catherine gave his parents a property close to Tsarskoe Selo. The domain began about two-and-a-half miles (four kilometers) from the empress's own and encompassed more than a thousand hectares. Happily, the topography was even more picturesque than at Tsarskoe Selo. It was densely forested with both deciduous and coniferous trees and was traversed by the winding Slavyanka River, whose banks were bordered by low hills. Nature herself seemed to have predestined the property for a landscape park.

After land had been cleared to accommodate them, two small palaces were rapidly constructed. Maria Fedorovna's was named Paullust (German for "Paul's Joy"), while the one intended for Paul himself was dubbed Marienthal ("Maria's Valley"). These sentimental names are typical of the couple's tastes. Note, however, that the two residences were situated more than half a mile from each other.

Maria Fedorovna immediately set about devising a garden. She was guided by two considerations: she wanted to keep pace with the very latest tendencies in garden design and create something "new and unusual," but she also wanted a result reminiscent of the gardens she had known in Germany. Her preferred mode, the Anglo-Chinese garden, had caught on there, having been brought from France by German travelers and given a further boost by the French publications of Le Rounas,

Girardin, and Watelet, which had become fashionable throughout Europe. Echoes of the Parc Monceau and the farm at Versailles quickly appeared at Pavlovsk in the form of ruins, little bridges, cottages, Chinese kiosks, and artificial waterfalls. These "follies" had been imported from Marie-Antoinette's garden to various residences of Maria Fedorovna's German cousins, the rulers of little principalities, and from there to the environs of St. Petersburg. It was by this route that the Old Chalet appeared in Pavlovsk—a rustic cottage with a windmill-like tower.

Work on the garden and its pavilions continued until September 17, 1781, when the owners departed Pavlovsk to begin a trip abroad. After touring Austria, Italy, France, and Germany, they returned to Russia on November 20, 1782. Officially they were traveling incognito as the Count and Countess du Nord ("of the North"), but their true identities were an open secret and they were received accordingly by all the courts they visited. French palaces and parks made an indelible impression on them, Versailles above all, but the grand duke was also particularly taken with Chantilly. These preferences were at odds with what was then being built at Pavlovsk. Cameron had been placed in charge of the work during their absence, probably because Catherine the Great wanted

to have an authentic English country house close to Tsarskoe Selo. Her son's new francophile taste led to conflict with Cameron soon after Paul's return, and eventually the architect was dismissed. Before this rupture took place, however, Cameron succeeded in creating a genuine masterpiece.

THE EXTERIOR OF THE PALACE. Pavlovsk Palace is situated on a low hill overlooking the Slavyanka River. A dam was built to create a large lake in which the building would be reflected. The plan was devised by Cameron in 1781 and the first stone was laid on May 25, 1782. A year and a half later the shell had been completed but the interiors remained unfinished. Work continued on them for several years, and in the first half of the nineteenth century they were refurbished numerous times. The exterior of the palace was also modified.

To obtain some idea of the original appearance of Cameron's palace, one should view the building's lake façade from the foot of the hill; from this vantage point the subsequent additions are all but invisible.

Cameron's conception derived from the English eighteenth-century Palladian tradition. His teacher, Isaac Ware, was close to Lord Burlington, the builder of Chiswick House. Cameron had seen many of Palladio's plans, which Burlington collected, and had studied some of the more famous English country houses, in all likelihood Kedleston and Sion House. His design for Pavlovsk, conceived as a Palladian villa but incorporating many English features, is the culmination of this strain of palace design and thus occupies a unique place among all the country houses of eighteenth-century European neoclassicism.

The first thing one notices about the palace is the way the floors are divided: the ground and main floors are of about equal height, while the third floor is very low. The central portion of the palace seems higher than the others because the continuous rustication of the ground floor sets it apart as the "pedestal" for the rest of the building. The projecting Corinthian colonnade of the court façade is the focus and anchor of the composition. The dominant rectangular form of the central block is countered, however, by the cylindrical shape of a culminating dome whose drum is surrounded by an exterior peristyle of sixty-four columns.

The exterior of the central block remains much as Cameron conceived it, but the galleries and wings were reconstructed. After becoming emperor, Paul I decided to give Pavlovsk a more important role and made it an official residence. Brenna added another floor to the semicircular galleries and the southern wing, linking it to the chapel and the gallery. After the fire of 1803, the northern wing (on the right) was remodeled by Voronikhin. In 1822–24 Rossi modified it again, adding another story containing a library.

THE INTERIORS OF THE PALACE. Although Cameron had no hand in the interior decor of the central block, he is responsible for its plan. The central rotunda, inscribed within a rectangle and known as the Italian Hall, rises the full height of the building. It is surrounded on all three floors by rooms occupying the balance of the structure's floor space. Enfilades extend along the lateral façades of both the first and second floors. Behind the court façade are a lower vestibule and an upper one. The lake side of the second floor is occupied by the large Greek Hall.

All of the main-floor rooms in the central block were decorated by Brenna in two stages: first during the late 1780s and then, after Paul's accession and in a more lavish style, between 1797 and 1799. At the very beginning of the nineteenth century Quarenghi refurbished a few of the rooms. After the fire of 1803 the entire palace was restored under the direction of Voronikhin, and it was at this point that Maria Fedorovna intervened, insisting on restoration of the previous interiors. Between 1805 and 1807 Voronikhin was allowed to design a few interiors of his own in rooms where the earlier decors were considered unremarkable, and one of the results was Maria Fedorovna's Lantern Study on the ground floor. The most important interior produced by Rossi was the library, completed in 1824, four years prior to the empress's death. After her demise the palace was regarded as a memorial of sorts, and no modifications were made save for a few small projects overseen by Stakenschneider. A truly heroic restoration effort was mobilized after World War II, however, and the superb results make Pavlovsk the most successful restoration project in Russia.

The vestibule was refurbished in accordance with Cameron's original design. Its detailing is consistent with the building's exterior: the floor is paved with the same flagstones as the entry stairs, and the walls are treated with continuous rustication. There are medallions bearing emblems of the signs of the zodiac, the lateral doors are mirrored to create a more expansive spatial effect, and the ceiling is a sumptuous vault in the Roman spirit. When Voronikhin restored this room after the fire, he decorated it with Egyptian statuary in typical Empire style.

From the upper vestibule one enters directly into the heart of the palace, the round Italian Hall, designed by Cameron but decorated by Brenna, who faced it in the pink faux marble that was so expertly done in Russia. In the center of the parquet floor is an enormous marble twelve-pointed star. The room's four doors are inlaid with precious woods. Between them are large, semicircular niches occupied by ancient sculpture. The intervening spandrels are decorated with marble Roman portrait medallions, and the lower wall treatment culminates in a frieze of rampant lions, birds, and fantastic foliage. An elegant chandelier designed by Voronikhin illuminates the room's many gilded details.

Beyond is the Greek Hall, conceived by Brenna and subsequently refurbished in a somewhat more severe style by Voronikhin. Around its periphery is a Corinthian colonnade, painted to resemble green marble, which establishes the room's ancient theme. Both the walls and their ornamental relief frieze are white. In addition to two mirrored mantels, there are six white niches for sculpture. In the center of the elaborate ceiling, which is framed by another garlanded frieze, is a painted trompe l'oeil dome. At either end of the Greek Hall are octagonal salons that were dedicated to Peace and War after Paul's accession.

These rooms provide access to the lateral enfilades, the southern belonging to Maria Fedorovna and the northern to Paul. The northern sequence consisted of a Tapestry Room, Paul's library, a small study, and a dressing room. The southern sequence consisted of Maria Fedorovna's library (adjacent to the Salon of Peace), a boudoir, a ceremonial bedroom, and a dressing room. All of these interiors were conceived in a monumental neoclassical style incorporating a great many ancient motifs, for the masters of the house wanted the decors and appointments

THE PALACE.
*Paintings Gallery,
decorated by Brenna.*

to reflect what they had seen in France. The gifts presented to the Russian couple by Louis XVI and Marie-Antoinette are to be found at Pavlovsk.

Ceremonial rooms were also installed in the galleries and wings of the main floor. The enormous square Throne Room, with its sumptuous, monumental decor, is suggestive of designs by Piranesi. The ceiling is decorated with a simple architectural mural executed after a sketch by Gonzaga. This room opens into the curved Paintings Gallery, from which one passes into the long Cavaliers Hall, effectively transformed into an exhibition space in the second half of the nineteenth century, when a great many statues were placed there. This room in turn communicates with the choir of the chapel.

On the ground floor there are also a few rooms decorated by Cameron: the New Study and the General Study, the billiard room, the old drawing room, a ballroom, and the French Room. These more modest but comfortable interiors predate Paul's accession and reflect his mother's control of his expenditures. Cameron opted for white color schemes and crisp detailing. At the special request of his patrons he made ample use of wallpaper and painted fabric, as was common in French decoration of the period.

THE CONCEPTION AND HISTORY OF THE PARK. Before Cameron's arrival, the park at Pavlovsk had been an "Anglo-Chinese" garden as defined in French books on gardening published in the 1770s, which is to say a composition in the picturesque mode with a great many exotic pavilions, or garden follies. Cameron set out to transform it into a typical English landscape park that would heighten the "genius of the place." This approach allowed considerable latitude, and Cameron opted for an idealized landscape charged with intimations of classical poetry and filled with pavilions and sculpture conceived along ancient lines.

According to Cameron's plan, the large palace was the focus of the composition and all axes were to converge upon it, but the "picturesque axis" of the design's many component parts was to be the winding Slavyanka River.

THE PARK AROUND THE PALACE. A triple promenade shaded by five rows of clipped linden trees imported from Holland led from the oval courtyard in front of the palace to a semicircular parade

However, a complete picture of Pavlovsk can be obtained only if one bears in mind that along the promenade between the Dairy and the aviary Paul's powdered guards often marched to a drumbeat very much at odds with the harmony of the muses celebrated elsewhere in the park. In 1801, behind the palace and overlooking the lake, Cameron built an elegant Ionic temple dedicated to the three graces surrounded by a small formal garden. The window of Maria's Lantern Study looked out on this temple ensemble, in which the statues of the graces were awash in a sea of white roses.

The parts of the park close to the palace closely reflect the tastes of the masters of the house, but Cameron was given a freer hand in the areas farther away, along the vale of the Slavyanka.

THE VALE OF THE SLAVYANKA. About twenty miles (thirty kilometers) from its source, the narrow Slavyanka River enters a landscape in which its banks become quite steep. A dam traversing the riverbed at this point marks the beginning of the park of Pavlovsk. Here, above the right bank and at the junction with the Tysva, Brenna built a neo-Gothic fortification known as Bip Fortress.

On the far side of the dam the banks have a gentler slope that makes them ideal for riverside walks. Closer to the palace are the "Swiss Mountains," a forested area distinguished by gentle hills and valleys. This was one of the first areas of the park to be designed by Cameron, who erected here, on an artificial rock, a classical obelisk commemorating the start of work on the site. It bore the inscription "The construction of Pavlovsk began in 1777." Farther on, a two-span stone bridge afforded access to a small island, effectively closing off the view of this portion of the Slavyanka. In the remainder of the vale the ancient themes of the park and its buildings were further developed.

On the other side of the bridge the river opens into a large lake overlooked by the palace. Its banks enveloped the paths that wound along the water's edge. The "family grove," where trees were planted in honor of births, marriages, and other events in the imperial family, occupied a small peninsula. It was meant to evoke the sacred woods of ancient mythology, and a green jasper Urn of Destiny was placed at its center.

On the left bank the hill inclines toward the lake, and it was here that the Apollo colonnade was built to showcase a copy of the Apollo Belvedere. Part of this structure collapsed during construction and it was left incomplete, being considered more evocative in its ruined state. This ensemble was the anchor of the park's Apollonian iconog-

ground for military reviews. Various landscape compositions were arrayed on either side of this promenade. Facing outward with one's back to the palace, to the left was a forested area whose winding paths followed the sloping banks of the Slavyanka. It was here, hidden in a thick wood, that the "Dairy" was located. Maria Fedorovna wrote, "It is quite close to my heart," and remarked that "it resembles the dairy in the park of His Highness the Duke of Wurtemberg."[2] It consists of a thatched cottage of earthen bricks outfitted with a stall for two cows as well as an elegant room furnished with feather-cushioned white-and-gold stools for comfortable seating while consuming the fresh milk. In 1786 Maria Fedorovna had Cameron build a monument to Frederika, her deceased sister, in the woods behind the Dairy. A sculpture memorializing her parents was also erected nearby.

The "rustic melancholy" of the left was in sharp contrast to the refined gaiety that prevailed on the right. As in French and German rococo gardens, there was an elaborate maze in which fantasy was given free rein, and at an angle to the triple promenade Cameron built a large aviary. The space between its rooms was enclosed by nets behind which flew parrots, nightingales, starlings, and quail. One of the rooms was full of flowering plants, prompting a poet to call it the "flowered boudoir." But there was room for melancholy here, too, for another room contained ancient tombstones brought from Italy, "on which tears are immortalized by engraving." In the words of one contemporary visitor, "Melancholy consumes the soul from the moment of arrival. . . . The pleasure is laced with pain."[3]

THE PALACE.
Chapel. View of
the iconostasis.
Decor by Brenna.

THE PARK.
LEFT *Pavilion of the Three Graces, built to plans by Cameron in 1801.*
BELOW The Three Graces, *sculpture by P. Triscorni inspired by an ancient statue in the Louvre.*
OPPOSITE *Detail of the Centaur Bridge designed by Voronikhin. In the distance, the lake façade of the palace.*

raphy, which focused on veneration of poetry, the muses, and the harmony of ancient art. Statues developing these themes also appeared in other areas, for example in both the New and Old Sylvias (see below) and in a small private garden. This implicit association of Apollo with Paul brings to mind Catherine's frequent representation as Minerva.

Beyond the lake the vale of the Slavyanka narrows and the two banks are joined by Voronikhin's Centaur Bridge. After passing through the so-called green corridor, where there is yet another island, bridges, another dam, and a waterfall, one reaches the valley where Cameron built a Temple of Friendship. His placement of this structure within one of the broadest bends in the Slavyanka reveals his sensitivity to the existing terrain, for it draws attention to the beauty of this part of the river. Situated at the valley's lowest point, the pavilion seems to emerge from the bottom of a beautiful bowl whose "sides" are covered with "reliefs" consisting of trees, dark green bushes, and the trembling foliage of poplars.

Pavilions resembling round classical temples were not infrequent in eighteenth-century gardens. Their most likely modern prototype was the Temple of Pan at Stowe, designed by William Chambers, but the building at Pavlovsk was modeled after the tholos at Delphi. It was originally designated the Temple of Gratitude in

acknowledgment of Catherine's gift of the property to Paul and his wife, but after the arrival in Russia of Joseph II, emperor of the Holy Roman Empire (traveling as Count Falkenstein) in the summer of 1780, it was rechristened the Temple of Friendship. The emperor wrote: "After lunch at the villa of the grand duke, or more precisely of the grand duchess, they obliged me to take part in the laying of the cornerstone of the Temple devoted to Friendship. I could hardly refuse. All this was accompanied by many kind words and professions of eternal friendship."[4]

The architect probably took the antique references quite seriously. In any event, this building provides one of Pavlovsk's most important neoclassical accents. In a similar vein, a nearby bridge over the Slavyanka, no longer extant, took the form of a "flying" ferry, as it was called in contemporary documents. When a kitchen was built near the Temple of Friendship to facilitate the consumption of light meals there, Cameron gave it the look of a hut made of wooden planks and branches.

The temple was Cameron's only architectural contribution to this part of the park. The rest of his work focused on landscape elements, accentuating the "wildness" of the area, the last to be designed by him in the 1780s. Later, at the beginning of the nineteenth century, he proposed to build several more pavilions farther downstream, including an artificial ruin in the Red Val-

ley (similar to the one at Stowe), an altogether fantastic construction.

Brenna continued to embellish Pavlovsk after Cameron's activity there had ceased. At the turn of the century he designed two formal sections not far from the palace: the Large Circles and the Grand Staircase leading to the valley of the Temple of Friendship. He also devised two larger areas with rather complex plans: Old Sylvia and New Sylvia, where a good deal of statuary was placed. The very valley of the Slavyanka was transformed. We have already mentioned Brenna's Bip Fortress, and at the other end of the vale he built the Pil Tower and an amphitheater, and he increased the size of the cascade. V. Taleporovsky rightly remarked: "Brenna sees the park at Pavlovsk with very different eyes than did Cameron, renouncing sentimentality, sweetness, and intimacy . . . he is even recasting the banks of the Slavyanka in front of the amphitheater into architectural forms."[5] This project was implemented during the reign of Paul I.

After Paul's death the park changed again. Between 1805 and 1808 the French architect Thomas de Thomon built a mausoleum in the form of a Roman temple—dedicated "to the beneficent husband," namely Paul—that was among the first Empire buildings to be built in Russia. This style was to appear elsewhere in the park. The most remarkable example was built by Voronikhin in 1807 be-

side the parade ground, at this point no longer used for military training: the Rose Pavilion, enlarged and decorated with murals in 1814 on the occasion of the return of Maria Fedorovna's son Emperor Alexander I from Paris. A rose garden was laid out around the pavilion, and an extensive picturesque garden was developed over a tract of several square kilometers in the White Birch area. Its remarkable plan was the work of Gonzaga, a gifted artist who had made a name for himself as a theatrical designer, above all in Venice. He arrived in Russia in the early 1790s, when his sets for both Moscow and St. Petersburg created something of a sensation. He occasionally organized festivities for Pavlovsk, where walls and ceilings were also painted after his designs.

Gonzaga turned out to be a remarkable landscape designer, and he introduced a picturesque theatricality to Pavlovsk. He began by installing a system of lakes in the northern area of the park, subsequently intervening in the distant part of the Slavyanka known as the Red Valley. But it was the White Birch section, a vast area covering 250 hectares, that earned him immortality in the history of Russian garden design. Working on an unprecedented scale, he devised landscape compositions incorporating

groves, meadows, forests, clearings, and roads. Over a period of twenty-five years, from 1803 to Maria Fedorovna's death in 1828, he cleared, planted, replanted, and pruned on this tract with extraordinary passion and perseverance. The area had always been exceptionally beautiful, but Gonzaga recast it to maximize its autumnal glory. Species of trees were deliberately juxtaposed so that the golden foliage and white trunks of the birches, the dark green needles of the firs, and the red leaves of the maples would create an inspired, vividly colored "canvas." In the words of Gonzaga himself, "The forms and colors of the trees impart quite tangible differences; there are gay trees, elegant trees, sad trees, [and] proud trees."[6] In his hands nature was made to submit to the laws of theatrical design.

DAILY LIFE AND FESTIVE OCCASIONS AT PAVLOVSK. An exchange of letters between the grand duchess and the overseer at Pavlovsk, the zealous Karl Kyukhelbeker, reflects the mood at Pavlovsk at the time: "The fruit trees are in bloom, the narcissi and hyacinths have already opened a little . . . and the lilies . . . which the gardener predicts will have marvelous flowers, and the rosebuds force me each time I see them to regret that this spring in the greenhouses is not visible to Your Highness. Even the beauties of the Italian climate now visible to Your Highness would not have left you indifferent to [the spectacle of] these plants struggling with so many difficulties, just as [your seeing] the precious remains of antiquity would not preclude your looking favorably upon the structures in your garden, built according to the rules of the masters of ancient Greece and Rome," the overseer wrote to Maria Fedorovna.

"I assure you, far from having spoiled Pavlovsk for me, Italy has led me to feel even greater affection for it. . . . My little familial corner, the Colonnade, the Temple at Pavlovsk give me greater pleasure than all the beauties of Italy," she answered him.[7]

In 1798 Pavlovsk was the site of a surprising ceremonial: the festival of "bonfires," organized by the knights of the Order of Malta as a ritual renunciation of all vanities. Emblems of earthly thought were burned on a "sacrificial altar" in accordance with medieval protocols sanctioned by the order, of which Paul had been elected grand master. Representatives had arrived in St. Petersburg with all their regalia, portraits bearing the symbolic emblems of the order, and, finally, chivalrous festivals.

By the morning of June 23, 1798, the guard regiments were at Pavlovsk. The knights of Malta arrived at the palace. "A few loads of wood, brushwood, and fir branches were brought, and nine bonfires were erected." The guard regiments lined up on three sides of the field around the bonfires, leaving open the side facing the palace. Around eight in the evening a procession emerged, with Paul I in the center. The knights carried torches and advanced two by two "solemnly and slowly . . . in plumed hats, red coats, and long black cloaks. . . . The knights circled the nine bonfires three times." Then the fires were lit. "Swirls of black smoke rose from the fir branches. When it disappeared the bonfires began to burn with a clear flame."[8]

After the death of Paul I such ceremonies ceased, and before long the Rose Pavilion became the traditional site of festivals, balls, and performances. These events were a constant topic of conversation in St. Petersburg's salons during the century's second decade. Voronikhin

THE PARK.
*Temple of Friendship.
Built between 1780
and 1783 to a design
by Cameron, it is
surrounded by sixteen
fluted Doric columns.
The metopes of the
frieze are decorated
with paired dolphins,
symbolic of friend-
ship, and wreaths of
grape leaves.*

and Gonzaga collaborated on some of these spectacles, in which many of the period's finest performers took part. The return of Alexander I was celebrated there in June 1814. For the occasion Gonzaga staged the wartime departure and then the return of militiamen to a rustic village, whose inhabitants responded to these goings and comings as one would expect. For this performance he devised an artificial landscape of exceptional perfection. The set, which remained in place for a time, took visitors by surprise. "I passed the Rose Pavilion and saw a marvelous village with a church, a master's house, and a country inn. I saw tall peasant *izbas* [huts], small lodgings with *terems* [towers] and, between them, wattle fences and gates, beyond which flower beds and little gardens were growing. . . . Suddenly a strange transformation took place before my eyes: it seemed as though an invisible curtain had been drawn over all the objects and hidden them from view. The closer I approached the more the charm dissipated . . . a few steps more and I saw the stretched canvas on which Gonzaga had traced the village; ten times I stepped back several paces to see everything as before."[9]

By the 1820s such sumptuous entertainments had come to an end. Contemporaries viewed the palace of Catherine's ill-loved heir as an image of the past. Pavlovsk became an aging witness of a vanishing time, an enormous, luxurious, but patriarchal residence. "When the weather is bad one remains in the palace and plays various games or keeps busy by reading, and boredom, a permanent inhabitant of palaces, dares not cast a glance here. There are hours when one works for the poor. Supper is served at ten o'clock in the evening, and then the gathering ends . . . In the larger world it is still very early, very noisy, but here it is already late and all is calm."[10]

THE PARK.
*View of the
White Birch area.*

THE PARK.
Aerial view of the
vale of the Slavyanka.
In the foreground,
the Pil Tower; in the
background, the
Temple of Friendship
and the palace.

THE PARK.
*Bip Fortress, built
between 1795 and 1798 by
Vincenzo Brenna.*

PETERHOF

Peterhof is the summer residence of the imperial family. From the eminence on which Peter the Great built it, on the edge of the gulf, one can see the Russian fleet in the Bay of Kronstadt; for here as elsewhere one cannot take even a single step without running up against the name of Peter the Great.

—Victor d'Arlincourt
Le Pélerin. L'Étoile polaire,
Paris, 1843

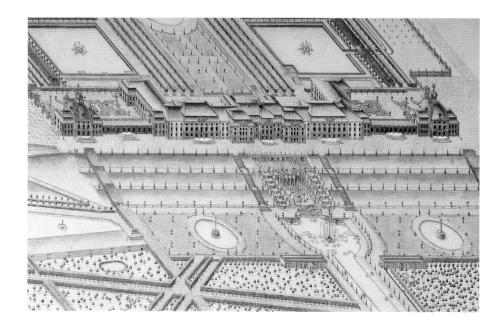

GREAT PALACE.
LEFT *Watercolor by P. A. de Saint-Hilaire, 1773. The palace is pictured here as it appeared after Rastrelli's expansion of 1745. It is situated between the Upper Garden, with its long, clipped promenades, and the Lower Garden, of which can be seen here the Great Cascade, the adjacent Samson Fountain, the beginning of the canal that runs to the sea, the round French and Italian fountains, topiary work, and a pair of arbors.* OPPOSITE *Southern façade facing the Upper Garden.*

UPPER GARDEN.
LEFT *Aerial view with the palace and the sea beyond. The first palace to rise on the site was begun in 1714 to designs by Peter the Great and completed, in somewhat modified form, in 1724. Its construction was overseen first by Leblond and then,* after his death in 1719, by Braunstein. The garden's central axis is dominated by three fountains, from the foreground: the Midway Fountain, the Neptune Fountain, and the Oak Fountain.*
BELOW *Statues adjacent to the Oak Fountain.*

The first mention of the palace dates from 1709. In his ukase, the emperor ordered built on the site "stone pleasure palaces of fine architectural quality."[2] The first small palace was erected in 1710–11. The main residence was completed in record time, like all projects undertaken on the shores of the Baltic after the Swedish defeat of 1709. The work was overseen by Johann Braunstein, a student of Andreas Schlüter, the famous Prussian architect of the early eighteenth century.

Jean-Baptiste-Alexandre Leblond, who commenced work at Peterhof in 1716, brought with him from Paris the French tradition of regular architectural ensembles. Unfortunately he died in 1719, but this gave him sufficient time to draw up a master plan for Peterhof. It showed the way to implement the tsar's desire for this seaside residence to be complemented by a "water garden," in which water would play the central role—spouting from countless fountains, cascading down waterfalls, flowing through canals, and running from the elevated ground of the Upper Garden through the Lower Garden and on to the sea. The existence of many natural springs in the imperial domain of Ropsha, situated some twelve miles (twenty kilometers) from Peterhof, made the "Water Plan" feasible. Accordingly, a canal was dug from that property to Peterhof to provide the water needed for the gardens.

Only the general concept of Leblond's master plan was implemented. After his death the Italian architect Nicolò Michetti began working at the site. His arrival during Peterhof's early years facilitated the coordination of work by German, French, and Italian masters, all of whom had been trained in different traditions; and in the first quarter of the eighteenth century Dutch garden designers were engaged to take part in the creation of the imperial gardens. This cosmopolitanism was not fortuitous or incidental. It is a sign of the degree to which no one model was followed in these projects. As Peterhof makes clear, Russian architecture of this period was eclectic, appropriating elements from many European architectural traditions.

The resulting ensemble made a strong impression on contemporaries, as evidenced by the journal of *Kammerjunker* Bergholtz, who witnessed the early-eighteenth-century construction campaigns firsthand. On August 13, 1723, he attended an "agreeable and sentimental" entertainment given by the emperor on the property. For the occasion, the famous boat made by Peter himself in his youth when he had become enthralled with the idea of building a Russian fleet arrived from St. Petersburg. "We reached Peterhof at about one-thirty. . . . No sooner had we arrived than we entered a marvelous large canal flowing right toward the palace. It is half a verst long [about

THE HISTORY OF PETERHOF AND ITS PERSONALITIES.

"At the sight of Peterhof one's thoughts turn involuntarily toward the period of Peter the Great . . . but while Peterhof is bound to the emperor Peter for founding it, the splendor of Peterhof belongs incontestably to the unforgettable Father of Your Majesty, our sovereign emperor Nicholas Pavlovich."[1] So wrote A. Geirot, author of the first detailed guide to Peterhof, to the reigning emperor Alexander II in 1868.

Since at least the late fifteenth century there had been a road along this sad coast of the Gulf of Finland (quite shallow here) that passed through a stunted forest and was used by the region's few inhabitants. In all likelihood it existed when the territory belonged to the merchant republic of Great Novgorod in the Middle Ages and then to the principality of Moscow before being conquered by the Swedes in the early seventeenth century. Neither the Russians nor the Swedes ever built anything of importance there.

The site of Peterhof was chosen because one day, during the period when the naval fortress on Kotlin Island was under construction, the emperor had ridden on horseback along the coast to this point, where he found it convenient to embark for Kronstadt. Accordingly the spot was deemed ideal for Peterhof, or "Peter's Palace."

GREAT PALACE.
*Ceiling of the main
staircase with painting
by Torelli.*

GREAT PALACE.
*Main staircase with
decor by Rastrelli.*

GREAT PALACE.
Throne Room.
Only the volumes
and parquet floor of
Rastrelli's original
design have survived.
The present decor was
realized by Georg
Velten between 1777
and 1779.

GREAT PALACE.
*Former Audience Room,
now known as the
Gilded Salon. Decor
by Rastrelli.*

half a mile] and wide enough to accommodate three little boats side by side. The emperor himself led the flotilla. . . . All the boats, which numbered about 115, lined up along both sides of the canal. When everyone had disembarked, the emperor began to guide . . . the distinguished guests all around, through the gardens, through the residences; the fountains overflowing with water were especially beautiful."[3]

On another occasion, Bergholtz brought some friends from Holstein to Peterhof and escorted them through the gardens in the emperor's absence. "The Lower Garden, through which runs a stone canal right against the principal block, is full of parterres and beautiful fountains. . . . The garden is surrounded by a great many beautiful and gay promenades running through groves. Two of the most beautiful, on either side of the garden, lead . . . to two pleasure palaces equidistant from the large palace on the hill. The one on the right is called Monplaisir; in its garden, also surrounded by a grove, there are a great many marvelous shrubs, paths, and parterres, a large stone-lined pond where swans and other birds swim, a special house for small birds, and various other amusing objects. The garden and the house of Marly on the left side of Peterhof . . . have already been begun."[4]

After the emperor's death his widow, Catherine I, continued to frequent Peterhof and organized many entertainments there.

Empress Anna Ivanovna was especially fond of Peter-

hof, where she spent most of her summers. Few lavish entertainments were held there during her reign, however, for she preferred to surround herself with a relatively small entourage, and her tastes in the way of amusement ran to jesters and dwarfs. She loved to go horseback riding along the garden's promenades, especially when she could be accompanied by her favorite, Biron, who was a splendid horseman. Sometimes they shot birds from the palace balcony. It was during her reign that the facilities and protocols of the imperial hunt were organized. To the east of the park, a menagerie encompassing nearly four square miles (ten square kilometers) was created and surrounded by a wall. Grouse hunts were organized in the forest, and a templelike pavilion was erected on a terrace near the sea to which deer were brought so the empress could shoot them. Exotic animals were kept on reserve for special occasions, including even tigers and buffalo. The peculiar institution of the imperial hunt continued at Peterhof for an entire century, until the middle of the nineteenth century. Regimental maneuvers were also organized in the preserve during Anna Ivanovna's reign. An earthworks fortress was built, and a demonstration of "how an enemy city is attacked and how it should defend itself" was presented for the empress's benefit. In this way military exercises entered the Peterhof tradition, as they had at Gatchina and Pavlovsk.

Empress Elizabeth Petrovna bestowed a new brilliance on Peterhof. She stipulated that in refurbishing

GREAT PALACE.
*Detail of former
Audience Room.
Decor by Rastrelli.*

the interiors her architects should "gild as much as possible," an instruction tellingly indicative of her personal taste. She took an interest in the fountains, too. Noting that they "played low," she set out to learn why, and as a result of her inquiry the complex water supply system was substantially modified. The wooden conduits installed in Peter's day were replaced by iron pipes. As a consequence of Elizabeth's interventions the fountains at Peterhof began to "play high" and its interiors sparkled as never before.

Even so, the empress's life at Peterhof was not all extravagant festivity. She was also attracted to the simple life of ordinary people. During the Seven Years War, Prussian standards taken in battle were brought to Peterhof, and a curious ritual ensued. Units of the guard would be assembled, an account of the battle read, and the enemy flags dragged along the ground before being brought into the Great Palace. When she grew weary of these triumphs, however, Elizabeth Petrovna would sometimes prepare her own meal in a "Dutch kitchen" built especially for her beside the small palace of Monplaisir. She was also devout and attended religious services with regularity. During her reign a chapel was built adjacent to the palace, effectively adding a wing to it. This proved insufficient for her needs, however, and in the summer a temporary country chapel was set up for her next to her beloved Monplaisir. The empress was also fond of

the theater, and she had one built at Peterhof. But the most important work undertaken between 1745 and 1755 was overseen by Bartolomeo Rastrelli, Elizabeth's "Oberarchitekt," or superintendent of buildings. Rastrelli transformed Peterhof into one of the most remarkable baroque ensembles in Russia.

Catherine the Great did not care for Peterhof and rarely went there. Even so, she decided to build a residence of her own on the property, one that would be distinct from those associated with Peter the Great and Elizabeth Petrovna. Accordingly, she built an enormous landscape park to the west of the formal gardens and two palaces, one for herself and another for the heir to the throne. Her new residence was called the English Palace, another instance of her Anglomania in the 1780s. An accomplished English garden designer, James Meders, was engaged to oversee the creation of the park, but when it came to the residence she one-upped the English Palladians by commissioning an Italian, Giacomo Quarenghi, to create her palaces in the "English Peterhof." Construction began in 1786 but was completed only in 1796, the year of the empress's death. The park still exists, but Quarenghi's palaces were destroyed during World War II.

Another of Catherine's projects should also be mentioned: her plan to transform all the properties situated along the road leading to Peterhof into country estates

GREAT PALACE. *Portrait Gallery. Originally known as the Italian Room, this was the baroque centerpiece of Peter the Great's original palace. Its first decor—of which only the ceiling survives—was contemporary with Peter the Great's study and was designed by Leblond, whose basic conception was carried out between 1719 and 1726 by Michetti. The present decor dates from the 1760s, when Catherine the Great commissioned Vallin de la Mothe to refurbish it. All of the portraits are by the same artist, P. Rotari, and all are of women, hence the room's nickname: Cabinet of Fashion and the Graces.*

GREAT PALACE.
*Peter the Great's
bedroom, adjacent to
his oak study. This is
the original decor; its
relative modesty reflects
the emperor's tastes.*

for the aristocracy. Relying on several books about English gardens, the empress herself drafted a set of "instructions" intended for the owners of these estates. They encouraged the imitation of nature and the creation of picturesque views, which Catherine hoped to see realized throughout the entire region along the Gulf of Finland. Unfortunately, the plan never progressed past the stage of "good intentions." As for Peterhof itself, in Catherine's old age it was rarely visited by the court and lost much of its brilliance.

Paul I, however, was convinced that he was in mystic communication with Peter the Great and that the ghost of the first emperor had foretold his destiny. Accordingly, he set about transforming Peterhof into a kind of memorial to his great-grandfather and installed his own study in the room where Peter's personal items were kept.

Paul's children regarded Peterhof in differing ways. Alexander I, who shared the tastes of his grandmother Catherine the Great, rarely resided there, using it only for occasional entertainments. The "Peterhof promenades" he organized were especially renowned. They took place on July 22, in honor of his mother, Maria Fedorovna.

Nicholas I, his younger brother and successor on the throne, preferred Peterhof to Tsarskoe Selo and spent his summers there. A curious pattern became established: if the reigning monarch was especially partial to Peterhof, his successor always preferred Tsarskoe Selo, and vice versa.

During the thirty-year reign of Nicholas I, from 1825 to 1855, the territory of Peterhof almost doubled in size and several new imperial residences were built. Especially noteworthy is the Alexandria complex, established on the former site of the eighteenth-century menagerie and named after the tsar's wife, Alexandra Fedorovna. Here the Scot Adam Menelas, assisted by I. Ivanov, built the so-called Cottage, a summer palace that was surrounded by a picturesque park full of romantic structures. The German architect Karl Schinkel designed a small Gothic chapel for the complex, in exchange for a small Byzantine church designed by the Russian architect Vasily Stasov in Potsdam.

Relations between Berlin and St. Petersburg were close during Nicholas's reign. Empress Alexandra Fedorovna was a Prussian princess, and Nicholas's sister, the

La vertu
ou
ſupreme
Pierre
Premier,
Empereur De
La Grande Ruſſie

GREAT PALACE. *Peter the Great's study. Detail of the Catherine I panel, carved in oak by Nicolas Pineau.*

GREAT PALACE.
*Peter the Great's
study, with oak
paneling carved by
Nicolas Pineau.*

grand duchess of Saxe-Weimar-Eisenach, lived in Weimar until her death. Family ties linked the imperial family to the ruling families of many other German principalities as well, which explains the German flavor of much of the "official romanticism" of the Russian court.

The emperor dreamed of being a "fearless and faultless knight," virile and gallant, an ideal reflected in Alexandria's coat of arms, devised by V. Zhukovsky: a crown of roses pierced by an upright sword.

Alexandria is a characteristic production of the 1820s and early 1830s, but the two other complexes built at Peterhof under Nicholas I, Colonists' Park and Meadow Park, date from the following two decades. Colonists' Park, formerly known as the "hunters' marsh," is situated to the south of the Upper Garden. It takes its name from German colonists to whom a portion of the land had been given after their arrival in Russia under Catherine II, who had encouraged their emigration. Nicholas's construction of a German village next to his own palace was a kindness toward his wife. The result was one of those idyllic tableaux of rustic peace and well-being typical of eighteenth-century gardens, examples of which we have already encountered at Tsarskoe Selo, Gatchina, and Oranienbaum.

A few pavilions were built in the park with belvederes that offered commanding views of the surrounding region, allowing the viewer to appreciate how the land-scaped gardens merged with the fields and forests to the south and the sea to the north. The Tsaritsa Pavilion, built by Andrei Stakenschneider about 1844 as a gift from the emperor to his wife, was exceptionally sumptuous. Nicholas probably intended it to remind her of the lavish constructions recently erected in her parents' park in Potsdam. This explains the choice of an "Italianate" idiom—a blend of Tuscan peasant architecture and formulas deriving from ancient Roman villas—developed by Schinkel and his students in the park at Sans-Souci. In this case, the building incorporated elements inspired by both Pompeian and Tuscan villas. In the center was a room suggestive of an ancient atrium, featuring a marble pool and a roof through which light could penetrate. There was also a small court resembling a Roman peristyle with an interior garden modeled after descriptions by ancient authors. Various marbles imported from Italy, Finland, and Siberia were used in the building, as were a few authentic Roman fragments, and a great many statues were placed inside, both genuine antiquities and nineteenth-century copies. A terrace was built in front of the pavilion for use in summer, when it was decorated with tropical plants, and around it was a "flowering carpet" appointed with bronze statuary, marble benches, and glass columns on marble pedestals. The pavilion was situated on an island in the middle of a lake, and visitors were ferried to it in Venetian

LOWER GARDEN.
*The Orangery, built
by Braunstein and
Zemtsov after a design
by Michetti. It was
begun in 1722, com-
pleted in 1725, and
remodeled in 1769.*

gondolas. The views afforded by the pavilion's tower were truly extraordinary.

An even smaller island was the site of another building: the Olga Pavilion, erected as a surprise gift for Grand Duchess Olga Nikolaevna and her husband, the king of Wurtemberg, when they visited Russia after their wedding. This building, featuring a three-story tower crowned by a roof terrace, is significant in the history of Russian architecture, for it resembles ancient residences in southern Italy.

A bit farther to the south is Meadow Park, realized between 1825 and 1857 by Wilhelm Ehrler and Pyotr Arkhipov, the same gardeners who executed Colonists' Park, after a design by Stakenschneider. It, too, was conceived along picturesque lines. The site featured vast fields, lakes dotted with islands, and groves. The principle of green masses arranged like theater wings, used so successfully by Pietro Gonzaga at Pavlovsk, was employed here. In these surroundings Stakenschneider built a small, Russian-style house; the Little Lake Pavilion, in the same style as the Tsaritsa Pavilion; and the Belvedere Palace, a Greek peripteral temple with Ionic columns atop a massive basement and preceded by a portico with four caryatids.

These landscape ensembles, whether filled with medievalizing images of a romantic cast, as at Alexandria, or conceived along Romano-Italian lines, as in Colonists'

and Meadow parks, convey some idea of the relatively relaxed way Nicholas I preferred to lead his private life. Even so, he never renounced the Romanov taste for soldiers, parades, and military drills. During the summer some surprising sights could be seen in these romantic precincts, as Geirot witnessed: "Among other things, Peterhof was greatly enlivened by the resumption in 1828 . . . of camp activities for the students of the military academies, who from that time on spent six weeks there every year living in tents between the Upper Garden and the English Garden [Alexandria, Meadow Park, Colonists' Park]. The New Village formerly located there was then moved behind Peterhof . . . and a site previously occupied by cultivated fields became a military field. In addition to being good for the health of these youths, camp life introduced them to the realities of military life. . . . In his early years, the heir . . . now His Majesty the reigning emperor [Alexander II], could usually be found among the ranks of the first cadet corps; he completed the entire march on foot in full military gear, and after arriving at the Peterhof camp he took part in roll call, exercises, and maneuvers, and spent his nights under the stars. The tsarevich made do with the modest provisions of the cadets and ate . . . with a wooden spoon from the communal pot. The boys developed the habit of keeping the tsarevich's spoons as souvenirs." And Geirot continues, describing with con-

LOWER GARDEN.
LOWER GARDEN.
Triton Fountain in
front of the Orangery.
The main spout emerges
from the mouth of a sea
monster whose jaw the
Triton is about to break.
The original design
dates from 1726, but the
fountain was recast
in 1875.

siderable enthusiasm "this temporary rapprochement between the imperial adolescent and the children of the poor nobility."[5] Of the many entertainments at Peterhof during the reign of Nicholas I, contemporaries retained most vividly in memory a lavish celebration in honor of Grand Duchess Olga Nikolaevna, queen of Wurtemberg. This event, which took place on the night of July 11, 1851, marked the apogee of nineteenth-century Russian court culture.

The most sumptuous period of Peterhof's history came to an end with the death of Nicholas I. His son Alexander II and his grandson Alexander III spent little time there and built very little on the property. When he was in residence, Alexander II generally stayed at the Farm Palace, built for him in 1838–39 by Stakenschneider, who incorporated into the new complex parts of the park "farm" devised by Menelas a decade earlier. This palace was situated in the Alexandria Park not far from the Cottage Palace. In the second half of the nineteenth century this part of Peterhof served as the private residence of the imperial family when its members wanted to vacation by the sea in the environs of St. Petersburg.

They took special care of it, and Nicholas II, the last emperor, continued this tradition. Another residence, known as the Lower Palace, was built for him in 1896 right on the shore of the Gulf of Finland, and this was the last to rise on the property. Designed by his court architect A. Tomishko in an eclectic vein, it was destroyed during World War II, which, as we have seen, caused considerable damage to the property.

Construction undertaken in the town of Peterhof during the middle years and second half of the nineteenth century played an important role in its development. Of the many available varieties of historicism, the neo-Gothic was considered the most fashionable. The Peterhof projects in this style included houses for members of the imperial family, built between 1830 and 1840 by the architect Joseph Charlemagne; a post office, erected by N. Benois and A. Kavos between 1850 and 1854; a stables and manège, also built by Benois between 1848 and 1855; and his New Peterhof train station, the last edifice in the "Gothic series," completed in 1859. Architecturally, this moment was characterized by a struggle between two tendencies: one rather freely evoking the

LOWER GARDEN.
One of the "Roman"
fountains, so called
because they were
thought to resemble the
tiered fountains in the
piazza of St. Peter's in
Rome. First envisioned
by Michetti in the
1720s, they were
actually built only
in 1738.

LOWER GARDEN.
*The Dragon Fountain,
also known as the
Chessboard Fountain.
Begun in 1722 by
Zemtsov in accordance
with an idea by Peter
the Great, it was
completed only in
1739. The final design
incorporates modifi-
cations introduced
by several architects.
The checkerboard
patterns evoke the
marble floors of Peter's
Monplaisir Palace.*

European Middle Ages, and another combining elements drawn from ancient Russian architecture with a
more archaeological Gothic idiom. The "Russian" style
eventually carried the day, for its appeal to national tradition proved irresistible.

Benois, born into a French family that had settled
in St. Petersburg, preferred an "authentic" Gothic that
was very different in feeling. His manège and train station employed elements borrowed from English and
French Gothic cathedrals, models that had nothing to
do with the functions of his own buildings, but the
results were nonetheless spectacular. These designs
established the presence of a European neo-Gothic
idiom in Russian architecture of the second half of the
nineteenth century. Benois was the founder of an artistic
clan that played a key role in Russian culture at the turn
of the century, comprising a pleiad of architects,
painters, sculptors, and art historians. A museum
devoted to the Benois family has recently been opened
next to the Great Palace at Peterhof.

THE GREAT PALACE. The Great Palace at
Peterhof as we know it today is largely the work
of Rastrelli, and thus it is a Russian baroque production of the mid-eighteenth century. Its history began
earlier, however, and older portions of the building were
incorporated into the interior of Rastrelli's design. In
1714 Peter the Great's first stone palace, known as the
Upper Palace, began to rise on the slope of a hill overlooking the sea, at the point where the present Lower
Garden begins. In 1716 Leblond, dissatisfied with what
had already been built, drew up a new plan for the
imperial residence. This was partially constructed before
Leblond's death about a year later and was completed
by his successor, the architect Braunstein. The building
burned in 1721, at which point Michetti undertook its
restoration and expansion. On either side of the central
block—the old Upper Palace—symmetrical wings with
linking arcades were built. Work on the interiors of
Peter's favorite residence continued until his death in
1725. French tapestries were imported to cover the walls
of the large room in the center of the building, and
the artist B. Tarsia was brought from Italy to paint the
ceiling. Empress Anna Ivanovna left the rooms of her
"Uncle Peter" as they were, but Elizabeth Petrovna
commissioned Rastrelli to completely recast the building, and the result was the palace as we know it today.

The wings and galleries built by Michetti were demolished, but the original central block was enclosed
within the new structure and given a new façade. By
1751 the palace had become a long building whose central three-story structure, covered by a hipped roof, was
flanked by two low galleries leading to the chapel (east)

ALEXANDRIA PARK.
*The Cottage. Given by
Nicholas I to his wife, it
was built between 1826
and 1829 to a design by
Adam Menelas, who
was inspired by English
neo-Gothic designs of
the period.*

and the so-called Arms Pavilion (west). These two buildings were identical from the outside save for one detail: the chapel's roof was topped by an Orthodox cross, whereas the pavilion's roof was crowned by a two-headed eagle, the emblem of imperial Russia. The use of these two emblems was significant, for they symbolized, respectively, faith and fidelity, Orthodoxy and autocracy. Similar schemes were used in other imperial palaces of the baroque era: at Tsarskoe Selo, for example, which also featured a chapel at one end and an "arms" pavilion at the other in the mid-eighteenth century.

Like all of Rastrelli's buildings, the Great Palace impresses by its scale, its gilding, its use of contrasting colors (white and yellow), and its wealth of decorative details. But these extravagant features do not diminish the architectural quality of the whole. Rastrelli's design has survived largely intact, but to the west, on the Upper Garden side, a low block was added perpendicular to the palace between 1779 and 1785, built to a classicizing design by Georg Velten. Between 1838 and 1840 this addition was refurbished in a neobaroque style by the architect Joseph Charlemagne. The palace suffered greatly during the last war, but a meticulous restoration campaign has now restored its façades to their original state.

The interior plan of the Great Palace is quite complex, an unusual departure for Rastrelli. But the complexity was a consequence of the incorporation of Peter the Great's palace. Its rooms in the building's center are easy to identify, for they are much smaller than those in the newer lateral wings. Here there are no uninterrupted enfilades extending the full length of the façades like those at Tsarskoe Selo. There are a few such sequences of rooms, of course, but they are much shorter. The approach to the chapel through the gallery is unusually grand, as is the immense ballroom in the opposite wing of the building.

The dates of the interior decor vary considerably. Most of Rastrelli's interiors were destroyed in the course of remodeling, but the four most important ones—the main staircase, the Audience Room, the ballroom, and the chapel—retain at least the broad outlines of his original conceptions. As in the Winter Palace and Tsarskoe Selo, the baroque master here indulged his taste for gilded sculptural ornament arrayed against a white ground that further enhances its brilliance. Slender gold moldings limn the basic structural elements, complemented by arabesques, vegetal motifs, rosettes, and plump putti. The sumptuous effect is further enriched by countless candelabra, ornately framed mirrors, and allegorical medallions painted on the walls and ceilings, also enclosed in lavish gold frames. Despite the stylistic similarity and profusion of these details, the results are anything but heavy. They offer a kind of précis

ALEXANDRIA PARK.
*The Cottage. Detail of
one of the cast-iron
porches. The treatment
on the back wall incor-
porates Alexandria's
coat of arms, a crown
of roses pierced by
a sword.*

of Rastrelli's baroque idiom, remarkable for its vivacity and optimism.

The era of Catherine the Great at Peterhof has two distinct aspects, corresponding to her tastes in the 1760s and 1770s. Between 1763 and 1770 the French architect Jean-Baptiste Vallin de la Mothe, invited to Russia soon after the empress's accession, refurbished the apartments at the heart of the building: the large room precisely at its center, hitherto known as the Italian Room, and the two rooms on either side. He might have been expected to produce classicizing decors, but he opted instead for the most extravagant rococo idiom. Doubtless Catherine approved. We have already discussed her youthful preference for such surroundings, which may reflect her intoxication at having attained power through her successful coup.

In the 1760s the sumptuous ceremonial rooms of the baroque era took on a different and altogether eccentric character. The Italian Room was transformed into a Portrait or Picture Gallery. It was also called on occasion the Cabinet of Fashion and the Graces, a title that suits it perfectly, for its ample walls were lined with more than three hundred portraits of beautiful young women, variously dressed but all manifestly carefree, and all painted by the same artist, P. Rotari. The original ceiling has been preserved but is of little interest. From this room one could access, as today, the two other rooms deco-

rated by Vallin de la Mothe for the young Catherine II, the Chinese Study and the Chinese Boudoir. Nineteenth-century descriptions of Peterhof assert that their walls and "all decorations and furnishings were authentically Chinese," but such was not the case. The only genuine Chinese things in them were porcelain tea services and some statuettes. Otherwise their decor was pure eighteenth-century chinoiserie, consisting of fantastic evocations of an imaginary China produced by a French artist for the empress's delectation. Especially notable are the large panels of black-and-gold lacquer framed by the squared arabesques considered Chinese in the eighteenth century. They were produced in Russia but modeled after designs on authentic Chinese lacquer, painted porcelain, and painted silk.

By the turn of the 1770s, however, Catherine was a different person; the experience of power and a series of military victories had changed her. The "rocaille princess" whose tastes ran to decorative extravagance, perhaps to counteract her natural seriousness, had been transformed into a "classical empress." Accordingly, the St. Petersburg architect Velten was commissioned to refurbish the ceremonial rooms: the Throne Room, the Banquet Hall, the first anteroom (dedicated to the naval victory at Chesme and thus known as the Chesme Room), the Divan and Partridge rooms, the ceremonial bedroom (known as the Crown Bedroom), and the

ALEXANDRIA PARK.
The Cottage. View of the main staircase with its Gothic trompe l'oeil decor painted by D. B. Scotti in 1828.

ALEXANDRIA PARK.
*The Cottage. Gothic
Room, general view
(left) and detail
(below). The ceiling
pattern evokes both
the work of the Adam
brothers and the
English Decorative
style. The bronze clock
on one of the corner
mantelpieces repro-
duces the façade of
Reims Cathedral, with
the clock face inserted
in its rose window.*

dressing room. In the Throne Room, Banquet Hall, and Chesme Room resolution, stability, and restraint reign. Painting and sculpture are relegated to subsidiary roles, and the iconography tends to be official and edifying. The Throne Room, for example, features reliefs glorifying justice and wisdom, whereas those in the Banquet Hall celebrate joy and abundance. After othe gilded turbulence of Rastrelli's baroque and the extravagance of rococo, these two spaces produce a rather glacial impression, but there is something fresh as well as majestic about them, perhaps the result of their having been among the first neoclassical interiors in Russia.

The Divan Room, the Partridge Room, the bedroom, and the dressing room are quite different. Their decors are much more welcoming, although still quite far from rocaille exuberance. There is little sculptural or architectural detailing in these interiors aside from gilded cornices and doors, a bit of paneling, and a few alcoves. Attention is focused instead on the draperies. Sumptuous fabrics were used: Chinese painted silk, produced in the early eighteenth century, as well as French materials woven to designs by Philippe de Lasalle. The fabrics covering the walls, the curtains, and the cushions arrayed on large divans and deep armchairs, combined with many sconces and candelabra to produce an effect of refined comfort.

ALEXANDRIA PARK.
*The Cottage. Dining
room. The furniture
and decor were exe-
cuted after designs by
Adam Menelas.*

WATERFALLS AND FOUNTAINS. A large grotto with waterfalls some 130 feet (40 meters) long was constructed in front of the Great Palace during the period of Peter the Great. Just beneath it, at the end of the canal that led to the sea, was the *kovsh*, or harbor, for the emperor's yachts. Construction of this project, conceived in part to strengthen the hill on which the palace was built, began in 1715. After arriving in Russia, Leblond continued the work but introduced a few modifications. Michetti, who succeeded him, significantly increased the number of sculptures ornamenting the waterfalls, partly in response to Peter's wish that the Great Cascade commemorate his victory over the Swedes. The final result is an enormous tiered ensemble incorporating two grottos, three cascades, and dozens of fountains and sculptures. Close to the palace a viewing terrace with a balustrade was built. Below it unfold, in turn, the arcaded face of one grotto; a second terrace, also surrounded by a balustrade, containing fountains and statues; and, lowest of all, a second, deeper grotto facing a large, circular fountain. On either side and in the center of these elements are three waterfalls that empty into the oval *kovsh*, which flows into the long, straight canal. The effect of all this was, and remains, quite dazzling.

Most of the sculptures for the Great Cascade were originally made of lead, cast in the workshops of Bartolo-meo Rastrelli the elder (the architect's father), F. Vassi, and the English builder G. Thomas. Many of the statues were produced after designs by Leblond, Michetti, and Zemtsov, the successive overseers of the palace's construction, but the series of allegorical depictions of the seasons were produced in Holland. In short, the statuary of the Great Cascade is stylistically heterogeneous, representing an array of European traditions. Even so, the design reflects the intentions of Peter the Great, who personally intervened in the ensemble's construction on several occasions.

The central focus of the design is the Samson Fountain, created after a maquette by Rastrelli the elder. All of the original statues had to be replaced in subsequent years, but the basic thematic conception was retained. The lead sculpture was already in a sorry state by the end of the eighteenth century, and bronze versions were cast between 1799 and 1806. The finest sculptors of the era took part in the project: Mikhail Kozlovsky, Ivan Prokofiev, Feodosy Shchedrin, Ivan Martos, Jean-Dominique Rachette, and Fedot Shubin. Many of them adopted a neobaroque idiom for the occasion, for example Kozlovsky in his new version of *Samson Breaking the Lion's Jaw.*

To the right and left of the cascades, three terraces dating from the period of Peter the Great make it possible to follow the water's descent to the Lower Garden. Michetti suggested decorating their retaining walls with water-spouting golden masks, an idea not realized at the time but implemented by Andrei Voronikhin at the turn of the nineteenth century. He transformed them into small, independent, stepped limestone cascades that culminate in round pools featuring a central jet of water. The cascades were subsequently remodeled in marble and granite by Stakenschneider.

Two large, round fountains were placed in flowered parterres at the bottom of the ensemble. They feature enormous vases and are called the French (east) and the Italian (west) fountains, a reference to the nationalities of the craftsmen who produced them in the first quarter of the eighteenth century.

More fountains and other waterworks extend all the way to the sea. The fountains along the Great Canal take various forms but all feature edifying sculptures inspired by the parables in a popular early-eighteenth-century Russian book entitled *The Spectacle of Human Life*, for example, "The Two Snakes," "The Mountain and the Mouse," and "The Hen and the Hawk." By 1735 there were twenty-two fountains in the proximity of the Grand Canal, each with no less than twenty jets of water and each with different figures.

Among the extant eighteenth-century fountains scattered through the Lower Garden, three are especially noteworthy: the Favorite, Adam, and Eve fountains. The

LEFT
ALEXANDRIA PARK. *The Gothic chapel, dedicated to Alexander Nevsky. Begun in 1831 by Adam Menalas to a design by the German architect Karl Schinkel, it was completed after Menelas's death by Joseph Charlemagne.*

THE TOWN OF PETERHOF. BELOW *The stables and manège. These neo-Gothic buildings, built by N. Benois between 1848 and 1855, are the most important structures in the town.* OPPOSITE *The Church of Saints Peter and Paul.*

first was inspired by a similar fountain at Versailles called the Ducks and the Water Spaniel. In the Peterhof version, a little mechanized dog runs through a basin in pursuit of four ducks to the accompaniment of sound effects reproducing the quacking of the ducks and the barking of the dog. The original was made of wood, but in 1730 a bronze version was cast. Unfortunately, all but a single figure of the group was destroyed in World War II, but it has since been reconstituted on the basis of the eighteenth-century drawings. The fountains of Adam and Eve are situated in large, round pools; fifteen jets of water spurt from their central pedestals. The figures of Adam and Eve are copies—made in 1718 in Venice by Giovanni Bonazza—of the celebrated statues by Antonio Rizzi then in the Palazzo Ducale. The fountains are surrounded by trellised structures dating from the 1720s.

In 1853–54 two Marble Bench fountains were erected in the Lower Garden to designs by Stakenschneider. Each consists of a long white marble bench, above which rises a basin of the same material. In one of the basins is a statue of Danae, a copy by Ivan Vitali after an original by Christian Daniel Rauch, and in the other is a nymph after an antique sculpture.

These fountains are situated in the central part of the Lower Garden. Another ensemble is to be found in the eastern part, south of the Monplaisir Palace. Aligned with its main axis, at the foot of a hill, is a large, open square with two fountains on one side and a cascade set into the hill's slope on the other. This area was designed in the first half of the eighteenth century by Michetti. At that time the hill was tiered, the square was planted with a "carpet" of flowers, and the whole was complemented by clipped bosquets. All that now survives are the two Roman fountains and their octagonal pools, so called because they were thought to resemble the large, tiered fountains in the piazza in front of St. Peter's in Rome. These fountains have since been modified several times by prominent architects, including Rastrelli, receiving their definitive form only in 1817.

The Dragon Cascade must be numbered among the most interesting features of the Lower Garden. It was conceived by Peter the Great himself along the lines of the small cascade in the park at Marly, which had made a strong impression on him during his trip to France. Michetti drafted the original design, but its realization was repeatedly delayed by changes of architect. In 1738 a variant devised by I. Blank was approved, but a year later it was decided to transform it into a Chinese fountain by adding dragons. The definitive design is extremely curious. Set into a bed of rough stones on a hill are four gently tilted and stepped platforms painted with a chessboardlike pattern of black-and-white lozenges. At the top, three brightly colored metal dragons spout water,

LOWER GARDEN. *Pyramid fountain, so called because of the low stepped pyramid from which the jets spray. Designed by Michetti in 1721 and operative by 1724, it was remodeled several times during the eighteenth century.*

MONPLAISIR PALACE. *Eastern façade of the bathhouse. Begun in 1714 and completed in 1722, this palace was Peter the Great's first residence at Peterhof.*

which then flows over the remaining platforms and into a rocky pool below. On either side are narrow staircases and marble statues.

The most notable feature of the eastern part of the Lower Garden is the Pyramid Fountain. Also erected in the 1720s, it was completed only in the following century. The original version was made of wood. It was then transformed into a marble step pyramid set within a rather large, rectangular marble pool surrounded by a high marble balustrade. Farther north, closer to Monplaisir, some "trick" fountains were installed. These begin to flow in unexpected places and at unexpected times. The first ones were built in 1723, but they were reconstructed countless times, notably in the 1780s and 1790s. Thanks to the work of contemporary restorers, these delightful water fantasies are once again operative. They include a Chinese Umbrella, from the perimeter of which water flows unexpectedly, a Settee, in front of which a "curtain" of water sometimes spurts up from the pavement without warning, and a Bench fountain conceived along the same lines, as well as the Little Spruce, Little Oak, and Tulip fountains, from

whose metal flowers and leaves water can be made to gush. Still more fountains were built around Monplaisir and the adjacent menagerie, among them the Sun Fountain with a rotating disk, the Bell Fountain with a statue of Bacchus, and the Shell Fountain in the Chinese garden.

Waterworks are to be found everywhere at Peterhof, and the western portion of the Lower Garden is no exception. In the environs of the Marly Palace is the longest of all the cascades: the Golden Hill, featuring twenty steps and surrounded by sixteen marble statues. With the four small triton fountains and the large, round fountains of the menagerie, it figures as part of the Garden of Bacchus created on orders from Peter the Great along the lines of that at Marly, outside Paris, which had made a strong impression on him. Michetti set out to build a precise replica, but as usual the design underwent subsequent modifications, notably under the direction of Zemtsov.

After this long enumeration of Peterhof's fountains, we turn to the small palaces built in the Lower Garden close to the shore: Monplaisir and Marly.

MONPLAISIR PALACE.
Great Hall.
OPPOSITE *General view.*
RIGHT *Detail of ceiling. The ceiling paintings were executed by P. Pillement in 1718, and the stucco work is by Rastrelli the elder.*

337

MONPLAISIR. Peter the Great himself chose the site of Monplaisir. His own sketches of the interiors and the surrounding formal garden survive, and the building was consistent with his tastes: its dimensions were not large, the rooms were comfortable, and—above all—it was situated by the sea. It afforded a sweeping view of the Gulf of Finland, and St. Petersburg could be discerned in the distance, the gilded spire of the Cathedral of Peter and Paul rising above it. In old guidebooks Monplaisir is often called "the little Dutch house," an allusion to Peter the Great's stint in an Amsterdam shipyard. It is difficult to name a specific Dutch model for the building's design, but the interior decor is consistent with Dutch fashions of the early eighteenth century.

Construction was begun in 1714 under the direction of Braunstein, and two years later the central portion of the palace was complete. The stucco work has been attributed to Rastrelli the elder, but Leblond played an important role in the conception of the decors, as did Peter the Great himself. More than once the emperor ordered additional work done because a new idea had come to him. Many accomplished artists contributed to the project, both Russian and foreign, including P. Pillement, J. Michel, G. Brumkorst, A. Cardassier, A. Zakharov, N. Lyubetsky, and D. Soloviev. Work was completed in 1723, and the building has

changed very little since then. Even in the eighteenth century it was perceived as a commemorative monument to Peter that offered singular insight into his tastes and way of life.

In the middle of the central pavilion is the Great Hall, surrounded by three smaller rooms. The floors of the Great Hall are paved with black and white marble in a canted checkerboard pattern, and the walls are lined with simple oak paneling into which Dutch and Flemish paintings from Peter's collection have been set, framed in black. All of this is consistent with what one would expect of a "little Dutch house," but the upper portion of the room is very different in character. A bracketed white cornice with decorative cartouches separates the walls from a high vault. In its corners are large terms of mythological figures whose Italian character is indicative of Rastrelli the elder's participation in the decor's realization. The intervening panels and the ceiling are decorated with elegant painted arabesque compositions and mythological figures by Pillement.

Of the six small rooms in the central pavilion (a pantry, a kitchen, and the Chinese Room to the east; the Maritime Room, a bedroom, and a secretary's office to the west), the most exotic is the Chinese Room, also known as the Lacquer Room. The galleries have oak paneling and checkered marble floors like those in the Great

MONPLAISIR PALACE.
One of the lateral galleries, which feature windows on both sides, creating an effect of lightness that is complemented by the airy arabesque design on the ceilings.

LOWER GARDEN.
Trick fountain,
nineteenth century.

LOWER GARDEN.
RIGHT *Sun
Fountain, 1723.*
FAR RIGHT *Chinese
Umbrella Fountain,
1796.*

Hall; their ceilings are painted with similar arabesque compositions against a white ground, and their walls, too, are decorated with Dutch paintings from Peter's collection. The small lateral pavilions, crowned by lanterns, are decorated in the same spirit.

Additional structures were built close to the eastern wing of the palace. A bathhouse outfitted with a square pool, a fountain, and baths, for example, was erected by Quarenghi in 1800 on the former site of a wooden building. In the second half of the nineteenth century another bathhouse was built nearby for the courtiers residing at Peterhof. The kitchen building, a single-story structure that included both cooking facilities and lodgings for the cooks, was erected between 1726 and 1732, and in 1748 Rastrelli added a banquet hall that was decorated with tapestries depicting tropical landscapes. On the western side of the palace, Rastrelli built the so-called Catherine Palace. This is much larger than the intimately scaled Monplaisir, a typically monumental production of the mid-eighteenth-century Russian baroque with massive proportions and abundant decoration on its façades. Originally its interior consisted of several public rooms, but in 1760 the "Dutch kitchen" was installed for Empress Elizabeth Petrovna, who loved to cook there.

A formal garden was planted around the palace in 1714–16, during the initial construction, and it of course included fountains, among them the Sheaf Fountain with many jets of water and four Bell fountains decorated with gilded statuary. In 1718–19 a menagerie was established nearby with a pond for swans and ducks, and an aviary.

MARLY AND THE HERMITAGE. The Marly Palace, with its surrounding formal garden, lakes, and fountains, constitutes an independent ensemble in the Lower Garden of Peterhof. Like Monplaisir, it reflects Peter's own tastes in architecture and garden design. Plans were drawn up by Braunstein at the end of 1720. The shell was finished by the following winter, and the interiors were completed in 1723. It retained its original form until it suffered damage during World War II, but it has since been restored to its former glory.

The western part of the Lower Garden nestles between a high embankment along the coast on one side and the slope leading to the Upper Garden on the other. This disposition lends a special intimacy to the Marly ensemble. The palace itself is not large; cubic in form,

THE GREAT CASCADE.
ABOVE *The Great Cascade and Samson Fountain at Peterhof, print after a drawing by Shotoshnikov, c. 1800.*
OPPOSITE *The focus of the Great Cascade is the Samson Fountain, created after a model by Rastrelli the elder. In the first half of the eighteenth century it was understood to represent the "Russian Samson" (Peter the Great) tearing to pieces the roaring Swedish lion (Charles XII). Many of the other statues, too, can be read as politically aggrandizing.*

it is perched between two pools, one rectangular and the other semicircular. Its delicate access bridges, elegant cast-iron balconies, and serene reflections conspire to produce a picture of harmonious calm that remains in the mind.

The plan features more rooms than might be expected: there are nine on each floor, so naturally they are quite small. The decors are restrained but of high quality, featuring marble floors, oak doors and windows, and square-tiled stoves. Originally, the walls in some of the rooms were lined with fabric or covered with paneling. The kitchen was "Dutch," with Delft tiles prominent in its decor. Many paintings and furnishings dating from the first half of the eighteenth century can still be seen there.

Not far from Marly but closer to the sea is the Hermitage, built to a design by Braunstein between 1721 and 1724. It, too, is a two-story building. The ground floor contained service facilities for the main room on the floor above, where intimate luncheons and suppers were served during the reigns of Peter the Great and, especially, his daughter Elizabeth. This din-

ing room occupied the entire floor, and in its center was a mechanism allowing the completely set dining table to rise from the kitchen below. The decor of wall-to-wall paintings dates from Rastrelli's remodeling of 1756–57.

THE COTTAGE. The vaguely neo-Gothic Cottage is a reflection of the picturesque taste prevalent in England in the late eighteenth and early nineteenth centuries, which left quite a few marks on Russian architecture. It resembles many designs proposed to English gentlemen in publications of the first quarter of the nineteenth century, in which Renaissance and neo-Gothic elements are combined to create a romantic image that was found especially appealing in the century's first half.

Menelas, who worked in turn for Catherine the Great, Paul I, Alexander I, and Nicholas I, built the Cottage toward the end of his life, between 1826 and 1829. The original design was symmetrical, but Staken-schneider's addition in 1841 of a dining room and cast-

LOWER GARDEN.
The Hermitage, built between 1721 and 1723.

LOWER GARDEN. *Dining room in the Hermitage. The ground floor consisted of a vestibule, a kitchen, offices, and a closet housing the "flying table." This device made it possible to prepare a meal below and lift it directly into the center of the room above, obviating the need for attending servants. Originally, a similarly conceived "flying chair" was used to lift the guests to the room. At the end of the eighteenth century it was replaced by a stairway.*

iron porch changed its character. It did not, however, diminish its charm. The building remains the finest reflection of the period of Nicholas I, and it reveals much about the everyday life of the court in those years, thanks in part to a successful restoration campaign.

In the center of the building is the main staircase, which serves all three floors. It is decorated with grisailles by the celebrated painter D. B. Scotti, who modeled his neo-Gothic designs after the stair at Strawberry Hill, Horace Walpole's country house near London. The staircase is accessed by a vestibule, to the left of which is the apartment of Empress Alexandra Fedorovna. All the first-floor rooms are arranged round the central staircase, starting with Alexandra Fedorovna's dressing room, bedroom, study, drawing room, and library. The latter is contiguous with a large salon, a dining room, and a small salon, which are not part of her private quarters. All these rooms are relatively small, and each has an intimate character established by its decor. Like most mid-nineteenth century interiors, they are filled with furniture, folding screens, paintings, candelabra, clocks, vases, shelves displaying porcelain, bookshelves, potted plants, and curtains. The furniture was made to Menelas's designs by the court furniture maker, G. Hambson. The interiors are Gothic in feeling, featuring lacy stucco ceiling designs inspired by the English Decorative style. Window sashes, niches, and

furniture encrusted with Gothic tracery add to the effect, as do many of the accompanying objects. The Gothic decor of the empress's study is especially successful, partly as a result of the integrated conceptions of its bookcases, table, and high armchairs. On a mantel is a remarkable bronze clock reproducing the main façade of Reims Cathedral, with the clock face occupying the place of its rose window.

The apartments of Nicholas I and the children's rooms are on the second floor. Above the first-floor drawing room is the emperor's study, also featuring a Gothic decor, and his adjoining dressing room and wardrobe. The children's bedrooms have no pronounced decorative character but are nonetheless quite attractive, for they are in the typical mid-nineteenth-century style executed to perfection. Especially noteworthy is a "study balcony" intended for use by the heir apparent and his brothers. Its walls are painted to resemble a military tent, like a similar room in Charlottenhof Palace in Potsdam.

The third floor contains servants' quarters and the Maritime Study of Nicholas I, which also has a martial theme, for its walls are lined with fabric suggestive of a campaign tent. From here the emperor could observe by telescope the maneuvers of his fleet in the Gulf of Finland. According to tradition, it was in this room that Nicholas I awaited news of the Anglo-French fleet's

LOWER GARDEN.
LEFT *Eve Fountain.
Its centerpiece is a copy
by Giovanni Bonazza
of the statue of Eve
carved by Antonio Rizzi
for the Palazzo Ducale
in Venice. Bonazza's
version was produced
in 1718 but installed in
the fountain only
much later.*
OPPOSITE *Marly
Avenue.*

approach toward Kronstadt during the Crimean War, which ended in a defeat for Russia that hastened the emperor's end.

The Cottage is perhaps his most significant memorial. It conveys something of his character, which was marked by restraint and devotion to the military as well as by commitment to family and a desire to acknowledge his humanity. He did not allow these last sentiments to affect his political decisions, but the serene self-confidence is reflected in these interiors, which tell us much about the state of mind prevailing in Russia at the last moment of its historical prosperity, and the beginning of its fall.

LOWER GARDEN.

OPPOSITE
Marly Palace, ingeniously situated between two pools.
RIGHT AND BELOW
Golden Hill Fountain, view looking down (right) and detail of its topmost level (below). Commissioned by Peter the Great from Michetti in 1721 and completed in 1735, it was modeled after a similar cascade in the gardens of Marly in France.

LOWER GARDEN.
ABOVE *Bell Fountain,*
commissioned in 1721 and
installed in 1732.
OPPOSITE *Embankment*
protecting Marly from the
Gulf of Finland.

LOWER GARDEN.
Marly Embankment.

CHAPTER 1

1. Vladimir F. Odoyevsky, *Works*, vol. 2, Moscow, 1981, p. 146.

2. N. A. Antsiferov, "Account of Years Past," in *The True History and Myths of Petersburg*, Petrograd, 1924, p. 12.

3. *Record from the Era of Peter the Great*, vol. 1, 1703–7, Moscow, 1903, pp. 73–74; S. P. Luppov, *History of the Construction of Petersburg in the First Quarter of the Eighteenth Century*, Moscow and Leningrad, 1957, pp. 16–17.

4. Igor E. Grabar, *History of Russian Art*, vol. 3, Moscow, 1903, p. 27.

5. H. Bruce, *Memoirs*, vol. 4, London, 1784, p. 42.

6. "Petersburg in 1720: The Account of a Pole," in *Russkaya Starina*, June 1879, p. 261.

CHAPTER 2

1. Georg Kraft, *Authentic and Circumstantial Description of the House of Ice Erected in St. Petersburg*, St. Petersburg, 1743, p. 3.

2. Ibid., p. 4.

3. Igor E. Grabar, *History of Russian Art*, vol. 3, Moscow, 1903, p. 180.

4. Boris R. Vipper, *Russian Baroque Architecture*, Moscow, 1978, p. 77.

CHAPTER 3

1. Denis Diderot, *From Petersburg, Complete Works*, vol. 10, Moscow, 1947, p. 98.

2. *Archives of the Senate*, vol. 10, St. Petersburg, 1902, p. 132.

3. Ibid.

4. Catherine the Great, *Complete Works*, vol. 12, St. Petersburg, 1892, pp. 583–84.

5. Alexander Sergeevich Pushkin, "The Bronze Horseman," translated by Walter Arndt, in George Gibian, ed., *The Portable Nineteenth-Century Russian Reader*, New York, 1993, p. 19.

6. *The Masters of Art on Art*, vol. 2, Moscow, 1958, p. 155.

7. *Publication of the Imperial Society of Russian History*, vol. 23, St. Petersburg, 1878, p. 85.

8. Ibid., p. 157.

9. Ibid.

10. Filipp Vigel, *Notes*, vol. 1, Moscow, 1928, p. 181.

11. *Russian Archives*, 1867, no. 5, p. 93.

CHAPTER 4

1. Varvara N. Golovina, "Notes," in *Russkaya Starina*, Moscow, 1992, p. 323.

2. Ibid.

CHAPTER 5

1. Filipp Vigel, *Notes*, vol. 1, Moscow, 1928, p. 125.

2. Alexander Pushkin, "The Snowstorm," in *The Captain's Daughter and Other Stories*, New York, 1936, p. 171.

3. Vigel, *Notes*, pp. 177–79.

4. Ibid.

5. M. Taranovskaya, *Carlo Rossi*, Leningrad, 1980, p. 23.

6. Ibid., p. 124

7. Ibid., p. 41.

8. Vigel, *Notes*, p. 182.

9. Ibid., vol. II, p. 85.

10. Ibid.

11. Osip Mandelstam, "The Admiralty," in *Selected Poems*, trans. by Clarence Brown and W. S. Merwin, New York, 1983, pp. 5–6.

12. Théophile Gautier, *Voyage to Russia*, Moscow, 1867, p. 180.

13. Ibid., p. 191.

14. Nikolai Gogol, "Nevsky Avenue," in *The Overcoat and Other Tales of Good and Evil*, trans. by David Magarshack, New York, 1965, p. 161.

15. Alexander Blok, *On the Islands*, in *Complete Works*, vol. II, Leningrad, 1980, p. 143.

CHAPTER 6

1. Fedor Dostoevsky, *Diary of a Writer*, as cited in N. Antsiferov, *Dostoevsky's Petersburg*, Petrograd, 1923, p. 73.

2. *The Architect*, 1872, no. 1, p. 7.

3. *The Architect*, 1882, no. 5, pp. 71–72.

CHAPTER 8

1. Alexander Pushkin, "The Nineteenth of October," in *Complete Works*, p. 288.

2. Nikolai Gumilev, "In Memory of Innokenty Annensky," in *Tsarskoe Selo in Poetry*, Petrograd, 1922.

3. "Letters from Catherine II to Grimm," in Alexander Benois, *Tsarskoe Selo in the Period of Empress Elizabeth Petrovna*, St. Petersburg, p. 12.

4. Mikhail Lomonosov, "Ode to the Empress Elizabeth," in *Tsarskoe Selo in Poetry*, p. 17.

5. Alexander Benois, *Complete Works*, p. 24.

6. E. Gollerbakh, *The Country Palaces and Parks*, Petrograd, 1924, p. 31.

7. Igor E. Grabar, *History of Russian Art*, Moscow, 1903, p. 370.

8. M. Voronov, G. Khodasevich, *Cameron's Ensemble in Pushkin [Tsarskoe Selo]*, Leningrad, 1990, p. 25.

9. E. Gollerbakh, in *Cameron at Tsarskoe Selo: Charles Cameron*, Petrograd, 1924, p. 40.

10. "Letters from Catherine II to Grimm," in M. Pylyaev, *The Forgotten Past of the Environs of Petersburg*, St. Petersburg, 1889, p. 462.

11. Ibid.

12. Ibid.

13. Alexander Pushkin, *Complete Works*, vol. 1, Moscow, p. 535.

14. In Gollerbakh, *The Country Palaces and Parks*, p. 32.

15. "Letters from Catherine II to Grimm," in *The Road Builder*, St. Petersburg, 1802, p. 20.

16. A. Khrapovitsky, *Notes*, Moscow, 1874, pp. 244–45.

17. Ch. de Ligne, *Letters*, vol. 2, Moscow, 1802, p. 108.

18. "Letters from Catherine II to Voltaire," in *Charles Cameron*, Petrograd, 1924, p. 41.

19. Central State Archives of Old Decrees, archive 14, inv. 1, no. 250, part 1, sheet 82.

20. Fedor Tyutchev, "Gently over the lake . . ." (1866), in *Tsarskoe Selo in Poetry*, p. 38.

CHAPTER 10

1. N. Shilder, "The Emperor Paul in His Acts and Orders," *Russkaya Starina*, November 1897, p. 43.

2. *Russkaya Starina*, Moscow, 1992, p. 432.

3. "Letters from G. Orlov to J.-J. Rousseau," in D. Kyuchariants and A. Raskin, *Gatchina*, Leningrad, 1990, p. 13.

CHAPTER 11

1. John Lowdon, *The Encyclopedia of Gardening*, London, 1827, p. 56.

2. "Letters from Maria Fedorovna," in Taleporovsky, *The Park at Pavlovsk*, Petrograd, 1923, p. 61.

3. E. Saint-Maure, *Anthologie Russe*, Paris, 1823, p. 247.

4. D. Kobeko, *The Tsarevich Paul Petrovitch*, St. Petersburg, 1882, p. 179.

5. V. Taleporovsky, *The Park at Pavlovsk*, p. 10.

6. Pietro Gonzaga, in Taleporovsky, *The Park at Pavlovsk*, p. 64.

7. Correspondence between Maria Fedorovna and Kyukhelbeker, Archives of the Pavlovsk Palace-Museum.

8. Ibid.

9. F. Glinka, "Letters from Pavlovsk to a Friend," in *Russian Messenger*, 1815, no. 63, p. 26.

10. *Pavlovsk 1777–1877*, St. Petersburg, 1877, p. 15.

CHAPTER 12

1. A. Geirot, *Description of Peterhof*, St. Petersburg, 1868, p. 1.

2. *Journal of Peter the Great*, vol. 1, St. Petersburg, 1770, p. 234.

3. F. Bergholtz, *Journal*, St. Petersburg, 1834, part 3, p. 184.

4. Ibid., part 1, p. 131.

5. Geirot, pp. 49–50.

Numbers in *italics* indicate illustrations.

A

Academy of Fine Arts (Mikhailov II), 130
Academy of Fine Arts (Vallin de la Mothe),
    91–92, *91, 92, 93*, 138; landing pier, *126*
Academy of Mines (Voronikhin), 128, 138
Academy of Sciences (Quarenghi), *10–11*,
    100, *124–25*, 138
Academy of Sciences Institute of Russian
    Literature, 137–38
Adam, Robert and James, Tsarskoe Selo,
    222–28
Admiralty (Korobov/Zakharov), *20, 24, 56–61*,
    65, 87, 129, 138–39, *140–47*, 159, 198
Admiralty Island, 20
Admiralty quarter, 56
Admiralty Square, *137*
Akhmatova, Anna, 192, 206–7
Alexander Column (Palace Square)
    (de Montferrand), *80, 148–50*
Alexander I, 107, 116, 122–36, 167, 170, 174,
    234, 270, 289, 319
Alexander II, *178–88*, 276, 310, 323
Alexander III, *178–88*, 276, 323
Alexander Institute (Velten), 94
Alexander Nevsky Lavra, 24, 102–4, *104–5*
Alexander Pavlovich. *See* Alexander I
Alexander the Great, 107
Alexandra Fedorovna, 319, 345
Alexandria Park, 332
Alexandrinsky Theater (Rossi), *156*, 167
Alexis, Tsarevich, 34, 245
Amiconi, G., painting, 69
Anichkov Bridge (Rossi), *169*
Anichkov Palace (Rossi), 100, *150–55*, 167,
    169
Anna I (Anna Ivanovna), 44–61, 76, 246, 270,
    316, 325
Anna Leopoldovna, 61–63
Annenhof Imperial Palace (Rastrelli), 63
Apollo Belvedere, 294–96
Architect, The (St. Petersburg architectural
    review), 178
Architect Rossi Street (formerly Theater
    Street), 130, *157*, 167
architects, Russian, 56
Archives of the State Council (Mesmakher),
    184
Argunov, Fedor, 76
Arkhipov, Pyotr, 322
Artillery Museum, 36
Art Nouveau, 180, 188, 194–202
Arts Square. *See* Mikhailovsky Palace Square
Astoria Hotel (Lidval), 180
Azovsko-Donskoi Commercial Bank
    Headquarters (Lidval), *198–99*

B

Baltic Station (Krakau), 184
Bank Bridge (Tretter), *86, 87*
Baranovsky, Gavriil, 194, 198
Baroque style, 32, 42, 61, 63, 65, 66, 84, 273
Barozzi, S., 262
Bazhenov, Vasily, 112–16, 174

Beggrov, A. K., 150
Behrens, Peter, 180
Bell Tower of Ivan the Great (Kremlin,
    Moscow), 66
Belogrud, Andrei, residences, *191*, 198
Beloselsky-Belozersky Palace
    (Stakenschneider), *158–61, 169*, 180
Benois, Alexander, 162, 198, 212
Benois, Leonti, 180
Benois, N., 323–25
Beretti, V., 159
Bestuzhev-Ryumin, Count Alexander, 65,
    150, 172
Bestuzhev-Ryumin Palace (Rastrelli/
    Bazhenov), 150, 172
Bestuzhev School, 199
Béthencourt, Augustin, 130, 134
Betsky residence (Vallin de la Mothe or
    Starov), 170
Biron, Ernst Johann, 52, 63, 316
Blank, I., 334–35
Blenheim Palace (England), 273
Blok, Alexander, 172, 192
Blondel, Jacques-François, 91
Blümentrost, Johann, 270
boathouse, *19*
Bogdanovich (poet), 206
Bolshoi Prospekt, 198
Bonazza, Giovanni, Peterhof, *334, 346*
Borman, Georgi, dacha of, 202
Bossay, Harald, *80*, 180, 256
Boullée, Etienne-Louis, 100, 129
Brasova, Natalya, 270
Braunstein, Johann Friedrich, 13, 32, 208,
    310, 322, 325, 338, 341–44
Brenna, Vincenzo, 110, 112–16, 130, 150;
    Gatchina, 269, 273, 274, 276, 278, 280;
    Mikhailovsky Castle, 112–16; Pavlovsk,
    284, 289, 290, 292, 294, 298
Bridge of the Imperial Stables, *88–89*
Bronze Horseman (Falconet and Collot),
    98–100, 128, 150
Brown, Lancelot, 107
Brumkorst, G., 338
Bruni, Nikolai, 188
Bryulov, Alexander, *80*, 134, *147–50*, 159
Bryulov, Karl, 134, 156; dome painting, *133*
Bunin, Ivan, 192
Bureau of Departmental Affairs (Bossay), 180
Bush, John, 230
Bush, Joseph, 174, 264

C

Cameron, Charles, 100, 144, 207, *218–30*,
    284, 289–98
Cardassier, A., 338
Castle Howard (England), 273
Cathedral of the Annunciation (Tressini),
    102, 104, *105*
Cathedral of the Ascension, or of the Savior
    of the Blood (Parland), *186–89, 188*
Cathedral of the Assumption (Kremlin,
    Moscow), 66
Cathedral of Peter and Paul (Tressini), *19*, 36,
    256

Cathedral of Prince Vladimir (Rinaldi), 98
Cathedral of St. Nicholas of the Sea
    (Nikolsky Cathedral) (Chevakinsky),
    46–47, 48, 65, 71–74; bell tower, *49*;
    interior, *50, 51*
Cathedral of the Transfiguration for the
    Preobrazhensky Regiment (Stasov), *170*,
    172
Cathedral of the Trinity for the Izmailovsky
    Regiment (Stasov), *85, 171*, 172
Cathedral of the Trinity of the Alexander
    Nevsky Lavra (Starov), 102–4, *104–5*, 159
Catherine (Griboyedov) Canal, 53, 58, 59,
    86, 160
Catherine I, 52, 208, 245, 316
Catherine II (the Great), 84–107, 112, 122, 147,
    167, 174, 207, 208, 212, 218, 220, 228–29,
    234, 247–53, 262–64, 270–71, 289, 318–19,
    328–30
Catherine Palace (Rastrelli), 341
Chalgrin, Jean-François-Thérèse, 129, 144
Chambers, William, 218, 296
Chaplin House (Beretti), 159
Charlemagne, Joseph, *80*, 323, 326
Charles XII, of Sweden, 18
Chernyshev Bridge, 85
Chesme Church (Velten), 90
Chesme Palace (Velten), 94
Chevakinsky, Savva, 56, 208; Cathedral of
    St. Nicholas of the Sea (Nikolsky
    Cathedral), 65, 71–74; Hermitage
    Pavilion, 223; Kunstkamera, rebuilt by,
    42; New Holland, 92–94; Sheremetev
    Palace, 76; Tsarskoe Selo, 204
Chiaveri, Gaetano, 34, 40
Chichiren residence, 159
Chinese Palace (Rinaldi), *246–57, 253*,
    262–64
Chizhov, Matvei, 167
Church of the Annunciation (Tressini), 102
Church of Saints Peter and Paul (Peterhof),
    333
Church of St. Catherine (Vallin de la
    Mothe), 94
Church of the Archangel St. Michael, 58
Church of the Maltese Order (Quarenghi),
    100
classicism, 34, 91, 100–107, 122–34, 136–37,
    140, 144, 159, 162, 172, 174, 178, 184, 234,
    276
Clausen, Nicholas, throne, 69
Clérisseau, Charles, 220–21
Collot, Marie-Anne, 98, 128; marble portrait
    medallion, 255
Commercial Galleries (Vasiliev), 199
Committee for Buildings and Waterways,
    129–30, 134
Condé, Prince of, 280
Convent of the New Maidens and the
    Resurrection. *See* Smolny Convent
Cottage (Menelas), *326–31, 344–46*
Court Stables (Stasov), 130, *170–72*
Coypel, Charles, 274
Currency Bank (Quarenghi), 100
Customs Houses (Lucchini), *10–11, 130, 137*

D

Dashkova, Princess, 167
Decembrists, 34, 134–36, 151
Delft tiles, 39, 42, 43, 344
de Montferrand, Auguste Ricard, 80, 130, 134; Alexander Column, 148–50; St. Isaac's Cathedral, 134, 150, 151–56; Winter Palace, 69, 76
Demut-Malinovsky, V., 140, 160; reliefs, 241
Derzhavin (poet), 206, 221
de Thomon, Thomas, 120, 129, 136, 151, 174, 298
de Waal, François, 34
de Wailly, Charles, 102, 174, 220
Diderot, Denis, 87
Dnepr, allegorical statue of, 122
Dom Knigi. *See* Singer Sewing Machine Company
Dostoevsky, Feodor, 104, 136, 178–80
Doyen, François, painting, 274
Duma (City Council), Tower of the, 142, 143
Dutch Church, 159

E

eclecticism, 178, 310
Efimov, Nikolai, 76, 180
Ehrler, Wilhelm, 322
Elagin, Ivan, 174
Elagin Island, 20, 172, 174; house of Alexander I (Rossi), 130
Elagin Palace (Quarenghi/Rossi), 172–75, 174
Eliseyev building (Baranovsky), 198
Elizabeth I (Elizabeth Petrovna), 52, 61–80, 84, 147, 167, 174, 208, 212, 214, 246, 316–18, 325, 341
Empire style, 128, 292
Engineer's Castle. *See* Mikhailovsky Castle
English Decorative style, 345
English Embankment, 8–9, 126–27
Eropkin, Pyotr, 52, 56, 61, 256
Ethnographic Museum (Svinin), 164
Europa Hotel, 164

F

Fabergé, headquarters of (Schmidt), 192
Fabritzky, New Holland, 56
Falconet, Etienne: *Bronze Horseman*, 98–100, 128, 150; *Bronze Horseman* (with Collot), 128
feather bed gallery, 162
Fedorovsky community, 238–40
Ferrara, Carlo, 32
Ferrari, G., 142
Ferster, Johann Christian, 32, 208
Field of Mars, 111, 112, 162, 170–72
First Russian Insurance Company (Benois), 198
five-cupola plan, 48, 66, 71, 103, 171, 172
flood of 1824, 137
Florentine palace style, 184
Fomin, Ivan, 202
Fontana, Carlo, 32

Fontana, Giovanni Mario, 32, 34, 42, 253, 256
Fontanka embankments, 91
Fontanka River, 13, 20, 61, 84, 87
Friedrich Wilhelm I, of Prussia, 214
Frolov, Alexander, 188

G

Gagarin, Prince, 194
Gatchina estate, 270–80; ownership history, 270–71
Gatchina Palace (Rinaldi), 91, 269, 271–76, 271–76; Marble Dining Room (Brenna), 272, 274; Paintings Gallery, 276; Throne Room (Brenna), 273, 274; White Hall, 274–75, 276
Gatchina Park, 271, 276–80; Eagle Pavilion, 276, 280; Island of Cupid, 279; Little Birch House, 278, 278; obelisk, 278; Pavilion of Venus, 278, 279; plan (Sergeev), 268; water park, 277
Gaugin, Alexander, 194, 198
gauptvakhta (engineers house), 36
Gautier, Théophile, 151–52
Geisler, M. F., 197
General Staff Arch (Rossi), 78–79, 81, 148
General Staff Headquarters (Bryulov), 64, 147–50, 198
Girardin, Louis de, 270, 289
Glinka, Mikhail, 147
Gogol, Nikolai, 136, 147, 156
Golitsyn, Prince, 48
Golovin, Gavriil, 172
Golovina, Varvara, 112
Gonzaga, Pietro di Gottardo, 284, 293, 299, 300–302
Gordev, F., reliefs, 160
Gorodskoy Island, 20
Gorokhovaya Street, 56, 144
Gostiny Dvor (or Merchants' Court) (Vallin de la Mothe), 94, 143, 162
Gothic chapel (Menalas et al.) (Alexandria Park), 332
Gothic style, 276, 345
Gould, William, 107
Grabar, Igor, 13, 24, 63, 100, 130, 264
Grabbe residence, 76
Great Novgorod, 18, 310
Greek-cross plan, 48, 66, 102, 103, 130
Green Bridge. *See* Police Bridge
Grekov, 44
Griboyedov Canal. *See* Catherine Canal
Grimm, Friedrich, 100
Guards Economic Society (Virrich), 198
Guestier, William, 130, 159
Gumilev, Nikolai, 192, 206–7

H

Hambson, G., 345
Hawksmoor, 273
Hay Market, 188
Heket, James, 271, 280
Hellenism, 130
Herbel, Nikolaus, 32, 40
Hermitage Museum. *See* Winter Palace (Rastrelli)

Hermitage Theater (Quarenghi), 39, 74, 77, 100
Hoffmann, Martin, 259
Horse Guards Manège (Quarenghi), 100, 150
House of the Emir of Bukhara (Krichinsky), 192, 199

I

Ice Palace, 48–52
iconostases, 36, 50, 118, 134, 135, 256, 295
Ilin, L., 199
Imperial Cabinet building (Chancellery) (Quarenghi), 100
Ivan (brother of Peter the Great), 52
Ivanov, Alexander Andreevich, 156
Ivanov, I., 234, 319
Ivan VI, 61–63
Izmailovsky Cathedral. *See* Cathedral of the Trinity for the Izmailovsky Regiment

J

Jacob, A., 274
Jacottet, 80
Jensen, J. I., door, 161
Joseph II, 298

K

Kachalov, 13
Kalmeier Clinic, 199
Kamennoostrovsky Prospekt, 195, 198
Kamenny Island, 20, 172, 174, 202, 203
Kavos, A., 53, 323
Kazan Cathedral (Voronikhin), 128, 129, 140–41, 159–60
Kedleston (England), 290
Kirov Theater. *See* Mariinsky Theater
Klein, A., 199
Klenze, Leo von, 76, 134
Klodt, Pyotr Karlovich, 40, 156, 169
Kochubei residence, 184
Kokorinov, Alexander, 91–92
Kokorinov, Alexander, 91–92
Kolokolnikov brothers, 74
Kolomna district, 61
Korobov, Ivan, 56, 71; Admiralty, 144
Kotlin Island, 20, 310
Kotomin residence (Stasov), 159
Kozlovsky, Mikhail, 170, 331; reliefs, 98
Kraft, Georg, 48
Krakau, A. I., 182
Krakau, Georg, 184
Krasovsky, A., 80
Krestovsky Island, 20, 172
Krichinsky, S., 192
Kronstadt Fortress, 13, 20, 253, 310
Kronverk fortification, 17, 36
Kronverk Prospekt, 198
Krylov, Ivan, 40
Kshessinskaya House (Gaugin), 198, 198–201
Kunstkamera (Mattarnovy and Zemtsov), 10–11, 24, 34, 40–42, 124–25, 138
Kurakin, Prince Alexander, 270
Kurland, 52, 63
Kutuzov, General, 122, 160
Kuzmin, R., 269, 273–74, 276

Kvasov, Andrei, 87, 208
Kyukhelbeker, Karl, 299

L

Lanskoy, Alexander, 147
Large Hermitage (Velten), 94
Lasalle, Philippe de, 330
Latin-cross plan, 102, 104, 140, 159
Latinism, 130
Laval residence (de Thomon), 151
Leblond, Jean-Baptiste-Alexandre, 32, 39,
    310, 318, 325, 331, 338
Ledoux, Claude-Nicholas, 94, 100, 107
Lermontov, Mikhail, 147, 206
Le Rounas, 289
liberalism, 134
Lidval, Fedor, 180, 194–99
Lion Bridge, 52
Little Hermitage (Vallin de la Mothe),
    71–73, 94, 180; Pavilion Hall, 72, 73
Loganovsky, A., 156, 244
Lomonosov, Mikhail Vasilievich, 104, 206,
    208
Louis XV, 202
Louis XVI, 293
Louis XVI style, 184
Lucchini, Giovanni, 130, 137
Ludwig, print by, 128
Lutheran Church (Bryulov), 159
Lutheran Churches of St. Catherine
    (Velten), 94
Lvov, Nikolai, 18, 36, 100, 102, 280
Lyalevich, M., 198
Lyubetsky, N., 338

M

Main Post Office (Lvov), 102
Makhaev, Mikhail, 44, 64
Maly Prospekt, 198
Mandelstam, Osip, 140, 146
Mannerism, 34
Marble Palace (Rinaldi), 94–101, 98, 111, 170
Maria Fedorovna, wife of Paul Petrovich, 222,
    228, 285, 289, 292
Marie-Antoinette, 293
Marienthal, 289
Mariinsky Palace (Stakenschneider), 136, 180
Mariinsky Theater (Kavos), 53, 53–55
Marly Avenue (Peterhof), 347
Marly Embankment, 351–53
Marly Palace (Peterhof) (Braunstein),
    341–44, 348
Martos, Ivan, 160, 331
Mattarnovy, Georg Johann, 32, 34, 39, 40, 123
Meders, James, 318
Meltzer House (Meltzer), 203
Menelas, Adam, 234, 319, 323, 332, 344–46
Mengs, Raphael, 100
Menshikov, Alexander Danilovich, 42, 52,
    208, 244–46, 253
Menshikov Palace (Great Palace of
    Oranienbaum) (G. M. Fontana), 242–43,
    253–59
Menshikov Palace (on Vasilievsky Island)
    (G. M. Fontana and Schädel), 24, 35–43,
    42, 138; bedroom of Varvara Arsenieva,
    40–43; salon, 38; vestibule, 36; Walnut
    Study, 39
Merchants' Court. See Gostiny Dvor
Mertens fur business headquarters
    (Lyalevich), 198

Mesmakher, Maximilian, 179, 182, 184, 195
Michel, J., 338
Michetti, Nicolò, 32–34, 56, 310, 318, 322,
    325, 331–32, 334–35
Mikeshin, Mikhail, 167
Mikhail Alexandrovich, Grand Duke, 270
Mikhail Mikhailovich, Palace of
    (Mesmakher), 184
Mikhailov II, Andrei, 130, 151, 162, 164
Mikhailov, V., 218, 230, 232, 233
Mikhailovskaya Street, 162, 164
Mikhailovsky Castle (Engineer's Castle)
    (Brenna), 111, 112–16, 113–19, 129, 162–64,
    170
Mikhailovsky Palace (Rossi), 144–49, 162–64,
    170; Salon of the White Columns, 146
Mikhailovsky Palace Square (Arts Square)
    (Rossi), 130, 162, 164
Ministry of State Property (Efimov), 180
Modern style. See Art Nouveau
modern-style house, 193
Moika embankments, 91
Moika River, 20, 61, 86
Monighetti, 208; staircase, 163
Monplaisir, 318, 338–41, 339; Chinese Room
    (Lacquer Room) (Brumkorst), 338–41,
    338; Great Hall, 336–37, 338
Moscow, 20, 65, 122, 188, 194, 310
Moscow (Nicholas) Train Station (Ton),
    169–70, 184
Moskovsky Prospekt, gates (Stasov), 172
M nich, Field Marshal, 34
Municipal Hospital of Peter the Great, 199

N

Napoleonic Wars, 122, 134
Nartov, A., 266
Narva Triumphal Gate (Quarenghi), 100
Natalya Alekseevna, 270
Nattier, Jean-Marc, 13
Naval Academy (Volkov), 138
Naval Museum, 137
Nechaev-Maltsev residence (Bossay), 180
Neelov, Ilya, 218, 230, 234, 238
Neelov, V., 218, 230, 232, 233
neobaroque style, 169, 178, 180, 198, 326,
    331
neoclassicism, 194, 198–202, 290, 292, 298
neo-Gothic style, 36, 90, 94, 101, 198, 234,
    323, 325, 326
neo-Renaissance style, 169, 198, 199
neo-Romantic style, 240
neo-Russian style, 138, 184
Nesterov, Mikhail, 188
Neva Embankments (Velten), 91
Neva Gate (Lvov), 18, 36
Neva River, 16, 20
Nevsky, Alexander, 18, 102, 104
Nevsky Prospekt, 24, 56, 86, 102, 140, 144, 148,
    150, 156–70
New Hermitage (von Klenze), 70, 75–77
New Holland (Vallin de la Mothe and
    Chevakinsky), 56, 92–94
New Holland Arch (Vallin de la Mothe), 57
Nicholas I, 136, 167, 169, 170, 188, 276,
    319–23, 344, 345–46
Nicholas II, 270, 323
Nicholas Station. See Moscow Station
Nikolaevsky Palace (Stakenschneider), 180
Nikolai Nikolaevich, Grand Duke, 180
Novodevichi (New Maidens Convent)
    (Moscow), 65–66

O

Oberkommandant, residence of, 36
October Revolution, 192
old Russian architecture, 66–71, 188, 325
Olga Nikolaevna, 322, 323
Opekushin, Alexander, 167
Oranienbaum, 24, 84, 91, 244–66; architects
    of, 256; under Peter III, 246–53;
    refurbishers of, 256. See also Chinese
    Palace; Menshikov Palace; Peterstadt;
    Sliding Hill Pavilion
Order of Malta, 270, 276, 300
Orlov, Grigori, 94, 98, 270–71
Orlovsky, Boris, 160
Orthodox Church, 65
Osner, Konrad, 36
Ostrovsky Square. See Theater Square

P

Paestum, Temple of, 136, 140
Palace Embankment (Neva River), 61, 177
Palace Square (Velten/Rossi), 64, 78–79, 130,
    147–50
Palladianism, 100–107, 128, 150, 202, 290
Palladio, Andrea, 56, 100
Pampel house (Schröter), 184
Parland, Alfred, 187, 188
Patersen, B., 128, 140
Paul I, 107, 110, 112–16, 170, 174, 206, 222, 228,
    234, 270, 280, 285–89, 290, 319
Paullust, 289
Pavlovsk estate, 284–302; creators of, 284–89;
    daily life at, 299–302; early years at,
    289–90; Old Chalet, 289
Pavlovsk Palace (Cameron/Brenna), 283–85,
    290–93; Chapel, 295; decorative vase,
    289; Dressing room of Maria Fedorovna,
    292; Greek Hall, 286–87, 292; interiors,
    290–95, 292–93; Italian Hall, 285, 292;
    Paintings Gallery (Brenna), 293, 293–94;
    restoration of, 292; rooms of Maria
    Fedorovna, 290–92; War Salon, 288
Pavlovsk Park, 293–99; Apollo Colonnade
    (Cameron), 298; Bip Fortress (Brenna),
    294, 298, 304–5; Centaur Bridge
    (Voronikhin), 296, 297; Cold Baths, 299;
    obelisk (Cameron), 294; Pavilion of the
    Three Graces (Cameron), 296; Pil Tower
    (Brenna), 298, 303; plan, 282; Slavyanka
    River vale, 294–99, 303; Temple of
    Friendship (Cameron), 296–98, 300, 301,
    303; White Birch section (Gonzaga), 299,
    302
Pavlovsk Regiment Barracks (Stasov), 130,
    170–72
Pechersky Monastery church, 138
Pel, A., 194
Pella palace (proposed) (Starov), 107
People's Will, 188
Peretyatkovich, Marian, 198, 199
Peter I (the Great), 12, 15–42, 52, 69, 172, 208,
    214, 244, 245, 270, 310, 334, 344; architects
    of, 24–34; Bronze Horseman (Falconet
    and Collot), 98–100, 128, 128, 150; daily
    life, 36–39; design of Summer Garden,
    39; palaces of, 36; statue of (Rastrelli the
    elder), 116, 147
Peter II, 42, 52, 245, 246; palace of, 42
Peter III, 84, 91, 174, 246–53, 259; palace of:
    see Peterstadt
Peterhof, town of, 323–25, 332

Peterhof estate, 24, 322–32; Alexandria complex, 319–21; Alexandria Park, 326–32; Belvedere Palace, 322; Colonists' Park complex, 321; Cottage (Menelas), 326–31, 344–46; English Palace and Park, 318; Farm Palace (Stakenschneider), 323; The Hermitage (Braunstein), 344, 344–45; history of ownership, 310–25; Lower Palace (Tomishko), 323; Meadow Park, 321, 322; Monplaisir Palace, 335–39; The Orangery, 322; Upper Garden, 308–9; Upper Palace, 325. *See also* Cottage; Marly Palace; Monplaisir

Peterhof Palace (Rastrelli), 306, 325–30; Arms Pavilion, 310; Audience Room (Gilded Salon) (Rastrelli), 316–17; facade facing Upper Garden, 307; interior decoration, 326–30; main staircase (Rastrelli and Torelli), 311–13; Peter the Great's bedroom, 319; Peter the Great's study, 320–21; Portrait Gallery (Cabinet of Fashion and the Graces), 318, 328; Throne Room (Velten and Rastrelli), 314–15, 328–30

Peterhof waterworks, 331–35; Bell Fountain, 350; Chinese Umbrella Fountain, 335, 341; Dragon Fountain (Chessboard Fountain) (Zemtsov), 325; Eve Fountain (Bonazza), 332–34, 346; Golden Hill Fountain, 349; Great Cascade, 342–43; Great Cascade sculptures and statues, 331–32; Marble Bench fountains (Stakenschneider), 334; Oak Fountain statues, 309; Pyramid fountain (Michetti), 334, 335; Roman fountains, 324; Samson Fountain, 331, 342–43; Sun Fountain, 335, 340, 341; trick fountains, 335, 340; Triton Fountain, 323

Peter-Paul Fortress (Tressini), 15, 17–19, 20, 24, 34–36, 87, 111, 124–25

Peter's little house, 39

Peterstadt (the palace of Peter III) (Rinaldi), 244–45, 259–62

Petrov, Vasily, 229

Pillement, P., 337, 338

Pilnikov, Grigori, 174

Pimenov, N., sculpture, 156, 240

Pimenov, S., 140, 160

Pineau, Nicolas, 320, 321

Piranesi, 293

Pokrovsky, V., 240

Police (Green) Bridge (Guestier), 60, 159

Polovtsov, Count: city residence of, 202; dacha of (Fomin), 202

Polovtsov House (Fomin), 194–95

Potemkin, Prince (Tauride Prince), 102, 104–7, 167

Pozzo, Andrea, 32–33

Prokofiev, Ivan, 160, 331

Przhevalsky, Nikolai, 147

Public Library complex (Rossi), 164

Pushkin, Alexander, 122, 134–36, 206, 230

Pushkin House, 137–38

Q

Quadro, Galeazzo, 32

Quarenghi, Giacomo, 71, 100, 128, 129, 144, 147, 167, 184, 222; Academy of Sciences, 100; Alexandrovsky Palace, 234; Anichkov Palace colonnade, 100; Church of the

Maltese Order, 100; Currency Bank, 100; Elagin Palace, 174; English Palace, 318; Hermitage Theater, 100; Horse Guards Manège, 100, 150; Imperial Cabinet, 100; Institute for the education of daughters of the poor nobility, 100; Monplaisir, 341; Narva Triumphal Gate, 100; Pavlovsk, 284, 292; Saltykov residence, 170; shopping arcade, 167; Stock Exchange, 100, 136; Winter Palace, 76

R

Rachette, Jean-Dominique, 331

Rastrelli, Bartolomeo, the elder, 331; Monplaisir, 338; statue of Peter the Great, 116, 147

Rastrelli, Bartolomeo Francesco, 61, 63–65, 91, 94, 102, 147, 184, 208; Annenhof Imperial Palace, 63; Bestuzhev-Ryumin Palace, 174; Catherine Palace, 341; Hermitage Pavilion, 223; Monplaisir, 341; Oranienbaum, 256; Peterhof, 318, 325–30, 344; Smolny Convent, 65–71; Stroganov Palace, 159; Tsarskoe Selo, 204, 212; Vorontsov Palace, 74; Winter Palace, 76–80

Rauch, Christian Daniel, 334

Razumovsky, Aleksei, 63, 65, 167

reformism, 122, 136

Reims Cathedral, 345

Renaissance Revival, 184

Renaissance style, 180, 202

Rezanov, Alexander, Vladimir Alexandrovich Palace, 184

Rinaldi, Antonio, 76, 91; Cathedral of Prince Vladimir, 98; Chinese Palace, 253, 262–64; Gatchina, 269, 271–76; Marble Palace, 94, 98, 170; obelisk (Gatchina), 278, 281; Oranienbaum, 256, 262–64; Peterstadt, 259; Sliding Hill Pavilion, 266; St. Isaac's Cathedral (not completed), 150; Tsarskoe Selo, 218, 230, 232

Rizzi, Antonio, 334, 346

rococo style, 34, 80, 98, 174, 184, 259, 262, 294, 328

Roerich, Nicholas, 192

Roman Baroque, 34

Rossi, Carlo, 130, 170, 174, 184; Alexandrinsky Theater, 167; Anichkov Palace, 167; Elagin Island house of Alexander I, 130; Mikhailovsky Palace, 162–64; Palace Square, 147–50; Pavlovsk, 284, 290, 292; Public Library complex, 164; Senate Square, 150–51; squares and streets designed by, 130, 147–51; Summer Garden, 40; Theater Square, 130; Theater Street, 130; Winter Palace, 80

Rotari, P., portraits, 318, 328

Rousseau, Jean-Jacques, 270

Rozenberg, A., 199

Rozenstein apartment house, 191

Rundbogenstil, 180

Rusca, Luigi, 162, 167, 229

Russian Bank of Commerce and Industry (Peretyatkovich), 199

Russian baroque, 80, 180, 256, 325, 341

Russian classicism, 80, 159, 169

Russian Hall of the Bank of Foreign Trade (Schröter), 188

Russian neoclassicism, 273

Russian style, 188, 325

Russo-Byzantine style, 188

Ruto, Domenico, 32

S

Sadovnikov, Vasily, watercolor, 66

St. Anne's Armenian church (Velten), 94

St. Catherine's Catholic Church (Vallin de la Mothe), 162

St. Catherine's church (Lvov), 102

Saint-Hilaire, P. A. de, 306

St. Isaac's Cathedral (de Montferrand), 8–9, 126–27, 129, 130–35, 134, 150, 151–56

St. Isaac's Cathedral (Rinaldi, not completed), 150

St. Peter Gate (Tressini), 18, 34–36

St. Peter's (Rome), 152

St. Petersburg: designs and plans for, 20–24, 32, 56–61, 87, 129–34; destiny of, 13; flood of 1824, 137; founding of, 16–20; islands, 172–74; maps of, 2, 16, 43; residential architecture, 159; return of capital to, from Moscow, 52; social organization in, 22–24; view of, 138

St. Petersburg Academy of Fine Arts (Vallin de la Mothe), 91–92

St. Petersburg Art Nouveau style, 194–99

St. Petersburg baroque, 66, 184

St. Petersburg classicism, 100, 156

St. Petersburg style, 34, 39

St. Petersburg University, 40

St. Stanislav Catholic Church (Vichonti), 130

Salon of the Muses (Torelli), 250–52

Saltykov residence (Quarenghi), 170

Savina House (Geisler), 197

Schädel, Gottfried, 32, 42, 256

Schinkel, Karl, 152, 319, 321, 332

Schlüter, Andreas, 29, 32, 39, 256, 310

Schmidt, K. K.: apartments on Khramovaya Street, 196; Fabergé factory, 192

Schreiber, Vladimir, 80, 184

Schröter, Victor A., 53, 184, 188

Schwertfeger, Theodor, 32, 40, 102

Scotti, D. B., 150, 329, 345

Semenov Bridge, 83

Senate (Schwertfeger), 40, 150

Senate and Synod (Rossi), 129, 151

Senate Square (Rossi), 128, 130, 150–51

Shchebuev, V., 156; paintings, 92

Shchedrin, Feodosy, 146, 331

Shcherbatov, Prince, 84

Shchuko, Vladimir, 198

Sheremetev, Boris, 76

Sheremetev Palace (Chevakinsky and Argunov), 76

Shubin, Fedot, 331; reliefs, 98

Shustov, Smaragd, 130, 151

Shuvalov, Count Ivan, 76, 91, 162

Shuvalov Palace (Chevakinsky), 76

Shuvalov Palace (Efimov), 180

silver galleries, 162

Singer Sewing Machine Company (Suzor), 198

Sion House (England), 290

Sliding Hill Pavilion (Rinaldi), 258–67, 266

Smolny Convent (Convent of the New Maidens and the Resurrection) (Rastrelli), 65–71, 102–3

Sokolov, E., 164

Sokolov, P., cast-iron griffins, 87; fountain, 241

Soloviev, D., 338

Sparrow, John and Charles, 271

Speransky, 122

Stakenschneider, Andrei, 136, 178–80; Beloselsky-Belozersky Palace, 159, 169, 180; Cottage, 344; Little Hermitage, 72, 73, 180; Mariinsky Palace, 180; Oranienbaum, 256; Pavlovsk, 284, 292; Peterhof, 321–22, 323, 332, 334

Stalin, 199

Starov, Ivan, 102–7, 147, 148, 159, 167, 170

Stasov, Vasily, 76, 130, 151, 170–72; Byzantine church (Potsdam), 319; Cathedral of the Transfiguration for the Preobrazhensky Regiment, 170, 172; Cathedral of the Trinity for the Izmailovsky Regiment, 172; Court Stables, 130, 170–72; Kotomin residence, 159; Moskovsky Prospekt gates, 172; Oranienbaum, 256; Pavlovsk Barracks, 130, 170–72; Smolny Convent, 66; War Ministry, 172; Winter Palace after 1837 fire, 80

Staub, V., 198

Stegelman house, 76

Stieglitz, A. L., 182

Stieglitz residence, 184

Stieglitz school (Krakau), 182–83

Stock Exchange: de Thomon's, 10–11, 120–21, 123, 129, 136; Quarenghi's, 100, 136

Strelna, 24

Stroganov, Count Sergei, 74, 128

Stroganov Palace (Rastrelli), 60–63, 74, 86, 159

Sukhozamet residence, 169

Sultanov, Nikolai, 188

Summer Garden, 24, 112, 119, 162, 170; Coffeehouse (Rossi), 31; Cupid and Psyche sculptures, 17th century, 30; gate (Velten), 33, 94; Grotto (Rossi), 13, 39; Peter the Great designer of, 39; sculpture, 32

Summer Palace (former, of Peter the Great) (Tressini), 21, 24, 28–29, 39, 112, 170; bedroom of Peter the Great, 27; gardens, 29; Green Salon, 23, 25; mirrors, 24; reliefs (Schlüter), 22, 39; tapestry in tsarina's bedroom, 26

Summer Palace of Elizabeth Petrovna, 45

Summer Theater (Shustov), 130

Suvorov, General, 167, 170

Suzor, Paul, 194, 198

Svinin, V., 164

Sweden, 18

T

Tarakanova, Princess, 34

Tardieu, P. F., 44

Tarsia, B., 325

Tauride Palace (Starov), 104–7, 106–9

Terebenev, Alexander, 146

Theater (Ostrovsky) Square (Rossi), 130, 164–67

Theater Street. See Architect Rossi Street

Thomas, G., 331

Toll (engineer), 230

Tolly, Barclay de, 160

Tolstoy, Leo, 178

Tomishko, A., 323

Ton, Konstantin, 126, 138, 169–70, 184, 188

Torelli, Stefano, 274; painting by, 250–53, 311

Toselli, Angelo, watercolor, 138

train stations, 184

Tressini, Domenico, 24–32, 56, 104, 208; Alexander Nevsky Lavra, 102; Cathedral of Peter and Paul, 36; Peter-Paul Fortress, 34; plan for Vasilievsky Island, 22; St. Peter Gate, 34–36; Summer Palace, 39; Twelve colleges, 40

Tressini the younger, 56

Tretter, G., 87

Trinity Bridge, 195

Trinity Cathedral (Zayachy Island), 20

Triscorni, P., sculpture, 150, 296

Trombara, Giacomo, 100

Tsarskoe Selo estate, 91, 206–40; aerial view, 204; Alexandrovsky Palace (Quarenghi), 234, 240; Alexandrovsky Park, 207, 238; Dragon Bridge, 238; Egyptian Gates (Menelas), 241; entry to courtyard, 206; history of construction, 207–18; map, 204; meaning of, 206–7; Sofia model village, 207, 232

Tsarskoe Selo Palace, 206–18, 208, 221, 222–29; Amber Room, 214–18, 214; garden facade (Rastrelli), 216–17; Grand Ballroom (Rastrelli), 210–12, 212–14; Green Dining Room (Cameron), 214, 215, 222, 228; Lyons Room, 228; main staircase (Monighetti), 209; Paintings Room, 214, 214; Salon, 213

Tsarskoe Selo Park, 218–22, 218–37, 229–34; Agate Pavilion (Cameron), 221, 222, 224–27, 231; Cameron Gallery (Cameron), 221–22, 228, 229, 231; Chinese Caprice, 218–20; Chinese Pavilion (Squeaking Pavilion), 218, 238; Grotto Pavilion (Rastrelli), 212, 222, 231; Hermitage Pavilion (Zemstov and Chevakinsky), 212, 220, 223; Large Chinese Bridge (Cameron), 239; Marble Bridge (Palladian Bridge) (Neelov), 230, 231, 232–34; Music Pavilion, 236; Turkish Bath (Monighetti), 230, 234–35; Upper Baths (Neelov), 218–19

Turgenev, Ivan, 206

Twelve Colleges (Tressini), 24, 40, 138

Tyutchev, Fedor, 206, 238

U

University Embankment, 8–9, 124–25, 138

urban planning, 87, 129–34

V

Valeriani, Giuseppe, painting, 223

Vallin de la Mothe, Jean-Baptiste, 56, 76, 91–94, 170; Academy of Fine Arts, 91–92; Church of St. Catherine, 94; Gostiny Dvor, 94, 162; Little Hermitage, 94; New Holland, 92–94; New Holland Arch, 56; Peterhof, 318, 328; St. Catherine's Catholic Church, 162

Vanbrugh, 273

Van Switten, Stephan, 34

Vanvitelli, Luigi, 91, 271

Vasiliev, Nikolai, 194, 199

Vasilievsky Island, 10–11, 20, 24, 32, 40–42, 61, 87, 136–40

Vasnetsov, Viktor, 188

Vassi, F., 331

Vavelberg Bank (Peretyatkovich), 198

Velten, Georg, 90, 92, 94, 100, 174; Academy of Fine Arts, 92; Alexander Institute, 94; bridge, 76; Chesme Palace, 94; gate to Summer Garden, 40, 94; Large Hermitage, 94; Lutheran Churches of St. Catherine, 94; Neva Embankments, 91; Palace Square and colonnade, 147–48; Peterhof, 326, 328–30; St. Anne's Armenian church, 94; Tsarskoe Selo, 218, 231–32, 238; Winter Palace Colonnade, 147

Vichonti, David, 130

Vigel, Filipp, 128, 130, 134

Viollet, A., 278

Virrich, Ernst, 194, 198

Vishnyakov, Ivan, 256

Vitali, Ivan, 156, 334

Vladimir, Grand Prince, 20

Vladimir Alexandrovich, Palace of (Rezanov), 177–81, 184

Voltaire, 232

Volynsky, Artemi, 52

von Bauer (engineer), 230

von Bolius, Hermann, 34

Voronikhin, Andrei, 63, 128–29; Academy of Mines, 128, 138; Kazan Cathedral, 128, 159–60; Pavlovsk, 284, 290, 292, 296, 298, 300; Peterhof, 332; Stroganov Palace, 74

Vorontsov, Count Mikhail, 74, 102

Vorontsov Palace (Rastrelli), 60, 74

Voznesensky Prospekt, 24, 56, 144

W

Ware, Isaac, 290

War Ministry (Stasov), 172

Watelet, 289

Winter Canal, 77

Winter Palace: first (1711), 24, 39; second (Mattarnovy) (1721), 39; third (1732) (Rastrelli), 76; fourth (1754): see Winter Palace (Hermitage Museum)

Winter Palace (Hermitage Museum) (Rastrelli), 64, 65, 66–67, 76–80; Ambassador's Staircase (Jordan Staircase), 68–69; Gold Salon (Schreiber), 80; Library of Nicholas II (Krasovsky), 80; Little Throne Room (de Montferrand), 69; Red Bedroom (Bossay), 80; restoration of Stasov and Bryulov, after 1837 fire, 80

Witte House (Virrich), 198

World War II, 214, 222, 264, 274, 276, 289, 318, 323, 334, 341

Wren, Christopher, 152

Y

Yusupov, Prince, 162

Yusupov Palace (Vallin de la Mothe and Mikhailov II), 162–69, 169

Z

Zakharov, Adrian, 56, 129, 130, 139, 140–47, 184, 280, 338

Zarudny, Ivan, 36, 256

Zayachy Island, 20

Zemstov, Mikhail, 34, 40, 56, 123, 208, 223, 256, 322, 331, 335

Zhukovsky, Vasily, 147, 206, 321